Cities in the Developing World

*Policies for Their Equitable
and Efficient Growth*

A WORLD BANK RESEARCH PUBLICATION

Cities in the Developing World

Policies for Their Equitable
and Efficient Growth

Johannes F. Linn

Published for The World Bank
OXFORD UNIVERSITY PRESS

Oxford University Press

NEW YORK OXFORD LONDON GLASGOW
TORONTO MELBOURNE WELLINGTON HONG KONG
TOKYO KUALA LUMPUR SINGAPORE JAKARTA
DELHI BOMBAY CALCUTTA MADRAS KARACHI
NAIROBI DAR ES SALAAM CAPE TOWN

Originally published in hardcover and paperback January 1983
Second paperback printing June 1985

EDITOR   James E. McEuen
PRODUCTION   Virginia deHaven Hitchcock
FIGURES   David C. Pyle
BOOK DESIGN   Brian J. Svikhart
COVER DESIGN   Joyce C. Eisen

Library of Congress Cataloging in Publication Data
Linn, Johannes, F.
  Cities in the developing world.

  Bibliography: p.
  Includes index.
  1. Underdeveloped areas—Cities and towns.
2. Cities and towns—Growth.   I. World Bank.
II. Title.
HT169.5.L56 1983   307'.14'091724   82-22401
ISBN 0-19-520382-8
ISBN 0-19-520383-6 (pbk.)

Contents

Tables and Figures

FIGURES

Foreword

THIS BOOK WAS ORIGINALLY WRITTEN as a background study for the *World Development Report, 1979*, the second of a series of annual reports produced by the World Bank's economic staff. Each year the best of these studies are separately published for the use of scholars and practitioners in specific fields. The present work is one of three monographs dealing with problems of industrialization and urban development, the main themes of the 1979 Report.

The unprecedented rate of urban growth in developing nations has created massive new tasks for national and local policymakers. This study by Johannes Linn delineates the major problems of adapting to the growth of cities in developing countries, and it discusses policies to increase the efficiency and equity of urban development. The areas covered include urban employment, income redistribution, transport, housing, and social services such as health and education. Linn evaluates the effectiveness of policy instruments such as public investment, pricing, taxation, and regulation. Some of these policies can be used in ways that improve both the efficiency and the equity of the development of cities, without a conflict between these goals.

As in other World Bank research studies, Linn takes a broad comparative view of his subject. His policy recommendations are soundly based in economic theory, but supported as well by a wealth of empirical illustrations drawn from the Bank's operational work.

> Hollis B. Chenery
> *Vice President*
> *Development Policy*
> *The World Bank*

xi

Preface

THE URBAN POPULATION OF DEVELOPING COUNTRIES is growing at a very rapid rate. Between 1975 and the year 2000, urban communities in developing countries will have to absorb close to 1 billion people.[1] The number of very large cities is also increasing rapidly. In 1950 only one city in the developing countries had more than 5 million inhabitants. By the end of this century, some forty cities are expected to be at or above this size. Such a pace of urban growth poses unprecedented challenges for national and municipal policymakers, particularly in the areas of urban employment, transport, housing, health, and education. This study addresses the question of how policy in these areas can be designed to improve both the efficiency and equity of urban growth; its conclusion is that many policies can be identified that simultaneously serve these twin goals.

Policies addressing the urbanization process must be formulated at the national, regional, and city levels. The primary concern of this study is the policy issues that arise and can be dealt with at the municipal level. National spatial development and the growth of any particular urban area, however, represent highly interrelated aspects of one and the same process of transformation experienced in all developing countries. The main implications of this interrelation are discussed in Renaud (1981).

A discussion of the institutional framework of urban government, administration, and finances—another aspect of urban policy—was purposefully set aside as lying largely beyond the scope of this volume. Urban government presents very difficult tasks under the best of circumstances; in the cities of developing countries the problems faced by urban authorities are monumental, whereas the resources to deal with them are exceedingly scarce. Since the public sector has a pervasive role in managing urban growth, the benefits from making urban governments more effective are substantial. Even the best urban development strategy comes to naught unless institutions exist to im-

---

1. In this book the word "billion" means one thousand million.

plement it. Improvements in the institutional framework are therefore a prerequisite for more efficient and equitable growth. This study addresses some institutional and fiscal questions in relation to specific areas of urban policy; the range and importance of issues regarding urban administration and finances, however, are so significant as to warrant a separate, comprehensive and detailed assessment of urban government. Such an assessment is currently under preparation (Bahl and Linn, forthcoming).

This volume thus takes as its primary theme the design of city-level policy for more efficient and equitable urban growth in developing countries. Such an analysis must begin with a diagnosis of the problem of urban policy in developing countries, which can be summarized as consisting of two interrelated phenomena. First, urban labor supply tends to expand as rapidly, if not in fact more rapidly, than urban labor demand; this limits the growth of urban wages and incomes, especially for unskilled workers. Second, the demand for urban services (including transport, housing, and public services) expands more rapidly than their supply; this leads to rising prices for urban land and housing, overcrowded housing, and shortages of public services, all of which affect the urban poor especially. Since these imbalances are largely the result of inefficient management of labor demand and service supply by governments, the efficiency and equity of urban development can be increased by improving the policies that create the imbalances. The present volume also analyzes policies concerning urban labor supply and conditions of service demand in considerable detail. The principal conclusions can be briefly summarized as follows.

Employment and Labor Market Policies

Because the urban poor are particularly affected by maladjustments in the labor market, the drawing of an employment profile of the urban poor is a first step in the analysis of employment and labor market policies. The commonly held notion that the poor are poor primarily because they are unemployed (or employed in marginal or "informal-sector" activities, untouched by government intervention) is found to be largely unfounded. The poor generally work many hours, often are found in formal-sector employment, and are frequently affected by government intervention. The primary reason for their poverty is that their productivity is too low to permit their earning a comfortable living.

An improvement in labor earnings must be sought principally through action at the national and sectoral levels that is directed toward improving the balance between the growth of labor supply and labor demand. A limited array of policy steps, however, can also be taken at the city level, and this would help increase the earnings of the urban poor. These policies include improvements in local administration, regulation, and taxation that would eliminate biases against low-income employment; public service investment and pricing measures designed to foster a greater labor intensity of service provision and improved operations of small-scale enterprises; urban land-use policies to permit increased participation of poor households in the labor market; and improved education and health services for low-income neighborhoods.

Fiscal System

More and better employment opportunities can raise the incomes of the urban population, particularly of the urban poor, only in the long term. Immediate alleviation of urban poverty must come through other public actions. Although the fiscal system in most countries has not been notably effective in reducing overall inequality, tax measures can be designed that reduce the burden of existing taxes on the lower-income groups and shift a greater share of the burden of higher tax revenues to those who can better afford it. Since the urban poor tend to pay about 10 percent of their incomes in taxes, the reduction of taxes bearing on the poor (mainly indirect taxes, in particular sumptuary taxes and local excise taxes) should be contemplated. To the extent that increased public revenues have to be raised, reliance on progressive taxes—such as urban property taxes, automotive taxes, and various types of benefit taxes—would be desirable. Nevertheless, the main potential of the public sector for improving the equity and efficiency of urban growth lies on the expenditure side of the public budget and in related regulatory and pricing policies for urban services, especially in the areas of urban transport, housing, and social services. Careful sectoral policy analysis, design, and implementation are required to ensure that public expenditures that are made ostensibly on behalf of the poor will actually reach them and that the welfare of as many of the poor as possible will improve. In the past, urban policies have frequently involved the bulldozing of slums, the banning of street vendors and traditional modes of transport, and the building of high-cost housing, subways, and limited-access highways, and all these measures served primarily the interests of the wealthier residents. In place of these approaches, urban investment, pricing, and regulation policies can and should be designed to assist those forms of transport, housing, sanitation, and other services that meet the needs of a majority of the urban population, including the poor, at costs they can afford.

Urban Transport

Urban transport is one of the areas selected for study in this volume. The function of urban transport is to provide the link between residence, employment, and amenities and to link consumers and producers in urban commerce. The available evidence on the determinants of demand and supply in urban transport in developing countries suggests that transport demand and costs vary directly with city size; the correct design of urban transport systems and of urban land use therefore gains importance as cities grow. The poor are particularly affected by transport policies because their adequate access to employment opportunities is critical and because they cannot afford to spend large shares of their limited income on transport.

The main transport policies appropriate for large cities in developing countries include support for walking and bicycling complemented by improved bus services in the poorest developing countries; a relatively heavier reliance on bus services and other intermediate motorized transport modes (for example, jitneys or vans) should be encouraged in the more advanced developing countries. Conventional investment strategies favoring costly rapid mass transit (for example, subways) and the private automobile are not likely to be in the interest of efficient urban transport in most developing countries, whereas curbs on the use of the private automobile in congested central cities will increase transport efficiency. Besides increasing the efficiency of urban transport, the policies proposed in this volume would also lead to transport systems that better serve the needs of the urban poor.

Urban Housing

In the area of urban housing, analysis must begin with a careful and comprehensive definition of housing. Such a definition would include not only the shelter structure but also the lot on which the structure stands, the infrastructure services available to the lot, and the access the lot has to off-site services (such as health and education services), employment opportunities, and other urban amenities. The importance of housing thus broadly defined for the economy of developing countries and their cities, as well as for the welfare of urban households, particularly the poor, can readily be demonstrated.

Once urban shelter has been correctly defined, analysis can address the urban housing problem in developing countries, and for this a review of the major determinants of housing demand and supply is useful. For determining urban housing demand, the structure and variation of private preferences for the major housing attributes (access, space, tenure, services, and shelter structure) are essential, as are the effects of urban population and income growth on the increase in housing demand over time. For urban housing supply, a recognition of the different roles played by various supply agents—in particular the role of public agencies in providing urban services and of the private sector in providing raw land and shelter structures—must be made. Also of importance are the various factors limiting increases in the housing supply, especially public policies restricing land conversion, provision of public services, and construction of shelter.

The urban housing problem—whose symptoms include land invasion and illegal subdivision, overcrowding, lack of basic services, poor access to employment opportunities, and rapidly rising land and housing prices—can then be seen as the inevitable result of a rapid increase in the demand for housing, which places a heavy strain on an inelastic housing supply. Since the failure of supply to adjust more quickly to changes in demand is in part attributable to inefficient public policies, and since the poor are especially hurt by these malpractices, a more appropriate urban housing policy can contribute to greater efficiency and equity.

On the basis of this diagnosis of the urban housing problem, it is possible to develop a strategy for providing improved housing for the poor. One can begin by estimating housing needs and the implied resource requirements at a global level by a "basic needs" approach; but since such estimates of housing needs have to be translated into specific policy prescriptions, a discussion of public policies designed to lower the cost and increase the supply of housing for the poor is necessary.

In direct public supply of housing services, urban governments generally can act only in a limited way through urban land acquisition. They must, however, undertake major activity in providing public services and must use low-cost technologies much more extensively than has commonly been done in developing countries—especially for water supply, sanitation and solid waste disposal, and neighborhood road construction. In general, governments should not get directly involved in shelter construction in most cities in the developing world because the private sector is relatively efficient in this area and because the public sector has generally not been successful. The exceptional experiences with public housing in Singapore and Hong Kong are very likely not replicable in most other developing countries.

The effects of public pricing and taxation measures on urban housing demand and supply must also be considered. Property taxation is potentially the most important among the tax instruments in this regard, but it is found in practice not to have a significant direct effect on urban housing supply in developing countries. Nonetheless, policymakers should avoid high taxes on buildings, eliminate taxes on property transfers, use special taxes on vacant land with caution, and view proposals for taxation on land value increments with some suspicion. In contrast, user charges have a substantial effect in encouraging an efficient allocation of demand and efficient investment patterns for urban public services. In general, estimates of the marginal cost of service provision can serve as a guide to efficient pricing, although the cost of administration will limit fine adjustments in the pricing structure, particularly in the case of limited consumption. General subsidies for urban public services should be avoided because their effects on efficiency, revenues, and equity will likely be undesirable. Selective subsidies, however, can be defended on grounds of externalities or alleviation of poverty, but they need to be carefully designed. In the case of water supply, for example, consideration must be given to the appropriate vehicle for reaching the most deserving households: subsidy of house connection is likely to be feasible and desirable in middle-income countries, but subsidy of standpipes will be preferable in low-income countries.

Regulation and control of urban housing in developing countries have on the whole done more harm than good. Regulations regarding urban land use, subdivision, and building standards are observed mainly in the breach; nevertheless, they can result in clouded land titles, the bulldozing of slums, and elevated standards for public housing programs. Rent controls are counterproductive to their goal of lowering rents because they tend to restrict the housing supply, impede mobility, reduce access of the poor to housing, and limit property tax revenues.

A comparison of conventional public housing programs in developing countries with low-cost urban housing projects supported by the World Bank shows that the latter are designed to reach those much lower in the income distribution, tend to avoid subsidies more successfully, and are likely to be more easily replicated to reach a much larger number of urban poor. A review of estimated economic rates of return indicates further that these projects not only serve the goal of alleviating poverty but also can earn respectable economic rates of return; thus they avoid any conflict with the goal of economic efficiency. The main explanation for this good performance lies in the low-cost service standards that are adopted in such projects. Yet a number of limitations on replicability remain even for these projects, particularly as regards the availability of urban land and the regularization of tenure, the overall housing strategy in a country, and the availability of general public revenues to support nonshelter components of urban projects.

Social Services

Finally, among the urban amenities important to the poor, social services play a major role. An analysis of these services must recognize the complexity of relations between education, health, nutrition, and fertility, as well as the important role and needs of women, infants, and children in urban life. The main problem for the poor is that they are trapped in a vicious circle in which low incomes induce poor education, health, nutrition, and family planning, which in turn act upon and reinforce each other, thus leading in the end to continuing low productivity and poverty.

For education in the urban setting, efficiency could be improved by a greater emphasis on public primary (or basic) education than on higher education, by a more aggressive, albeit selective, use of school fees, and by a restructured curriculum that would provide more functional training. Similar measures would also serve the interest of the urban poor, but special emphasis needs to be placed on reducing the private cost of education to them (for example, out-of-pocket expenses) and on increasing the physical accessibility of schools.

Health and nutrition problems are particularly serious among the urban poor, even when compared with rural dwellers, and it is not clear that public health systems always serve the urban poor better than the rural poor. In attempting to deal with urban health and nutrition problems, the conventional policy bias in favor of modern curative health care needs to be replaced by a focus on preventive, or basic, health care. The central role of women in contributing to the health of poor families through appropriate hygienic and nutritional practices must be recognized. These measures will serve to increase the efficiency and equity of the health care system.

In sum, the challenges presented by the rapid growth of cities in the developing world are great and troublesome. The severity of the problems, however, need not overwhelm those in charge of managing the rapid growth of urban populations. The conclusion of this study is that policy instruments exist, and have been tested, by which many of the urban ills in developing countries may be redressed. Certainly, governments cannot hope to eliminate all manifestations of urban poverty and inefficiency, but they can begin to make inroads against them on many fronts—at a minimum, by eliminating those policies that have commonly served to compound the difficulties associated with rapid urban growth and, more positively yet, by supporting and encouraging many of the policies that can simultaneously serve to increase efficiency and equity in urban development. The progress that has been made in many developing countries over the recent years in replacing many of the counterproductive, conventional policy approaches with imaginative new departures can be taken as a hopeful sign that further changes of this kind are possible. Indeed, that this volume can go beyond mere speculation about the beneficial effects of the policies it proposes and supports is a credit entirely to those many people whose creativity in thought and whose courage in implementation have led to the rich body of experience that is reviewed and analyzed here.

Acknowledgments

MANY INDIVIDUALS have assisted in the preparation of this study. Helpful comments on early drafts were contributed by Shankar Acharya, Michael Bamberger, Anthony Churchill, Fred Golladay, Gregory Ingram, Paul Isenman, Douglas H. Keare, Rakesh Mohan, Bertrand Renaud, Lyn Squire, and Alan Walters. Two anonymous reviewers provided additional helpful suggestions. Throughout the volume extensive use is made of the written work of my colleagues at the World Bank. Without access to this extensive body of evidence, the study could not have been completed in its present form. Edward Ebere Eule, Aeran Lee, and Ravi Trehan provided excellent research assistance. Banjonglak Duangrat, Anita Economides, Mary Ann Heraud, Mattie McCarter, and Gladys Tivel assisted with their outstanding secretarial help in producing the draft of the manuscript.

Cities in the Developing World

*Policies for Their Equitable
and Efficient Growth*

1

Overview

IN 1950 APPROXIMATELY 20 PERCENT of the population in developing countries lived in urban areas. In 1975 this proportion had reached an estimated 31 percent, and by the year 2000 some 45 percent of the people in developing countries will live in cities and towns (World Bank 1979a, ch. 6). This rapid urbanization process has been accompanied by the explosive growth of the large cities in these countries. For example, in the mid-1970s Mexico City and Sao Paulo each grew by over half a million people annually, while cities such as Jakarta and Seoul grew by over a quarter of a million people each year.[1] Small and medium-size cities are also growing rapidly—in some countries, in fact, more rapidly than the largest cities—but it is in the largest cities that the difficulties of adjusting to rapid growth and increased size tend to become most visible.

The populations of such metropolitan areas as Mexico City (whose population exceeded 10 million in 1975) and Buenos Aires, Sao Paulo, Rio de Janeiro, Cairo, Seoul, Jakarta, Calcutta, and Bombay (each with populations well in excess of 5 million) compare in size with the national populations of some medium-size and large developing countries.[2] In income and production, these large cities are even more important than their populations indicate if the high concentration of economic activity in urban areas is considered. For example, in 1973 the city of Bogota accounted for some 12 percent of the population of Colombia but contributed approximately 20 percent of the country's gross national product (GNP) (Linn 1979a). For South Asia, it has been observed that the GNP of any large Indian city-region is as great as the national GNP of Sri Lanka or Nepal (1978 World Bank data compiled by E. Bevan Waide).

Because of the sheer size of their populations and economic activity, the large cities in developing countries deserve the attention of politicians, planners, and economists. The efficiency with which the cities and towns in developing countries allocate their resources will increasingly determine the overall performance of these economies, particularly in the middle-income countries such as Argentina, Mexico, Colombia, Brazil, Algeria, Egypt, and the Republic of Korea (henceforth referred to as Korea), in which some two-thirds or more of the national population are expected to live in urban areas by the year 2000 (Beier and others 1975). What is more, although the incidence of poverty in developing countries is higher in rural than in urban areas (see table 1-5 for poverty indicators), the absolute numbers of the poor in cities and towns are large. In Manila, for example, 1.5 million people were classified as living in absolute poverty in the early 1970s (1975 World Bank data); in Brazil, some 600,000 people currently live below the poverty threshold in Rio de Janeiro and Sao Paulo, some 1.7 million people in the remaining urban areas (Pfeffermann and Webb 1979). For moral and political reasons, a policy of general poverty alleviation must also come to grips with the problems of the poor in urban areas, where poverty is particularly visible and troublesome because of its spatial concentration.

Purpose and Scope of the Study

This study assumes that urbanization will continue at a rapid pace in developing countries for the foreseeable future. Even if it were desirable and feasible to slow down this process of transformation, urbanization and the growth of large cities would continue into the future under all but the most extreme and unlikely policies.[3] It therefore becomes increasingly important to search for policies that improve the efficiency of resource allocation in urban areas and alleviate urban poverty.

The purpose of this volume is to contribute to this search by taking a comprehensive look at the state of the art of economic analysis of urban problems and policies in developing countries. Such an overview must cover a large range of issues, including employment, housing, public services, and fiscal policy, and this study had to go to some length to do justice to these issues. To make the task manageable, a number of restrictions were placed on the scope of the analysis. First, the study emphasizes the policies for efficiency and equity in the growth of *cities* and thus largely neglects rural-urban linkage as well as purely rural issues.[4] Second, it focuses to a significant extent on policies that can be implemented *at the city or project level* rather than on national policies affecting urbanization trends and patterns.[5] Third, the study does not address in a comprehensive manner questions of urban public administration, management, and planning.[6]

The views presented in this volume draw on a large array of studies spanning a wide spectrum, from analytical and quantitative research results to highly subjective evaluations by practitioners in the field. The record of experience gathered by the World Bank in its research and lending operations has been particularly useful. Although much of this record is already in the public domain, a systematic overview has so far not been presented on the scale provided within this volume.

Some Dimensions of the Urban Policy Problem

The rapid urbanization process and the explosive growth of cities in developing countries can be interpreted as either a success story or a failure. On the positive side, average incomes in cities are generally higher than in the countryside, and proportionally fewer people live in poverty in urban compared with rural areas.[7] Considering the scale of population movement to the cities, this influx has been absorbed remarkably smoothly by cities that have provided employment, means of livelihood, and a modicum of basic services for many. Migrants on balance appear to be "satisfied with their new lives, primarily because life is 'better' in the city than it was in their home communities."[8] On the negative side, urban unemployment and underemployment are frequently cited; the disastrous living conditions in city slums are evident even to the casual observer; and congestion and pollution in the large metropolises of developing countries tend to be as bad as they are in the cities of developed countries. Both of these perspectives contain elements of truth, but in isolation each misses important dimensions of urban development in the developing world. The purpose of this section is to provide a summary of the most important of these dimensions.[9]

Before reviewing the available statistics, however, a brief but important note of caution must be expressed regarding the usefulness of cross-country comparisons of statistics dealing with the dimensions of urban development in developing countries. First, there are inherent weaknesses in many of the data bases, relating especially to biases in surveys and the noncomparability of definitions across countries. Table 1-1 gives a vivid demonstration of bias in the case of housing statistics in Bogota: because of a more complete coverage of households in Bogota, the 1973 census figures differ drastically from those derived from a large, but evidently biased, household survey carried out during the same year. Often there exists no possibility to check survey figures against census data, and biases may therefore remain undetected. As regards noncomparability of definitions, estimates of housing needs are particularly problematic, as are estimates of poverty or underemployment (see Webb 1976, for examples). Second, global statistics for the urban sector in developing countries can easily be misinterpreted because they tend to gloss over important differences within this sector. For instance, it is useful to distinguish between large, medium-size, and small cities in reporting such

Table 1-1. *Characteristics of Housing in Bogota, Colombia*
(percent of households)

Characteristics	1973 Census	Survey
Type of dwelling		
Independent house	49.2	62.6
Apartments	8.8	17.4
Room	1.2	20.0
Inquilinato (leased)	38.9	n.a.
Other	1.2	n.a.
Number of rooms occupied by household		
1	43.98	20.77
2	21.20	21.50
3	9.40	19.55
4 or more	18.85	38.20
No reply	6.61	n.a.
Water connection		
Exclusive piped water	33.21	83.02
Shared piped water	62.44	13.28
Other	4.35	3.70
Mode of tenure		
Owner-occupied	26.32	52.02
Rental	58.43	42.35
Squatter	0.59	n.a.
Other	14.66	5.37

n.a. Not available.
Source: Valverde (1978), table 1.

variables as household incomes, poverty levels, service access, and the like. But even this is not enough: cities of similar size within the same country can exhibit vast differences in these statistics.[10] Furthermore, within urban areas neighborhoods differ in employment opportunities, availability of services, and conditions of health and nutrition. Examples will be cited below. Care needs to be taken, therefore, in basing urban policy design on broad data aggregates for the urban sector or for urban areas, and the conclusions derived from cross-country comparisons can only relate to very broad characterizations of urban development and cannot serve for specific policy analyses or prescriptions. On the basis of this understanding, a review of the evidence may proceed.

Employment and Incomes

The principal measurements of how well urban areas in developing countries have absorbed the rapid population influx are estimates of urban unemployment and underemployment rates. Tables 1-2 and 1-3 summarize the available statistics as compiled by Squire (1981). The salient feature of table 1-2 is that open unemployment rates tend to be higher in urban than in rural areas. Squire further points out that open unemployment in urban areas is a more serious problem for those fifteen to twenty-four years old than for the total labor force, for females than for males, and, at least up to a postsecondary level of education, for the more educated than for the less educated. Visible underemployment (that is, people working less than full time and wishing to work more hours) in general is small, whereas estimates of "invisible" underemployment (that is, people working full time at low wages) show that substantial portions of the urban labor force may be affected in developing countries. But, as Squire observes, invisible underemployment is really a measure of low productivity and poverty and as such is related to other measures of poverty that will be discussed below.

Average household incomes tend to be systematically higher in urban than in rural areas and tend to be positively associated with city size (table 1-4). Poverty indicators show that the incidence of poverty varies considerably between regional groupings (table 1-5). Urban poverty is particularly prevalent in South Asia, where the incidence of poverty is estimated to be higher in urban areas than in rural areas.[11] In all other regional groupings, the proportion of average urban population in poverty does not exceed 28 percent, whereas portions of the rural population in poverty exceed 40 percent every-

Table 1-2. *Urban and Rural Unemployment Rates in Selected Economies*

Economy	Year	Unemployment rate (percent) Urban	Rural	Ratio of urban to rural unemployment rates
Korea	1965	12.7	3.1	4.1
Panama	1967	9.3	2.8	3.3
Chile	1968	6.1	2.0	3.1
Indonesia	1971	4.8	1.8	2.7
Taiwan	1968	3.5	1.4	2.5
Venezuela	1968	6.5	3.1	2.1
Philippines	1967	13.1	6.9	1.9
Trinidad and Tobago	1971	16.5	8.7	1.9
Tanzania	1965	7.0	3.9	1.8
India	1972–73	6.7	3.9	1.7
Malaysia	1967	11.6	7.4	1.6
Syria	1967	7.3	4.6	1.6
Sri Lanka	1968	14.8	10.4	1.4
Iran	1966	5.5	11.3	0.5

Source: Squire (1981), p. 68.

Table 1-3. *Estimates of Underemployment in Selected Economies*

Country or region	Year	Rate of under-employment (percent)	Definition of underemployment
Visible underemployment			
Chile (metropolitan area)	1960	28.0	Employed persons wanting to work longer
Colombia (urban areas)	1967	2.0	Persons working less than 32 hours per week and seeking more work
Tanzania (urban areas)	1971	5.0	Number working short hours
Invisible underemployment			
Brazil (Sao Paulo)	1970	34.6	Those earning less than the official minimum wage
Dominican Republic (Santo Domingo)	1973	60.0	Based on stability and level of earnings
El Salvador (metropolitan area)	1961	21.0	Those earning less than the considered absolute minimum
Kenya (Nairobi)	1970		
Male		13.6	Those earning less than
Female		31.8	K Sh200 a month
Mexico	1969	37.6–44.8	Includes those working short hours or earning less than the official minimum wage and most unpaid family workers
Peru (urban areas)	1971	42.0	Based on hours worked and minimum wage
Philippines (urban areas)	1971	14.0	Methodology not clear
Tanzania (urban areas)	1971	41.0	Number earning less than urban minimum wage
Africa	1970	39.0	Includes those employed
Asia	1970	26.0	part time or whose pro-
Latin America	1970	20.0	ductivity is particularly low.

Note: "Visible underemployment" describes those working less than full time who wish to work more hours; "invisible underemployment" describes those working full time at low wages.
Source: Squire (1981), p. 72.

Table 1-4. *Urban Household Incomes across Cities
in Relation to Average National Incomes for Selected Economies*

Colombia (1970)	
Bogota	1.39
Cali	1.29
Cartagena	0.99
Malaysia (1973)	
Metropolitan areas (≥75,000 pop.)	2.15
Large urban areas (10,000–74,999)	1.04
Small urban areas (1,001–9,999)	0.89
Rural areas (≤1,000)	0.68
Peru (1971)	
Lima metropolitan area	2.11
Urban coast (excluding Lima)	1.39
Rural Sierra	0.48
Turkey (1973)	
Ankara	1.23
Istanbul	1.64
Izmir	1.58
Cities (≥100,000 pop.)	1.17
Cities (50,000–100,000)	1.02
Zaire (1970)	
Bukaru	0.84
Kinshasa	1.00
Kisangani	0.60

Note: The national average for each economy, except Zaire, was 1.00; the average for Kinshasa, Zaire, was 1.00.

Sources: Turkey, 1977 World Bank data; Colombia, Linn (1976a); Zaire, 1973 World Bank data; Peru, Thomas (1978); Malaysia, Meerman (1979, using his definition 1).

where except in Europe, the Middle East, and North Africa. As in the case of average incomes, average poverty indicators vary with city size (table 1-6). As a proportion of total city or regional population, the lowest incidence of poverty is generally found in the largest city, but this incidence increases as one passes to medium-size and small towns.

Housing and Access to Infrastructure Services

The difficulty of defining and measuring housing conditions across countries and cities has already been mentioned. Estimates of the incidence of slum and squatter areas in selected cities of developing countries must there-

Table 1-5. *Global Poverty Indicators: Regional Averages*

Region	Absolute poverty (U.S. dollars per capita)		Population below poverty (percent)		Relative poverty (U.S. dollars per capita)	
	Urban	*Rural*	*Urban*	*Rural*	*Urban*	*Rural*
Sub-Saharan Africa	108.8	74.1	26.8	47.6	124.4	59.6
North Africa, Middle East, and southern Europe	n.a.	194.9	18.2	24.2	295.1	309.2
South Asia[a]	80.2	67.2	50.3	44.6	n.a.	39.8
East Asia and Pacific[b]	140.8	112.8	27.7	40.4	n.a.	76.8
Latin America and the Caribbean	251.9	200.6	24.8	65.2	403.1	258.0

n.a. Not available.

Note: Table shows population-weighted geometric means, excluding the extreme values of the indicator and the most populated country in each group. The poverty levels shown in the table are defined as follows: *Absolute poverty* is that income level below which a minimal, nutritionally adequate diet plus essential nonfood requirements is not affordable. *Relative poverty* is that income level less than one-third of the per capita personal income of the particular economy. *Estimated population below poverty level* is that portion of the population who are either "absolute poor" or "relative poor," whichever is greater.

Source: World Bank estimates as of September 1978.

a. Identical to "low-income Asia" group in table 1-8, except that Indonesia is not included.

b. Includes economies of Indonesia, Hong Kong, Singapore, Fiji, Taiwan, Laos, Papua New Guinea, and Western Samoa, in addition to economies in "middle-income Asia" listed in table 1-8.

fore be taken with a large grain of salt (table 1-7). Similarly, what spotty information is available on the number of persons per room (table 1-8) cannot give much of an impression of the relative severity of the housing problem across cities and countries because the definition of a room varies from census to census and from survey to survey. A broad pattern shows that the incidence of slums and squatter areas is highest in sub-Saharan Africa and in Latin America. Overcrowding, as measured by the number of persons per room, appears to be relatively high in Asian countries and in sub-Saharan Africa. The variability within regional groupings and within individual members of these groupings, however, is so large that broad regional categorizations are not very useful. Moreover, as will be discussed at length in chapter 5, the definition of the urban housing problem in developing countries needs to be carefully considered, and no simple measurement of housing needs or deficits is likely to be very helpful for urban housing policy.[12]

Somewhat less difficult and controversial are estimates of access to urban infrastructure services, in particular to safe water supply, excreta disposal, and electricity. And yet even here problems arise. Table 1-8 shows the

Table 1-6. *Global Poverty Indicators: Distribution within Selected Economies*

Country and area	Households in poverty	
	Percentage of total households in region	*Percentage of total poor households*
Brazil (1974–75)		
Brazil	32	100
Metropolitan areas	11	9
Other urban areas	23	25
Rural areas	55	66
Malaysia (1973)		
Malaysia	36	100
Metropolitan areas	12	2
Large urban areas	40	13
Small urban areas	48	11
Rural	51	74
Peru (1971)		
Peru	28	n.a.
Lima metropolitan area	8	n.a.
Urban coast	12	n.a.
Rural Sierra	41	n.a.

n.a. Not available.
Note: Uniform definitions apply within each economy but not necessarily across economies.
Sources: Brazil, Webb and Pfefferman (1979); Malaysia, Meerman (1979); Peru, Thomas (1978).

Table 1-7. *Incidence of Slums and Squatter Areas in Selected Cities*

Region and country	City	Slums and squatter settlements as percentage of city population	Year
Sub-Saharan Africa			
Cameroon	Douala	80	1970
	Yaounde	90	1970
Ethiopia	Addis Ababa	90	1968
Ghana	Accra	53	1968
Ivory Coast	Abidjan	60	1964
Kenya	Nairobi	33	1970
	Mombasa	66	1970
Liberia	Monrovia	50	1970
Madagascar	Tananarive	33	1969
Malawi	Blantyre	56	1966
Nigeria	Ibadan	75	1971
Senegal	Dakar	60	1971
Somalia	Mogadishu	77	1967
Sudan	Port Sudan	55	1971
Tanzania	Dar es Salaam	50	1970
Togo	Lome	75	1970
Upper Volta	Ouagadougou	70	1966
Zaire	Kinshasa	60	1969
Zambia	Lusaka	48	1969
North Africa and Middle East			
Iraq	Baghdad	29	1965
Jordan	Amman	14	1971
Lebanon	Beirut	1.5	1970
Morocco	Casablanca	70	1971
	Rabat	60	1971
Turkey	Ankara	60	1970
	Istanbul	40	1970
	Izmir	65	1970
Low-income Asia			
Afghanistan	Kabul	21	1971
India	Calcutta	33	1971
	Bombay	25	1971
	Delhi	30	1971
	Madras	25	1971
	Baroda	19	1971
Indonesia	Jakarta	26	1972
	Bandung	27	1972
	Makassar	33	1972
Nepal	Katmandu	22	1961
Pakistan	Karachi	23	1970
Sri Lanka	Colombo	43	1968

Region and country	City	Slums and squatter settlements as percentage of city population	Year
Middle-income Asia			
Hong Kong	Hong Kong	16	1969
Korea	Seoul	30	1970
	Busan	31	1970
Malaysia	Kuala Lumpur	37	1971
Philippines	Manila	35	1972
Singapore	Singapore	15	1970
Latin America and the Caribbean			
Brazil	Rio de Janeiro	30	1970
	Belo Horizonte	14	1970
	Recife	50	1970
	Porto Alegre	13	1970
	Brasilia	41	1970
Chile	Santiago	25	1964
Colombia	Bogota	60	1969
	Cali	30	1969
	Buenaventura	80	1969
Ecuador	Guayaquil	49	1969
Guatemala	Guatemala City	30	1971
Honduras	Tegucigalpa	25	1970
Mexico	Mexico City	46	1970
Panama	Panama City	17	1970
Peru	Lima	40	1970
	Arequipa	40	1970
	Chimbote	67	1970
Venezuela	Caracas	40	1969
	Maracaibo	50	1969
	Barquisimeto	41	1969
	Ciudad Guayana	40	1969

Note: Definitions of "slums" and "squatter areas" vary from region to region and from city to city; therefore, these data only present the roughest of impressions of the housing problem in these cities.

Source: Grimes (1976).

availability of electricity in homes, and table 1-9 reports estimates of the proportions of urban and rural populations with access to water supply and excreta disposal (with access quite broadly defined).[13] In general, urban areas are much better serviced than rural areas, and urban areas of Latin America, Europe, the Middle East, and North Africa are better provided with these services than are urban areas of Asia and sub-Saharan Africa.[14] According to the data available, the number of people with access to water supply has

(*Text continues on page 19.*)

Table 1-8. *Persons per Room and Access to Electricity in Urban Areas, 1960, 1970, and Recently*

Region and economy	Persons per room					
	1960		1970		Recently	
	Urban	Rural	Urban	Rural	Urban	Rural
Sub-Saharan Africa						
Ethiopia	2.7					
Ivory Coast	2.5[b]					
Kenya	2.5[c]					
Liberia	1.7[d]					
Malawi			1.9[e]			
Mauritius	1.8[f]	1.9[f]				
Nigeria	3.0					
Sierra Leone					2.0[c]	
Sudan			2.5[g]			
Zambia			2.6	2.6		
North Africa, Middle East, and southern Europe						
Algeria			2.8[h]			
Cyprus	1.3	1.6	1.0		0.8	1.0
Egypt	1.6					
Greece	1.4	1.6	0.9	1.0		
Iran			2.2	2.4		
Jordan						
Lebanon	2.2		2.1			
Morocco	2.1	2.3	2.1	2.6		
Portugal	1.0	1.1				
Romania			1.3	1.4		
Spain	0.9					
Syria	2.5	3.2				
Tunisia			2.7	3.6		
Turkey	2.0		1.9			
Yemen					1.8[j]	3.1
Yugoslavia	1.7	1.5	1.3	1.5		
Low-income Asia						
Indonesia			1.6	1.6		
Nepal	2.0					
Pakistan	3.1	3.1				
Sri Lanka	2.1[k]	2.0[k]	2.7	2.5		
Middle-income Asia						
Hong Kong						
Korea	2.8	2.4	2.7	2.2		
Malaysia	2.3		2.3[l]	2.8[l]		
Philippines			2.1	2.4		
Singapore			2.9[l]			
Taiwan						
Thailand						

Access to electricity (percentage of dwellings)					
1960		1970		Recently	
Urban	Rural	Urban	Rural	Urban	Rural
58.2[a]					
		16.0[e]			
81.9[f]	20.0[f]				42.4
27.5					
		12.0[h]			
90.4	21.5			99.0	
37.8					
81.5	13.5	97.6	77.0		
		69.0	4.0		
39.0	1.0				
	71.0				
85.4[i]	31.0[i]	68.4		55.0	
88.5	27.4				
		86.0	27.0		
97.5	84.0				
87.7[c]	10.5[c]	84.7	10.2		
	2.0		18.0		
				56.5[j]	
92.7	36.1	98.4	80.1		
		75.5	39.1		
30.2					
35.9[k]	2.3[k]	34.5	2.8		
100.0					
67.3	12.0	92.3	30.0		
		84.7[l]	30.0[l]		
		60.4	7.0		10.0
			88.0[l]		
		63.0[m]	13.0		

(Table continues on the following pages.)

Table 1-8 *(continued)*

Region and economy	Persons per room					
	1960		1970		Recently	
	Urban	Rural	Urban	Rural	Urban	Rural
Latin America and the Caribbean						
Argentina	1.3	1.7	1.4			
Barbados	1.2		1.0			
Bolivia						
Brazil			1.0	1.2	1.2[f]	1.2[f]
Chile	1.6	2.0	1.3	1.7		
Colombia						
Costa Rica	1.3[k]	1.7[k]			1.4	
Dominican Republic	1.6	1.2				
Ecuador	2.1[c]	2.8[c]				
El Salvador			3.8			
Guatemala	1.9[n]	3.1[n]			1.6	2.7
Guyana	1.7		2.1			
Haiti			2.2	2.1		
Honduras	1.8	2.7				
Jamaica	1.6	2.0				
Mexico	2.6	3.4	2.2	3.2		
Nicaragua	2.2[k]	3.2[k]				
Panama	2.1	2.6	1.8	2.5		
Paraguay	2.6[c]				1.7	3.1
Peru	2.0	2.7				
Surinam	1.7[n]					
Trinidad and Tobago	1.6	1.8	1.7			
Uruguay	1.5[k]					
Venezuela	1.6		1.5			

Note: Unless otherwise noted, "1960" refers to any year between 1959 and 1961; "1970" to any year between 1969 and 1971; and "recently" to any year between 1973 and 1977.

Source: World Bank estimates as of September 1978.

a. Addis Ababa only.
b. 1956–57 instead of 1960.
c. 1962.
d. Monrovia only.
e. 1967.
f. 1972.

| Access to electricity (percentage of dwellings) | | | | | |
| 1960 | | 1970 | | Recently | |
Urban	Rural	Urban	Rural	Urban	Rural
84.7	19.0				
76.0k	8.0k				
		75.6	8.4	77.9	12.5
86.3	24.0				30.0
83.0	8.0				
93.5k	32.0k				50.0
57.7	3.0				
78.5c	6.0c				12.0
60.4		73.0	7.0		14.4
56.0n	4.0n			67.8	5.4
56.7	2.0				
		80.7	28.0		
71.0	4.0	76.7	7.0		
82.7	11.0	90.4	16.0		
33.2c	1.2c			41.5	1.2
50.7	4.0				
70.8	30.0				
88.0k	29.0k				

g. 1965.
h. 1966.
i. Brick buildings only.
j. Only in the major cities of Samor, Gaiz, and Hodaidah.
k. 1963.
l. West Malaysia.
m. Bangkok metropolitan area.
n. 1964.

Table 1-9. *Percentage of Population with Access to Water Supply and Excreta Disposal: Regional Averages*

	Access to water		Access to excreta disposal	
Region	Urban	Rural	Urban	Rural
Sub-Saharan Africa	66.3	10.4	70.3	14.2
North Africa, Middle East, and southern Europe	74.3	64.4	94.0	93.0
South Asia	66.3	17.2	66.9	2.5
East Asia and Pacific	58.3	9.8	66.6	14.8
Latin America and the Caribbean	78.0	34.9	80.3	25.4

Note: Estimates are based on information for years between 1973 and 1977, in accordance with availability of data.

Source: World Bank estimates as of September 1978.

Table 1-10. *Estimated Rural and Urban Infant Mortality Rates in Selected Economies*
(Annual deaths per thousand live births among children under 1 year of age)

Economy	Number
Chad	
Rural	164
Urban	134
Guinea	
Rural	218
Urban	189
Morocco	
Rural	170
Urban	105
Pakistan	
Rural	138
Urban	100
Philippines	
Rural	85
Urban	75
Tunisia	
Rural	120
Urban	80
Turkey	
Rural	168
Urban	113

Source: Basta (1977).

Table 1-11. *Intake of Selected Nutrients and Energy
in Urban and Rural Areas of Nine Developing Economies, 1960–70*
(amount per capita daily)

Economy	Energy (calories)	Protein (grams)			Fat (grams)
		Total	Animal	Vegetable	
Bangladesh (1962–63)					
Rural	2,254	57.4	7.9	49.5	17.2
Urban	1,732	49.5	12.1	37.4	25.0
Brazil (1960)					
Rural	2,640	79.2	29.7	49.5	60.0
Urban	2,428	74.0	30.7	43.3	63.0
Chad (1965)					
Rural	2,467	90.1	10.5	79.6	62.9
Urban	2,113	73.3	23.9	49.5	52.2
Dahomey (1966–67)					
Rural	2,142	51.0	7.0	44.0	47.4
Urban	1,908	52.0	10.0	42.0	46.2
Korea (1969)					
Rural	2,181	66.9	5.1	61.8	15.8
Urban	1,946	62.8	10.9	51.9	19.5
Morocco (1970–71)					
Rural	2,888	84.0	12.0	72.0	n.a.
Urban	2,521	70.0	19.0	51.0	n.a.
Pakistan (1965–66)					
Rural	2,126	69.8	7.9	61.9	40.3
Urban	1,806	58.4	9.8	48.6	40.0
Trinidad and Tobago (1970)					
Rural	3,011	81.7	31.8	49.9	84.0
Urban	2,550	83.6	43.3	40.3	95.8
Tunisia (1965–67)					
Rural	2,315	63.7	7.4	56.3	55.2
Urban	2,550	67.7	15.0	52.7	77.5

n.a. Not available.
Source: Basta (1977).

increased in recent years; much of this improvement in access, however, appears to have been counteracted by deterioration in the quality and reliability of water supply (World Bank 1980e). As a result, a substantial portion of urban populations in developing countries do not have the benefit of safe water or excreta disposal, with consequent effects in poor health and nutrition for these urban dwellers.[15]

Table 1-12. *Food Intake and Demographic, Socioeconomic, and Health Characteristics for Nonsquatter and Squatter Urban Areas in India and Pakistan*

Country and city	Parameter	Nonsquatter area (city or high-income average)	Squatter area	Notes on squatter settlement
India				
Calcutta	Mean cost of daily diet (in paisas) of children 3–5 years old	108.8	49.4	
Calcutta	Mean energy intake, daily diet of children 3–5 years old (calories)	960 ± 321	789 ± 237	Group with monthly income ≤20 rupees per capita
Calcutta	Mean vitamin A intake, daily diet of children 3–5 years old (international units)	709 ± 843	410 ± 678	Group with monthly income ≤20 rupees per capita
Calcutta	Average per capita energy intake (calories)	1,422	1,061	Group with monthly income ≤20 rupees per capita
Calcutta	Average per capita protein intake (grams daily)	45	34	
Calcutta	Average per capita intake of vitamin A (international units)	2,139	1,400	
Madras	Death rate per 100,000 population from:			
	Dysentery	7.6	21.8	Marina city section
	Tuberculosis	16.4	37.5	
Pakistan				
Karachi	Population to dispensary ratio	12,800:1	62,100:1	Mahmoodbad, Karangi Baldia; total pop. 0.2 million
Karachi	Hospital beds per 1,000 female population (15–49 years old)	2.07	0.49	Average of five slums
Karachi	Primary schools: minimum percentage of children 5–9 years old not enrolled	57	80	Nonsquatter average from old city and federal area; squatter areas were North Karachi and Mahmoodbad

Source: Basta (1977).

Table 1-13. *Characteristics of Nonsquatter and Squatter Urban Settlements in Manila, Philippines*

Parameter	Nonsquatter	Squatter	Notes on squatter settlement
School dropouts before high school (percent)	20	35	
Hospital bed to population ratio	1:300	1:4,000	Squatter settlements surveyed are Tondo, Malabon, and Navotas (pop. 714,924)
Infant mortality rate (per 1,000 live births)	76	210	Tondo and Navotas Port area (pop. 2,100)
Birth rate (per 1,000 pop.)	33	177	Tondo and Navotas Port area (pop. 2,100)
Neonatal mortality rate (per 1,000 live births)	40	105	Tondo and Navotas Port area (pop. 2,100)
Tuberculosis rate (per 100,000 pop.)	800	7,000	Greater Tondo area (pop. 0.4 million)
Gastroenteritis rate (per 100,000 pop.)	780	1,352	Greater Tondo area (pop. 0.4 million)
Third-degree malnutrition (percent of population surveyed)[a]	3	9.6	Tondo area nutrition survey of 6,000 households (Operation Timbang)
Second-degree malnutrition (percent of pop. surveyed)[a]	21	37.5	Tondo area nutrition survey of 6,000 households (Operation Timbang)
Anemia (percent of pop. surveyed)	10	20	Tondo area nutrition survey of 6,000 households (Operation Timbang)
Per capita energy intake (calories)	1,700	1,550	Tondo area nutrition survey of 6,000 households (Operation Timbang)
Typhoid rate (per 100,000 pop.)	33	135	Tondo area
Diphtheria rate (per 100,000 pop.)	48	77	Tondo area
Measles rate (per 100,000 pop.)	130	160	Tondo area
Clinical signs of vitamin A deficiency (percent of pop. affected)	50	72	Cebu City

Source: Basta (1977).

a. Malnutrition is defined according to the standard weight-for-age classification (also referred to as Gomez classification).

Health and Nutrition

Health conditions on average tend to be better in urban than in rural areas of developing countries. In 1960, for instance, the crude death rate for rural areas in developing countries was estimated as 21.7 per thousand and for urban areas as 15.4 (World Bank 1980c, p. 12). More recent comparisons of infant mortality between urban and rural areas tend to confirm the existence of an urban-rural health gap (table 1-10). However, Lee and Furst (1980, p. 25) conclude in their own survey of infant and child mortality statistics that "the high mortality rates of the lower socioeconomic class of urban populations are more comparable to their rural counterparts than their fellow urban dwellers of the upper class." For nutrition, Basta (1977) has shown for selected countries that in energy intake the rural dwellers tend to fare better than the urban dwellers, although this pattern is reversed for intake of protein and fats (table 1-11). More important, however, is the convincing evidence he provides for a number of cities in developing countries: the health and nutrition levels of the slum populations are vastly below the city average, and either close to or even below average rural levels (tables 1-12 and 1-13). Lee and Furst (1980) confirm these general findings on the basis of additional data for Brazil, Sri Lanka, India, and Thailand.

Table 1-14. *Distribution of Medical Doctors between the Capital and Remaining Regions of Selected Countries, 1968*

| Country | Number of people per medical doctor | | |
	Nationwide	*Capital city*	*Remaining regions*
Haiti	14,700	1,350	33,300
Kenya	10,999	672	25,600
Thailand	7,000	800	25,000
Senegal	19,100	4,270	44,300
Ghana[a]	18,000	4,340	41,360
Tunisia	6,486	2,912	10,056
Colombia[a]	2,220	1,000	6,400
Guatemala	4,860	875	22,600
Iran	3,750	906	6,220
Lebanon	1,470	650	3,000
Jamaica	2,280	840	5,510
Panama	1,850	760	4,400

Source: World Bank (1975a).
a. Major urban centers instead of capital city.

The availability of curative health services as reflected by the ratio of population to medical staff and hospital beds is, in general, significantly higher in urban than in rural areas (tables 1-14 and 1-15). There is reason to believe, however, that the urban poor have little access to these services, and in any case this type of medical care does not meet the urgent need of the poor for preventive care (see chapter 6).

Education

Cross-country data on comparative levels of literacy and educational status for urban and rural areas in developing countries do not appear to be readily available (Webb 1976), although there can be little doubt that urban dwellers

Table 1-15. *Persons per Hospital Bed, 1960, 1970, and Recently*

Region and economy	1960 Urban	1960 Rural	1970 Urban	1970 Rural	Recently Urban	Recently Rural
Sub-Saharan Africa						
Benin			360.0	1,620.0	280.0	1,440.0
Botswana					40.0	2,970.0
Burundi			70.0	730.0		
Cameroon						
Central African Republic			500.0	450.0		
Chad			130.0	1,870	330.0	1,910.0
Comoros			60.0	1,280.0		
Congo						
Ethiopia			350.0	15,370.0		
Gabon			150.0	90.0		
Gambia						
Ghana			770.0	790.0	490.0	870.0
Guinea	240.0	2,640.0	280.0	1,020.0		
Ivory Coast			250.0	1,650.0		
Kenya						
Lesotho	70.0	720.0	70.0	710.0		
Liberia						
Madagascar			170.0	520.0	240.0	500.0
Malawi			190.0	1,520.0		
Mali			780.0	1,560.0		
Mauritania			500.0	5,320.0	600.0	3,628.0

(Table continues on the following page.)

Table 1-15   *(continued)*

Region and economy	1960		1970		Recently	
	Urban	Rural	Urban	Rural	Urban	Rural
Mauritius			160.0	470.0	160.0	700.0
Niger			350.0	4,250.0	160.0	3,460.0
Nigeria			400.0	18,450.0		
Rwanda					40.0	1,840.0
Senegal			390.0	1,300.0	380.0	1,156.0
Sierra Leone						
Somali						
Sudan					290.0	2,270.0
Togo						
Upper Volta			300.0	2,580.0		
Zaire			90.0	1,070.0	110.0	1,000.0
Zambia			340.0	330.0		
North Africa, Middle East, and southern Europe						
Algeria						
Cyprus						
Egypt			290.0	2,110.0	250.0	2,090.0
Greece						
Iran			400.0	2,070.0	500.0	890.0
Iraq					310.0	5,520.0
Jordan			740.0	5,750.0		
Lebanon						
Libya			70.0	10,010.0		
Morocco			460.0	2,980.0		
Oman						
Portugal						
Romania	50.0	620.0	50.0	770.0	60.0	730.0
Spain						
Syria						
Tunisia			280.0	930.0	2,301.0	1,040.0
Turkey	190.0		200.0	5,890.0	210.0	5,750.0
Low-income Asia						
Afghanistan			1,090.0	9,650.0		
Bangladesh						
Burma			250.0	15,820.0	250.0	6,070.0
India						
Indonesia			1,130.0	1,890.0		
Laos						
Nepal						
Pakistan	370.0	22,850.0	500.0	12,390.0	560.0	12,360.0
Sri Lanka			130.0	570.0	140.0	600.0

Table 1-15   (continued)

Region and economy	1960 Urban	1960 Rural	1970 Urban	1970 Rural	Recently Urban	Recently Rural
Middle-income Asia						
Hong Kong	350.0[a]	530.0[a]	240.0	300.0	250.0	340.0
Korea						
Malaysia			80.0[b]	5,600.0[b]	110.0[b]	980.0[b]
Philippines						
Singapore			220.0	8,500.0	250.0	3,390.0
Taiwan						
Thailand			280.0	1,380.0	290.0	1,140.0
Latin America and the Caribbean						
Argentina			140.0			
Barbados			70.0	110.0[c]	90.0	170.0[c]
Bolivia			200.0	2,400.0		
Brazil						
Chile			220.0	1,160.0	240.0	590.0
Colombia					320.0	9,670.0
Costa Rica			100.0	4,440.0	40.0	
Dominican Republic			150.0	2,680.0	220.0	3,580.0
Ecuador			190.0	4,740.0		
El Salvador			230.0		250.0	
Guatemala						
Guyana	60.0	1,834.0	70.0	1,401.0	70.0	1,300.0
Haiti					290.0	5,270.0
Honduras			150.0	11,810.0		
Jamaica						
Mexico			780.0	1,310.0		
Nicaragua			220.0	2,310.0	220.0	
Panama			170.0	1,530.0	149.0	1,240.0
Paraguay			240.0	5,830.0		
Peru			410.0	3,450.0	340.0	1,300.0
Surinam					100.0	860.0
Trinidad and Tobago	90.0		60.0		60.0	
Uruguay						
Venezuela			280.0	650.0	300.0	770.0

Note: Unless otherwise noted, "1960" refers to any year between 1959 and 1961; "1970" to any year between 1969 and 1971; and "recently" to any year between 1973 and 1977. Blank cells indicate unavailable data.

Source: World Bank estimates as of September 1978.

a. 1962.

b. West Malaysia.

c. Government hospitals only.

Table 1-16. Comparison of Educational Efficiency in Urban and Rural Areas of Latin America: Successful Completion of Primary Education

Country	Percentage of entrants completing primary schooling			Years taken to produce a primary school graduate				Input:output ratio		
	Total	Urban	Rural	Ideal	Total	Urban	Rural	Total	Urban	Rural
Colombia	27.3	47.3	3.7	5	11	8	66	2.4	1.7	13.2
Dominican Republic	30.4	48.1	13.9	6	14	9	27	2.3	1.6	4.5
Guatemala	25.4	49.6	3.5	6	14	10	70	2.3	1.6	11.6
Panama	62.3	80.7	45.3	6	9	8	12	1.5	1.2	1.9
Average percentage of entrants completing	39	51	22							

Source: World Bank (1974).

Table 1-17. *Availability of Complete Primary Schools in Urban and Rural Areas*

Parameter	Number of countries	Complete schools (percentage of total)	
		Urban	Rural
Countries by per capita GNP (U.S. dollars)			
I—Up to $120			
(excluding India)	9	53	36
India		57	49
II—$121–250	7	72	32
III—$251–750	16	77	62
IV—$751–1,500	2	89	56
V—Over $1,500	6	100	99
By major regions			
Africa	16	79	54
Asia (excluding India)	9	94	66
India		57	49
South and Central America	10	88	34
Europe	5	98	99

Note: Table shows percentages of the total number of primary schools in each category (rural and urban) that offer the complete number of grades.
Source: World Bank (1974).

on average are better educated than rural dwellers—in part because of better educational services in urban areas (tables 1-16, 1-17, and 1-18) and in part because of selective migration of the better educated young people from rural to urban areas (Findley 1977). As in the case of health care, however, there is reason to believe that access to and use of educational services by school-age children is lower in the low-income areas of cities in developing countries than it is in the higher-income areas. The limited evidence available on this point is presented in chapter 6.[16]

Diagnosis of Urban Problems and Policy Approaches

Problems of urban development differ across geographic and municipal entities. Some common elements may nevertheless be found in attempting to provide a diagnosis of the evident difficulties that occur as cities grow rapidly throughout the developing world. In attempting such a diagnosis of what constitutes the "urban problem" in developing countries, it is important first to define the objectives according to which the prevailing urban trends will be evaluated.

Table 1-18. *Primary School Enrollment by Income Group*
(percent)

Country	Boys (age 5–9)		Girls (age 5–9)	
	Poorest households	Richest households	Poorest households	Richest households
Sri Lanka (1969–70)	70.3	89.8	65.8	81.9
Nepal (1973–74)				
11 towns	29.5	77.8	15.3	71.2
India (Gujarat state, 1972–73)				
Rural	22.7	53.9	8.6	50.9
Urban	42.1	77.7	30.8	69.5
India (Maharashira state, 1972–73)				
Rural	24.6	54.6	16.6	52.9
Urban	40.4	86.3	42.1	87.0

	Both sexes (age 6–11)	
Colombia (1974)		
Large cities	69.6	94.6
All urban	62.0	89.5
Rural	51.2	60.0

Note: Enrollments are expressed as a percentage of the number in the age group. Poorest and richest refer (in the case of India, Nepal, and Sri Lanka) to the bottom and top 10 percent of households ranked by expenditure per person, and (in the case of Colombia) to the bottom and top 20 percent of households ranked by income per person.

Source: World Bank (1974).

One common objective found among those in charge of designing urban policies in developing countries is the goal to make cities serve more effectively the preferences of the better-off sections of the urban population. This elite may tend to view the growth of slums as an infringement on the beauty of their city; to regard street vendors, pedestrians, and overcrowded buses as a nuisance impeding the mobility of private automobiles; and to perceive educational and health care needs as unmet requirements of more advanced facilities for higher education and curative (in contrast to preventive) medicine. The policy prescriptions that may flow from this diagnosis of the problem include the following: the "beautification" of cities through slum removal;[17] construction of high-cost public housing projects; the banning of street vendors from commercial districts; the construction of limited-access highways and high-cost rapid transit facilities (especially subways), often accompanied by a banning of slower, traditional transport—but not of private cars—from major, congested streets; and the expansion of subsidized univer-sities and modern city hospitals. Although this picture may seem a caricature, it is not far from the results of conventional urban policy in many cities of developing countries.[18]

An alternative set of objectives calls for an increase in the overall efficiency of urban growth and for the alleviation of the poverty affecting substantial portions of the population in the cities of the developing world. With these objectives in mind, one would begin by analyzing the urbanization process as the interaction between forces of demand for and supply of goods and services in cities (in particular transport, housing, and public services) and labor, capital, and land. The diagnosis of the urban problem would then include, for instance, the observation that the demand for unskilled labor is not expanding quickly enough to provide employment at rising wages to a rapidly increasing labor force, whereas the demands for land, capital, trans-port, housing, and public services are expanding more rapidly than their supplies (creating increased prices or shortages for factors of production and services). Policy analysis would therefore focus on the question of how the demand for labor, and in particular for unskilled labor, can be increased relative to the growth in labor supply, and of how the demands for scarce urban land, housing, and services can be contained efficiently and equitably while at the same time an attempt is made to expand supplies more rapidly (especially for the urban poor, who are most disadvantaged in their access to available supplies of urban amenities.)

The policy instruments used in implementing this second strategy would include trade, fiscal, and capital market policies designed to augment the demand for unskilled urban labor, the elimination of impediments to the functioning of the urban labor market, and a concurrent attempt to curb the growth in the urban labor supply through family planning programs and policies to accelerate rural development. These instruments would also in-clude the elimination of subsidies for urban public services. Such subsidies tend to lead to excessive demands for urban road space by automobile users, for high-cost public housing and infrastructure, and for higher education and modern curative health care. At the same time, the emphasis of public involvement in supplying transport, housing, and services would have to shift to areas such as low-cost urban infrastructure and basic education and health programs in which private supply responses are least able to meet the increases in demands associated with rapid urban growth. Moreover, the existing array of public regulations, controls, and tax instruments, which frequently inhibit private and public supply responses, would have to be amended to minimize interference.

A Conceptual Framework for Urban Policy Analysis

Figure 1 demonstrates how concerns for efficiency and poverty may overlap or conflict with each other. Assume that the two demand curves, D_p for poor consumers and D_r for rich consumers, show each group's willingness to pay

Figure 1. *Relation of Public Service Provision, Fiscal Dividend, Externalities, and Subsidies in the Urban Setting*

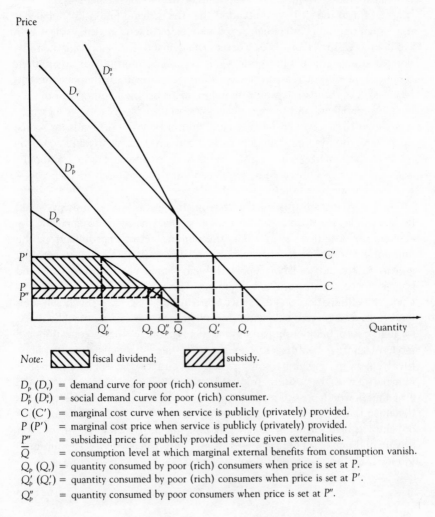

Note: ▨ fiscal dividend; ▨ subsidy.

D_p (D_r) = demand curve for poor (rich) consumer.
D_p^s (D_r^s) = social demand curve for poor (rich) consumer.
C (C') = marginal cost curve when service is publicly (privately) provided.
P (P') = marginal cost price when service is publicly (privately) provided.
P'' = subsidized price for publicly provided service given externalities.
$\overline{Q}$ = consumption level at which marginal external benefits from consumption vanish.
Q_p (Q_r) = quantity consumed by poor (rich) consumers when price is set at P.
Q_p' (Q_r') = quantity consumed by poor (rich) consumers when price is set at P'.
Q_p'' = quantity consumed by poor consumers when price is set at P''.

for a particular urban good or service and thus reflect the marginal private benefits received by each group.[19] Furthermore, assume that in addition to private benefits, there are external benefits associated with the consumption of the good or service. These external benefits can consist of increases in productivity, consumption benefits, or cost savings for other individuals (or firms) because of reduced public health hazards, increased education of the population, or the like. Such externalities can also be of the "basic needs" variety; that is, they can reflect the satisfaction that some individuals, especially among the higher-income classes, may derive from seeing the fundamental requirements of poor consumers met.[20] These external benefits are added to private benefits, creating two social demand curves D_p^s and D_r^s that reflect, respectively, the sum of marginal private and external benefits of consumption of the service under consideration by the poor and by the rich. Note that marginal external benefits are assumed to decline with increases in consumption and to vanish for consumption in excess of $\overline{Q}$. This assumption is made because many external benefits, such as those derived from improved general health and education levels, can probably be met by providing services at certain basic levels of quality and quantity. The same is true, of course, for basic needs externalities.

Next, consider the two horizontal curves labeled C and C'. These reflect the marginal costs of service provision, with C the cost curve for the service when it is publicly provided and C' the cost curve when the service is privately supplied.[21] The difference in costs for public and private provision of services may derive from economies of scale associated with the public sector's ability to build large production and distribution networks (especially in the case of public utilities) or from the elimination of monopoly rents that might be charged where the service is provided by private sector suppliers.

If it is then assumed that the government wishes to ensure efficient resource use by marginal cost pricing, the government would, in the absence of external benefits, charge a price $P = C$ to all consumers.[22] Despite the fact that marginal costs are covered by the price charged, consumers derive a benefit from public as compared with private service provision, which for each consumer is equal to the area bounded by the vertical axis, by the two cost curves C and C', and by his private demand curve (for the poor consumer, the upper shaded area in figure 1). This benefit has been termed "fiscal dividend" by some public finance economists (McLure 1975). If one then also allows for the existence of externalities, efficient pricing requires that the price to poor consumers be lowered to P'', which would ensure a consumption level of Q_p'' at which marginal social benefit D_p^s equals marginal social cost C. This means that the poor consumer, in addition to his fiscal dividend, also reaps the benefit of a subsidy (the lower shaded area in figure 1). No subsidy, however, should be paid to the rich consumer as long as the rich consumer's private demand curve D_r intersects with the public cost curve

C to the right of $\overline{Q}$, even though external benefits are derived from his inframarginal consumption. A subsidy to the poor consumer might also be justified on general equity grounds; that is, in the interest of income redistribution. For instance, P'' might be charged to the poor consumer even in the absence of external benefits. In this case, however, there is a loss in efficiency that is reflected by the difference between the total subsidy paid (the lower shaded area in figure 1) and the increase in consumer benefits (the area bounded by the vertical axis P, P'', and D_p). There is also a loss in government resources equal to the amount of the subsidy.

The primary concerns of subsequent chapters can now be succinctly described in relation to the framework of figure 1. Chapter 2 discusses ways to raise the disposable incomes of the poor through increased employment and productivity. In other words, it addresses the question of how the demand curve D_p can be shifted to the right through increased incomes, thus increasing the welfare of the urban poor. Another way of achieving the same goal is to reduce taxes paid by the poor or to make income transfers to them through the fiscal system. The scope for this approach to poverty alleviation is discussed in chapter 3. The remaining chapters deal with investment, pricing, and regulatory policies for specific urban goods and services, in particular, transport (chapter 4), housing (chapter 5), and social services (chapter 6). Each of these three chapters examines basically the same set of questions.

First, how can public investment policy be designed to reduce costs to the poor consumer, and how can the benefits of the greatest possible "fiscal dividend" derived from public intervention be shared among as many of the poor as possible? These benefits do not need to be the result of subsidies and are not necessarily associated with losses in efficiency. On the contrary, efficiency is increased when public intervention lowers costs by eliminating monopoly rents or by reaping economies of scale. The existence of such a fiscal dividend is, however, not always ensured by public intervention. The following chapters will cite examples where the private sector appears to be more efficient in providing services—as in the case of bus service, housing construction, and even garbage disposal—as long as it is not inhibited by public interference.

The realization of fiscal dividends for the poor requires a conscious attempt to reduce service costs and standards; substantial capital outlays in service provision, particularly where investments are lumpy, as is the case with many urban services; and the redirection of public investment expenditures and their fiscal dividends from the rich to the poor. Examples cited below include investment in primary education rather than in university training, and in low-cost rather than high-standard water and sewerage systems; road investments supporting pedestrian, bicycle, and bus traffic rather than those directed mainly toward private automobile traffic; investments in slum improvement programs rather than in public housing benefiting high- and middle-income groups. There is, however, a question concerning the extent to which the fiscal dividend generated by such investments for the poor actually stays with the poor. If investments are site or location specific, they may in part lead to land price and rent increases; thus, in the case of rental tenure of the poor, some of the fiscal dividend may be passed on to the landowners. Yet additions to the stock of serviced land will also lower the land value and rents on existing properties, so that some of the benefits are passed on to other renters. These questions are discussed further in the chapters that follow.

Efforts to increase the overall availability of public resources through improved public pricing and taxation are also required. This raises the possibility of a conflict between rich and poor beneficiaries of public programs, but this conflict is minimized to the extent that public investments for the poor can also be justified on grounds of externalities, including the basic needs externalities enjoyed by the wealthier segments of the population.

Second, how can service prices be designed to increase the efficiency of resources by preventing excessive demand for public services; to increase the revenues available for maintaining and expanding urban services to the poor; and to raise the incomes of the poor by selective subsidies, which may be justified on grounds of either economic or basic needs externalities? These three goals may at times involve tradeoffs, particularly where subsidies for general poverty alleviation are concerned, since they are likely to conflict with the goals of efficiency and revenue.

Third, how can governmental regulations and controls be designed not to raise unnecessarily the cost of public or private urban service provision but to preserve any beneficial effects, such as controlling negative externalities of private actions, they may have? An important issue in analyzing controls and regulations is to ascertain for whom they eliminate negative externalities and for whom they raise the cost of service provision. In many cases, regulations and controls serve to eliminate negative externalities perceived by the rich and lead to cost increases at the expense of the poor.

The preceding paragraphs suggest that there are cases in which the efficiency of resource allocation in cities can be improved while at the same time urban poverty is alleviated. The analysis in the subsequent chapters tends to support this claim, but this does not imply the absence of tradeoffs or conflicts. At a minimum there remains the tradeoff between alleviating poverty and increasing efficiency on the one hand, and continued subsidy of publicly supplied, high-cost urban amenities for the better-off on the other. For example, removing obstacles that impede the operations of small-scale enterprises, street vendors, and the like is likely to reduce the sales by large firms and established retail stores. Similarly, removal of subsidies to private automobiles using congested city streets can improve the efficiency of the urban transport system and the quality of public transport for lower-income groups, but it also reduces the welfare enjoyed by those who have to substitute public transport for the private automobile. Along the same lines, elimination of subsidies for higher education, modern curative medical care, and high-cost housing, in favor of investments in basic education and health care and in low-cost urban infrastructure, will improve efficiency and help to alleviate poverty but may also reduce the welfare of the better-off.

Although this tradeoff between benefits for the rich and for the poor does not pose problems on ethical grounds to those concerned with improving the lot of the poor, the practical problems of implementing policies oriented toward efficiency and poverty alleviation should not be underestimated if these policies reduce benefits currently enjoyed by the economic elite, whose members often are also the political elite. To overcome the objections of these elites and to enlist their support, an appeal to altruistic sentiments—the political basis for a basic needs strategy—is needed. An alternative is to impress upon the elite groups that in the long term a high degree of urban inefficiency coupled with extensive poverty will undermine their ability to continue leading the good life, either because of revolutionary upheavals or because the inefficiencies will become so pervasive as to stifle economic opportunities for everyone.

The remainder of this study will not have much to say about how this message can be imparted to those in control, although at various points steps that can be taken to reduce the adjustment costs for the established interest groups will be suggested. Instead, it will be assumed that the underlying political and economic forces favoring increased urban efficiency and poverty alleviation will be strong enough to support policies that work in this direction. Although this assumption may border on political naivete, it is necessary if policy prescriptions that are of broad applicability are to be made for cities in the developing world. In support of this approach, one might also add that urban policy in developing countries seems to be becoming more progressive; that is, it increasingly seeks to improve efficiency and alleviate poverty, if the evidence collected in this volume is to be trusted.

Notes to Chapter 1

1. Based on unpublished city population estimates and projections of the United Nations Population Division. See also Hauser and Gardner (1980).

2. In 1976, thirty-five of ninety-two developing countries had less than 5 million inhabitants and fifty-four had less than 10 million inhabitants ("World Development Indicators, 1978," table 1, annex to World Bank 1978b).

3. Renaud (1981) addresses the question of whether it is desirable and feasible to slow down the pace of urbanization and spatial concentration of population and economic activity in developing countries. See also World Bank (1979), chapter 6, and Hauser and Gardner (1980).

4. The question of rural-urban linkage is discussed in other studies—for example, in Renaud (1981).

5. These issues are dealt with in Keesing (1979), Renaud (1981), and Squire (1981) in relation to trade policies, national spatial policies, and national employment policies, respectively.

6. See Bahl and Linn (forthcoming) for an extensive treatment of these issues.

7. As Thomas (1978) has demonstrated, however, care must be taken in making such income comparisons because price levels may be substantially higher in urban than in rural areas.

8. Findley (1977, p. 23). In support of this observation, Findley cites a study of migrants in six cities in developing countries; in all but one city (Seoul), at least two-thirds of the migrants were satisfied relative to the former life of themselves and their children and were unwilling to return to their places of origin.

9. Population growth data are not discussed in this paper; see Renaud (1981) and Hauser and Gardner (1980) for population estimates and projections.

10. For example, in Colombia the city of Cali (926,000 inhabitants) was estimated in 1972 to have only 15 percent of households with insufficient public services, whereas Barranquilla (725,000) had 70 percent. For Cucuta (220,000) the proportion was 92 percent, whereas for Manizales (202,000) it was only 36 percent (Linn 1979a).

11. In absolute terms, however, the number of rural poor in South Asia exceeds that of the urban poor by a factor of almost five, given that the population remains predominantly rural in that region (World Bank 1980d, table 1).

12. See also Follain, Lim, and Renaud (1979) for a discussion of the difficulties of cross-country comparisons of housing crowding.

13. For water supply in urban areas, this definition includes standpipes located no more than 200 meters from the house; in rural areas, the limit is a reasonable amount of time spent on fetching water, which is obviously a rather loose criterion. For excreta disposal, any household system, such as pit latrines and waterborne sewerage systems, is included.

14. As regards differences in access to services by city size, Meerman (1979), Selowsky (1979b), and Thomas (1978) have found that service access tends to increase with city size in Malaysia, Colombia, and Peru.

15. Data collected by the United Nations show a more differentiated picture for service access, which confirms in essence the data presented here, but also show that "modern" services (that is, in-house water connections and flush toilets) are particularly scarce in the low-income countries (sub-Saharan Africa and low-income Asia), even for urban households (United Nations 1976).

16. See also the figures for the percentage of school dropouts before high school in Manila and its Tondo area in table 1-13.

17. This term was actually used in Khartoum (International Labour Office 1976).

18. For documentation, the reader is referred to the World Bank's experience as reported in sector papers on urban housing, transport, education, and health (World Bank 1974, 1975a, 1975b) and to subsequent chapters in this volume.

19. For the present purposes, the possibility that private benefits exist which are not reflected in users' willingness to pay is not considered; it could, however, be easily introduced as an additional consideration.

20. For a discussion of this type of externality, see Harberger (1978).

21. For simplicity, it is assumed that C and C' are identical and constant for each consumer or consumer group.

22. There are well-known limits to the rule that marginal cost pricing leads to efficient resource allocation; for a recent summary, see Ray (1975).

2

Employment and the Urban Poor

THE MAIN CAUSE OF URBAN POVERTY is the severely limited income earned by the poor through gainful employment. Policies designed to increase the employment and wages of the urban poor must therefore be given foremost attention. Although this chapter concentrates on the scope for increasing the labor earnings of the poor, it does not attempt to present an exhaustive analysis of urban employment issues and policies. Other recent surveys permit a more comprehensive understanding of urban employment and labor market problems.[1]

The approach chosen here is quite eclectic in two respects: the focus throughout will be on the relations between urban employment and the urban labor market on the one hand and urban poverty on the other; primary attention will be given to those policy instruments that can be deployed at the level of an individual city or investment project. The effect of nationwide policies, although not entirely neglected, is not pursued in detail. As will become obvious in the ensuing discussion, this narrow view of urban poverty and local policies has two principal limitations: first, urban poverty is intricately linked with the overall national and urban economy; second, nationwide policies are likely to provide the driving force over the long term for solving the urban employment problem in the developing world. Nonetheless, the approach used here was chosen because the aspects emphasized in this chapter get easily lost in the shuffle of the typical macro-oriented studies of urban employment and labor markets.[2]

To provide a better overview of the relation between urban employment, the urban labor market, and the urban poor, the employment characteristics of the poor must first be considered. The primary determinants of urban employment—the supply and the demand for labor, the transactions costs and imperfections that affect the operations of the urban labor market—must be analyzed. Finally, the implications for policy must be reviewed.

Employment Characteristics of the Urban Poor

Although it may amount to setting up a straw man, a brief review of what may be called the conventional employment profile of the urban poor is a useful starting point for analysis. This profile draws on the popular notion that the urban labor market may conveniently be separated into a "formal" and an "informal" sector. These sectors are taken to be largely without linkage to each other and are thought to possess characteristics that, in stylized fashion, can be summarized as in table 2-1. Although not all of these characteristics are always attributed to the formal and informal sectors, respectively (and yet other characteristics may enter if more than employment is analyzed), the contrasting elements shown in table 2-1 are frequently at the heart of popular views of the urban labor market.[3] A review of recently compiled evidence on urban labor markets in developing countries, however, leads to a different and much more complex picture than the simple dichotomy between formal and informal labor markets that table 2-1 suggests.

First, *urban open unemployment is not the primary cause of the urban poverty problem.* The urban poor cannot afford to remain without some form of employment, since they do not have any alternative source of subsistence. In most countries and cities, open unemployment can be attributed to the relatively well-educated younger members of the urban middle- and higher-income groups who can rely on family support while they search for jobs that they find commensurate with their training and wage expectations.[4]

Table 2-1. *The Conventional View of the Urban Labor Market*

Formal sector	Informal sector
High and middle income	Poor and very poor
Low unemployment	High unemployment
Industry, business, government	Artisans, services, petty trade
Large-scale operations	Small-scale operations
Wage employment	Self-employment and family employment
High-skill employment	Low-skill employment
Restricted entry	Easy entry
Regulated	Unregulated
Taxed	Untaxed
Native population	Recent migrants
Productive employment	Residual (unproductive) employment
Mainstream	Marginal

Second, *the principal income earners of poor urban households are found in virtually all types of employment*: in large, medium, and small firms; in wage employment as well as in self-employment or family employment; in the government and in the private sector; and in all urban activities.[5] Table 2-2 provides an illustration of the diversity in employment patterns of the urban poor. Furthermore, the poor are not necessarily those who have most recently migrated to a city, and migrants do not tend to enter into what are considered typical informal sector activities, such as street vending, shoe-shining, and the like, in disproportionate numbers (Findley 1977, Mazumdar 1976, Peattie 1979). In fact, urban poverty appears to be associated with two principal employment and household characteristics. One kind of urban poor household is characterized by low (and often irregular) earnings of the principal income earner and by a high dependency ratio because of the large household size relative to the number of earners (Beier and others 1975; Sant'Anna, Merrick, and Mazumdar 1976). The other kind of urban poor household is represented by what may be called the "floating migrant," usually

Table 2-2. *Employment Profile of the Urban Poor: Selected Cases*
(percent)

Occupational group	Case					
	Bangkok	Chile	Caracas	Lima	Belo Horizonte	Malaysia
By status						
Employees	57	73	71	59	65	57
Self-employed	43	27	29	41	35	43
By sector						
Agriculture	29	n.a.	*	1	3	15
Manufacturing	30	n.a.	26	24	17	18
Commerce	17	n.a.	29	15	15	19
Construction	*	n.a.	10	11	11	8
Transport	3	n.a.	8	7	7	12
Government	} 8	n.a.	} 16	11	13	11
Services		n.a.		18	23	18
Domestics	5	n.a.	*	*	10	*
Others	7	n.a.	11	12	—	—

n.a. Not available.

*Sectors included within other sectors listed.

— Not applicable.

Note: Definition of poverty varies by case, but for most it corresponds to about the bottom two deciles and refers to per capita family income. Malaysia, Caracas, and Chile distributions are of household heads only; others include secondary earners.

Source: Webb (1976).

young, single males who still have close ties with their rural homes and who "float" into and out of the city in response to urban labor availability and seasonal labor surplus in the countryside. This floating migration has been observed, for instance, in the Sahelian countries of Africa (Cohen 1978) and in Bombay, India (Mazumdar 1979). In general, it is probably the first kind of household that accounts for the overwhelming proportion of the urban poor.[6]

Third, *entry to the activities carried out by the poor and to the jobs held by them is not always unrestricted, nor are these activities or jobs necessarily unregulated or untaxed by government.* Sociological research on street vending, shoeshining, sale of lottery tickets, and small-scale retailing and manufacturing has shown that entry to these activities may in fact be quite restricted, particularly where locational advantage is a major determinant of earnings (for instance, in street vending) and where government restrictions on these activities at choice locations (near churches, government buildings, central squares, and the like) limit the number of jobs that are available.[7] Moreover, government regulation or control extends quite far down the ladder in the hierarchy of employment opportunities generally available to the poor, as will be obvious to anyone who has ever studied local government ordinances relating to licensing, safety and hygienic regulations, and the like for all types of urban activities.[8] Similarly, tax payments or license fees are legally required for informal sector activities in most cities.[9] Of course, the degree of evasion of these taxes and license requirements is generally substantial,[10] but even where licenses are not obtained or taxes and fees are not paid, the risk of official sanctions often seriously interferes with the mode of operation of informal sector activities.[11] The main point to be made here is that public action may have a considerable effect on informal sector employment and activities, and this effect is usually of the negative kind: restrictions on the location for these activities or on the conditions under which they may be carried out, taxation, or the threat of enforcement of regulations and taxation, and occasional interruptions of the activities and the imposition of fines. One exception is Malaysia, where a supportive approach to informal sector trading appears to have been taken.[12]

Fourth, *the activities carried out by the poor, or the jobs held by them, are often quite closely linked to the activities of the "modern" sector.* Apart from the fact that some of the poor have low-paid jobs in the modern sector or in government, and that government regulation and taxation extends its long arm to informal sector activities such as street vending, there are important input and output linkages found in many cities of developing countries between formal and informal sector activities. Subcontracting is widespread, for instance, in Indian cities (1978 World Bank data compiled by E. Bevan Waide and Christine I. Wallich) inputs from modern sector wholesalers or markets are typically required even for street vending, small stores, and artisan and repair shops (Bromley 1977; Peattie 1979; Fapohundar, Reijmerink, and van Dijk 1975); even the outputs generated by scavengers ("pickers") on municipal garbage dumps quickly find their way into modern sector enterprises and activities (1977 World Bank data compiled by Alfredo Sfeir-Younis). Capital requirements, especially for working capital, are frequently met—at exorbitant prices—by modern sector suppliers of inputs (Bromley 1977), and basic operating equipment such as for rickshaws is often provided, again at costly prices, by well-off intermediaries (Cousins 1977).[13] Moveover, it has been observed that there may be something of a life cycle in the occupational patterns of the poor. As children or young adults they begin to contribute to household earnings through jobs in informal sector activities. With increasing age, experience, and (sometimes) education or training, they may move into formal sector employment (for example, in the construction sector); later, because of age or failing health, they return to informal sector activities (Peattie 1979, Webb 1976). The reverse pattern may also prevail because in quite a few urban cultures self-employment in small trading or artisanry is thought preferable to wage employment in formal sector enterprises (Peattie 1979).

Finally, *it is not correct to view all, or even most, of the activities carried out by the urban poor as representing "residual," "unproductive," or "superfluous" employment.* As was pointed out earlier, many poor are employed in modern sector activities, albeit at low wages and with low productivity. Moreover, although this has not been proven in any rigorous fashion, it is quite likely that at the low income levels prevalent in many developing country cities—and given the poor transport and storage systems, as well as the absence of broadly dispersed automobile ownership—there is a role to be played by the long and diversified chain of intermediaries in production and distribution.[14] Similarly, solid waste has a high value relative to people's incomes: scavenging on public waste dumps becomes an economically viable activity. Indeed, the view of informal sector activities as basically unproductive, undesirable, and unworthy of public support—if not in fact worthy of public scorn and efforts at eradication—reflects a profoundly noneconomic view of this sector. For an economist, who accepts the test of the market as a prima facie criterion for productivity, all informal sector activities that provide employment to the poor are "productive." Only the introduction of value judgments regarding the nature of the output (for example, that street vendors provide an ungainly sight to the upper-income groups) leads to the notion of informal sector activities being unproductive, superfluous, or undesirable.[15] In other words, the objectives of policymakers crucially determine their responses to the informal sector and, indeed, to practically all manifestations of urban poverty (including slum settlements and the like). If the objective is to minimize the visibility of these manifestations and of the impact of urban poverty on the middle- and higher-income classes, then, of course, informal sector activities, and in particular employment in this sector, are viewed as "unproductive," "undesirable," and as something to be repressed and eradicated wherever possible. But if the objective of public policymakers is to assist the urban poor to make the best of a bad situation—that is, to try to maximize their welfare within the constraints set by national resource availability and the limits on outright resource redistribution—then informal sector activities must be viewed as extremely important contributions worthy of public support and encouragement (see Perlman 1976).

One of the primary conclusions of the review of the employment characteristics of the urban poor is therefore *that one should not start by defining informal sector activities—such as street vending, shoeshining, scavenging, artisanry, and street-corner repair work—as negative phenomena.* Indeed, unless strong economic or social arguments exist to the contrary, these activities ought to be recognized as valuable, interfered with as little as possible, and supported where resources permit, so that they may operate on an equal footing with their formal sector competitors.[16] Of course, this potential competition is part of the reason certain informal sector activities are restricted or suppressed (especially in the prime urban locations). Given the resistance of entrenched interest, it may not be easy to introduce the positive and supportive view of the informal sector that is called for, especially if local government action is required to do so.[17] For this reason it may be desirable to address the issue through national legislation. Such a course may also be important in achieving uniformity across cities, thus avoiding local governments' adoption of a "beggar-thy-neighbor" policy in this area by which they try to attract the "elite" activities from other cities by providing an environment substantially free from the "nuisance" of competition of informal sector activities.

Another implication of the employment profile of the urban poor as summarized above is that *the urban poor are a very heterogeneous group as regards their employment characteristics.* In this respect they are quite different from the typical rural poor, who are found among the landless laborers and the small-scale farmers and who usually form rather homogeneous groups across relatively easily identifiable geographic areas. The rural poor therefore represent a fairly identifiable target group whose income-earning capacity may be increased through uniformly applied measures such as land reform, improved agronomic technologies, better farm prices, extension services, input or marketing cooperatives, and the like. Although none of these measures is easy to implement for reasons that need not be spelled out here, the fact remains that it is much more difficult to identify the urban poor as a target group when trying to improve their income-earning capacity through measures such as input or marketing cooperatives, extension services, and support of small-scale enterprises. The kinds of activities of the urban poor vary widely, the technologies involved are diverse, and the same kinds of activities are carried out both by the wealthy and the poor segments of the urban population. As a result, it becomes very difficult to identify one or a few urban poverty target groups along the dimensions of employment or economic activity and to provide effective assistance, even where such target groups have been identified (Webb 1976). This is not to imply that city- or project-specific, target-group-oriented measures should be abandoned if on balance there is reason to believe that such measures increase the demand for certain labor categories and activities carried out by the urban poor, that they improve the quality of the labor which the poor supply (and thus increase the poor's productivity and wages), or that they reduce transactions costs and market imperfections which reduce the employment or real wage of the poor. Rather, the point is that, in general, the "leakage" from these measures, defined as positive effects on wealthier groups and possibly negative effects on other poor groups (who may be competing with the benefiting labor or activity category), may be significant. This makes general measures designed to increase the demand for labor, to raise the productivity of labor, or to reduce labor market imperfections through appropriate macroeconomic policies more attractive, since it may well be that these policies are as effective—in the number of beneficiaries and in the amount of administrative costs incurred—in reaching the poor as are the so-called target-group-oriented programs.[18]

One argument that is at times leveled against macroeconomic policies to increase urban employment is that they fail to "trickle down" to informal sector activities, and thus to the poor. Apart from the fact that the poor are not exclusively employed in the informal sector, it was argued above that *there is considerable linkage between the activities usually identified with each of these two sectors.* Although the exact extent of job creation may be subject to argument,[19] there is reason to be fairly optimistic on this score, especially if the transactions costs and market imperfections affecting the creation of informal sector jobs are reduced to a minimum.[20]

Urban Employment and Labor Markets

Any partial approach to the analysis of employment and labor market problems is fraught with pitfalls, because of the important linkage that exists between different employment and skill categories, between different labor market segments (within cities as well as between cities and rural areas), and between different determinants of labor supply and demand. Although a general equilibrium analysis of labor market interactions may be required to permit a conclusive evaluation of the effects of alternative policy instruments designed to improve the employment prospects of the urban poor, this section does not develop such a general equilibrium approach.[21] Its purpose is to survey briefly the major determinants of urban labor supply and demand and to discuss some of the transactions costs and imperfections often marring the workings of the urban labor markets in developing countries. Wherever possible, important linkages and indirect effects of policies will be highlighted.

Over the long term—and there can be little doubt that most employment policies will need considerable time before becoming effective—the goal of employment and labor market policies must be to increase (shift) the demand for urban labor more rapidly than the increase in the labor supply taking place simultaneously at all skill levels, but particularly at the lower end of the skill distribution. At the same time it is important to reduce transactions costs, which cut into the real wage earned by labor, and also to reduce market imperfections that hinder the mobility of labor—in particular, the upward mobility of those employed in occupations with low productivity and wages.

Urban Labor Supply

The size and distribution of a city's labor supply are determined by a number of well-known factors that will be only briefly summarized: the natural population growth in the city, the net migration to (or from) the city, the participation rate of the labor force, and the human capital embodied in the labor force (that is, the availability of skills and the health of the labor force, both of which affect the quality of the urban labor supply).

NATURAL POPULATION GROWTH. The first determinant of urban labor supply is the city's natural population growth, which in turn is determined by the city's fertility and death rates. Improved health and nutrition would tend to reduce the death rate, whereas greater efforts at family planning—as well as the effects of rising incomes and higher levels of education—might induce secular declines in the urban fertility rate. There is some reason to believe that the declines in fertility on balance outweigh the decline in the death rate, particularly in urban areas, and thus lead to a gradual decline in the natural growth rate of most cities in developing countries.[22] Because somewhere between 40 to 60 percent of the population growth in cities of developing countries is due to natural growth rather than to immigration (Findley 1977), national and urban governments should pay at least as much attention to policies that can help control the natural population increase in urban areas as they pay to policies that deal with the problem of rural-urban migration. This is of particular relevance in Latin America, where the average percentage of urban population growth accounted for by natural population growth is expected to reach some 75 percent in the period 1980–90 (Findley 1977). Measures directed toward reducing fertility, in particular, "education, extension, and service provision for family planning become increasingly feasible within the confines of urban areas. Many of the inhibiting forces such as religions and social traditions are weakened. Economic sanctions are reversed; an additional child can be a clear economic liability in the city and a long-term asset to the social security system in rural areas" (Beier and others 1975, p. 46). These considerations imply that it may be easier to reduce fertility in urban than in rural areas, provided that serious efforts are made at introducing family planning policies. This is an area in which the role played by city-level authorities can be very important and the scope for project-specific action is considerable, but these opportunities have often been neglected in national family planning programs.[23]

MIGRATION. Migration is the other important determinant of urban population growth, and thus of the growth in the urban labor force. The usual focus is on the net migration from rural to urban areas, but also of importance are the urban-to-urban migration flows that take place in many developing countries. The latter phenomenon is particularly important from the perspective of the smaller towns and intermediate-size cities that may be facing a net migration outflow.[24] The evidence on migration determinants is well documented and need not be reviewed in detail here (see Findley 1977, Squire 1981). Suffice it to say that migrants tend to respond mainly to perceived differences in economic opportunities between their original location and their final destination. In particular, the superior availability of jobs and the expectation of better education facilities for children are major reasons for migration to the cities. Migrants are relatively young and tend to be well educated and highly motivated relative to the population at the point of origin.[25] Cities that receive migrants thus are not, on balance, burdened with a flood of uneducated, unskilled, and unmotivated individuals and households, although there is little doubt that rural-urban migration tends to keep urban wages (particularly among the skill groups to which migrants belong) below levels that would prevail in the absence of migration. The selectivity of migration in terms of education, skill, and motivation—an effect that has been diagnosed as creating problems in the rural areas—has similar, and possibly more far-reaching, effects on the stagnating smaller and intermediate-size cities, where the most mobile individuals and households tend to be from the well-educated and highly skilled groups. Their departure for the large and dynamic cities may prevent the building up of a diversified labor supply, the lack of which keeps away private investors and retards improvements in the quality of local management and public administration, generally weak in smaller towns.

Two main points may be derived from this discussion of migration. First, migration is one of the aspects of urban labor markets in which the interaction between labor demand and supply is most pervasive. Increases (or declines) in urban labor demand will affect migration, and thus the labor supply in the aggregate and in its composition. Whether migration responses are "excessive"—that is, whether more migrants move into the city than is warranted by the availability of employment, thus increasing urban under- or unemployment—is an issue that cannot be resolved here.[26] Second, if migration is to be slowed down, the problem needs to be addressed through nationwide policies geared to change, to the extent possible, the size and composition of migration flows (see Renaud 1979 and Preston 1979 for discussions of such policies). There is little that can or should be done at the level of the individual city to affect or control migration flows. Indeed, such commonly found measures as restrictions on informal sector activities and employment, the bulldozing of slums or squatter settlements, the forceful relocation of slum dwellers to peripheral rural areas, the withholding of urban infrastructure or social services (when these could be provided within the resource constraints of the low-income beneficiaries and the local authorities) have all been shown not to affect migration flows significantly. They do, however, seriously impede the efficiency of large segments of the urban factor and goods markets, destroying valuable capital stock, and wreak havoc with the lives and welfare of the majority of the urban population affected by those policies (Yap 1975, Findley 1977).

By implication, one may also conclude that a constructive approach to the absorption of the growing urban population at the individual city level— for instance, by encouraging rather than hampering informal sector activities and employment and by improving instead of destroying slums—will not by itself stimulate migration to any great extent. In fact, other measures designed to increase the efficiency of the urban economy, in particular the pricing of public services at marginal social cost (including not only public utilities, but also the use of scarce urban road space), may have much more important, albeit indirect effects on migration. By reducing the effective subsidies which private investors can reap by investing in the large cities, one may lead them to consider investment locations elsewhere and thus to contribute to an increased availability of jobs outside the large cities.[27] The scope for increased efficiency in the provision and use of urban public services will be extensively studied in the following chapters. The main point to be made here is that the effect on migration of local actions is likely to be minimal and therefore should not determine the policies pursued.

PARTICIPATION RATE OF THE LABOR FORCE. The participation rate of the labor force determines what proportion of the working-age population actually offers its services in the labor market. This variable is again crucially linked to the labor demand side because some of the important determinants of the labor force participation rate, such as the opportunities for employment and the level of wages offered, are economic.[28] More important in the present context are two further considerations. First, public action at the city level may be important in raising the transactions costs associated with finding and keeping employment. Lowering or raising these transactions costs may have important effects on whether certain potential labor groups enter or drop out of the labor market. Studies of urban labor markets have indicated that the labor force participation rate of secondary income earners, and especially of women, is quite sensitive to transport costs, licensing require- ments, and the like.[29] Second, the poor households are particularly in need of secondary employment opportunities and at the same time are especially sensitive to transactions costs, given that the margin between the (low) money wage they earn and the opportunity cost of staying at home is generally extremely slim and can easily be outweighed by transport costs, licensing requirements, risks associated with illegal (that is, unlicensed) work, and so on. City- or project-specific actions to reduce transactions costs—for ex- ample, appropriate land use planning, a rational transport policy, and sensible (that is, minimal) licensing requirements—may especially affect the labor participation rate of poor income earners and thus increase their family incomes.

HUMAN CAPITAL. The final determinants of the labor supply considered here cover factors that are usually referred to as human capital. These include the education and skill level of the population, as well as its health and nutritional status, and largely determine the composition and quality of the labor supply. The basic difficulty with these factors is that, although they are important for national and urban policy intervention, our understanding of their implications is still extremely limited. This is not for lack of research or information on many aspects of human capital formation, but rather because of the extremely complex set of interrelations at work.[30] In particular, we have only little firm knowledge on the relation between investments in education, health, and nutrition on the one hand and labor productivity and employment on the other. Much of the quantitative data available suffer from the fact that results were derived from partial equilibrium analyses, which do not allow for the complexities of the general equilibrium framework in which the policies operate. The available data must therefore be interpreted with caution.

Education and training affect the skill level and the expectations of the labor force, increase productivity in occupations commensurate with workers' acquired skill levels, and influence the reservation wage of job seekers at- tempting to locate jobs commensurate with their expectations. The last effect may indeed become a problem where education of a certain type (usually higher education)[31] has created a surplus of a particular type of labor, and therefore open unemployment, because the individuals concerned are willing (and able) to remain unemployed in the hope of getting a high-prestige and well-paying job rather than to move down the employment ladder to a lower-paying job with less prestige.[32] As was mentioned before, this is not a problem generally affecting the poor or very poor, although in some cases poverty is associated with open unemployment of one or more members of a household.

More typical is the case where the upward mobility of the low-income groups is limited by their lack of the skills, training, and education that would permit them to find jobs with higher productivity wages. Indeed, many of the studies on urban wage determination have found that much, if not most, of the wage differentials in the urban labor market may be explained by basic human capital variables (see Mazumdar 1979; Mazumdar and Ahmed 1978; Sant'Anna, Merrick, and Mazumdar 1976). This supports the hypothesis that there are substantial private (and presumably social) returns to education and training.[33]

The extent to which education—broadly defined to include all types of formal and nonformal education and training—can contribute to solving the problem of urban poverty differs from country to country, as does the kind of educational programs or efforts required. For example, in Latin America literacy is at such a high level, particularly in urban areas, that continued heavy investments in primary education are probably not of high priority. Instead, a combination of expanded and improved secondary education and of improved and flexible educational facilities for out-of-school children and adolescents should be emphasized. In contrast, for many other developing countries where illiteracy is still of major proportions, the expansion of primary school education is crucial, albeit in combination with other schemes to reach the urban poor, particularly the adolescents. The main point about educational policy is that in each country one needs to identify those skill classes to which a given amount of investment in education will contribute most in releasing bottlenecks, and in moving large numbers of low-skilled individuals to higher-skill jobs, without generating unemployment or reducing wages at the higher skill levels to the extent that additional education is no longer worthwhile. This is, of course, a very difficult task, and the only generalization for overall education policy that may be feasible at this point is that in many if not most countries a move toward increased emphasis on improvements in the skills, education, and training of the poor is likely to be a move in the right direction, given the heavy emphasis in the past on educational programs primarily benefiting the rich.

More will be said about education in chapter 6. It is enough to conclude the discussion here with the comment that urban authorities may have considerable scope in shaping educational programs so that they are—or are

not—of benefit to the poor.[34] Although basic educational policies, investment strategies, curricula, and financing mechanisms are controlled by the
national (or state) government, urban authorities often have considerable
latitude in deciding on such issues as the location, staffing, and in some cases
even the program and curriculum design of educational facilities within the
urban area, particularly if innovative experiments are being conducted at the
city level.

The effect of educational policies on the quality and composition of the
urban labor supply is, of course, a matter of long-term development. The
same holds true for health and nutrition programs, especially when these are
designed to reach pregnant or lactating women and young children. It is well
established that improved health and nutrition help increase the productivity
of the labor force by reducing absenteeism and stimulating effort and motivation while on the job (see World Bank 1975a).[35] The main uncertainty
relates to the extent of the increases in productivity; the extent to which
increases in productivity are actually translated into income increases where
unemployment and underemployment are prevalent; and the appropriate
measures to achieve improvements in health and nutrition levels. These
problems cannot be explored in great detail here, but two points should be
made. First, ill health and poor nutrition are problems that affect primarily
the poor in developing countries and reduce their welfare—not only their
incomes but also the general quality of life. Thus, one may be satisfied with
a "rough and ready" calculus of the productivity gains that are a result of
improved health and nutrition levels, as long as one can be sure that a
country's or city's health and nutrition programs actually reach the poor. The
focus, as with most "basic needs" public policies, must thus be on program
design and implementation (see chapter 6) so that the primary goal, in this
case improved health and nutrition of the poor, is achieved. If one can be
reasonably certain on this count, then one can also be quite confident of the
desired effects on employment and productivity. The second point to be made
here is that, as in the case of education, although basic health and nutrition
policies are set at the national level and are executed often through national
agencies, local authorities in many cities play a major role in these areas
either as providers of services in their own right or as executing agents of
the national (state) government.[36] There may thus be considerable scope for
improvement even within a particular city and project.

Urban Labor Demand

The basic question to be answered in this section is how the urban labor
supply can be absorbed with increased labor earnings so as to increase the
incomes especially of the poor, who have to rely virtually exclusively on

labor earnings derived from low-productivity occupations. Increasing the demand for labor is of particular importance where under- or unemployment among the lowest skill levels is a prevalent phenomenon and where the scope for measures designed to raise the productivity of the urban poor (especially through improved education, health, and nutrition) is limited by the absence of an effective demand for the services of the improved labor supply. Of course, demand- and supply-oriented policies must go hand in hand, since the urban employment problem is rarely one restricted to either demand or supply limitations. Usually, bottlenecks in the availability of specific labor skill categories coexist with relative abundance of labor supply in other categories. The special and difficult task of employment policy in developing countries is to identify these distinct categories correctly and to design policy measures that will provide for supply and demand adjustments that are appropriate for, and limited to, each of these labor skill categories. The heterogeneity of the urban labor market, as compared with the rural labor market, which was previously commented on, significantly complicates this task. Furthermore, demand and supply conditions vary across countries, over time, and even within countries across regions and cities. This point has already been emphasized for the supply side in the context of the discussion of education policies, but it also applies to the demand side. For example, it may well be the case that in the largest cities of developing countries there is a relative oversupply of skilled and highly educated individuals, while in the intermediate and smaller towns and in the rural areas there is a dearth of highly skilled labor and management relative to the potential demand. In all but a few cases, however, it is probably true that increased demand for low- and unskilled urban labor would tend to improve the incomes of the poor by increasing the extent of their employment as well as by raising their wages. Since unskilled labor is a factor of production in abundant supply in developing countries, policies designed to increase the demand for it should have a high priority, on grounds not only of equity and poverty alleviation but also of efficient resource allocation.

The remainder of this section discusses various determinants of urban labor demand: the overall growth of the economy, the growth of industrial and service activities, the choice of technology, and the growth and management of particular urban areas.

OVERALL GROWTH OF THE ECONOMY. The overall growth of the economy is a powerful determinant of labor demand: a high growth rate will lead to more rapid labor absorption throughout the economy in urban and rural areas alike (Squire 1981). Furthermore, any structural adjustments to improve the composition of labor supply and to reduce the inefficiencies generated by market failures in the labor market as well as in the goods and other factor markets are made easier when the economy grows rapidly, since the resistance by groups with entrenched interests in the status quo (for example, in the form of restricted entry, government regulations, and the like) is likely to be less difficult to overcome when total employment grows rapidly. Conversely, when an economy stagnates, labor absorption is a much more pressing problem, and structural adjustments become much more difficult to implement. Korea and Brazil are good examples for the growth economies, where the labor absorption problem, although not entirely absent, has been a relatively minor problem and where structural adjustments have been undertaken at least to some extent.[37] At the other end of the spectrum are, for instance, the countries of the Sahelian region in Africa, where—because of the dismal economic growth prospects (which are mainly explained by the extreme ecological difficulties encountered in recent years in the agricultural sector and by the absence of a strong and dynamic industrial base)—the labor absorption process in the rural and in the urban areas is likely to be very constrained (Cohen 1978). Policies geared to improve the economic growth of a country are therefore important elements of an employment strategy, whether the concern is with rural or urban employment.

Macroeconomic policies, however, are clearly not enough to solve the general employment problem of developing countries, nor specifically the problems encountered in the absorption of urban labor supply. Furthermore, although economic growth is to some extent a matter of general macroeconomic policies, there can be no question that the structure of the economy, especially as regards the elements of labor demand and supply and the efficiency of the labor markets, plays a significant role in determining the economic growth performance of a country, particularly in the long term. The composition of the labor supply and its determinants were discussed above. The composition of labor demand and the efficiency of the labor market will be discussed in the remainder of this section.

THE GROWTH OF INDUSTRIAL, SERVICE, AND GOVERNMENT ACTIVITIES. The demand for urban labor is generated by those activities which take place within urban areas, especially those of industry, services, and the government sector. It is universally observed that economic development (defined as rising per capita incomes), urbanization, and the growing importance of industry, services, and government in total output go hand in hand (for evidence, see Renaud 1981 and Preston 1979). Policies designed to generate a rapid and sustainable growth in these activities will therefore also lead to a rapid growth in the demand for urban labor. Trade protection, exchange rate and tax policies, public investment strategies, and credit policies all have been used in various combinations to speed the transformation from a predominantly agricultural to a predominantly industrial economy supported by large service and government sectors. Whether such policies have been oriented toward import substitution or export promotion, the basic result has been an accelerated growth of industrial, service, and government activities, and with this has come an increased demand for urban labor.

Evidently, however, this set of policies has not "solved" the urban employment problem, although it may have helped improve the overall employment problem in some countries. Whether rural or urban development strategies can absorb the overall labor supply in the most efficient manner can be debated. The three major reasons rapid industrialization and urbanization in most parts of the developing world have not solved the urban employment problem, however, seem clear. First, there is the interaction of the labor demand side with the labor supply side, particularly the rapid migration flows from rural to urban areas in response to increased demand for urban labor. Second, industrialization and the related growth in the urban-based service and government sectors do not equally affect all urban areas. The largest cities, and especially capital cities, tend to attract a larger share of these activities than do intermediate cities and smaller towns; this generates extensive increases in labor demand in the former, but not to the same extent in the latter. The differential, and some would argue lack of balance, in these patterns of industrialization has led to different sets of employment problems in these two kinds of urban areas—in part because of the selectivity of the migration process alluded to above in the discussion of the effects of migration on labor supply. Third, and probably most important, in many developing countries economic policies have fostered a pattern of industrialization and urban development that appears to have stunted the growth in demand for urban labor, especially the demand for the unskilled labor in relatively abundant supply in both the urban and rural areas of developing countries. These policies and their consequences are discussed next.

CHOICE OF TECHNOLOGY, SCALE OF ENTERPRISE, AND LABOR INTENSITY. Beier and others (1975, p. 49) neatly summarize the problem posed in urban labor absorption:

> The paradox of the import-substitution type of development strategy is that, while it discriminates severely against the agricultural sector and appears to be partly responsible for the fast growth of large urban centers (together with high population growth rates), it has led to excessive patterns of dualism within the urban sector and has made the absorption of the new urban dwellers more difficult, not easier.

The authors go on to review the consequences for the urban labor market of conventional policies on trade protection, exchange rate overvaluation, and capital markets. A good case is made that these policies have tended to "result in capital-intensive projects with high capital costs making heavy demands on foreign exchange and low capacity to generate foreign exchange. They make heavy demands on the real savings of the economy and do not generate real savings" (Beier and others, pp. 49–50). By implication, the demand for labor, especially for low-skill labor, languishes,[38] and low wages and underemployment are thus preserved for the labor force in these low-skill grades.[39] Rather than dwelling on these points (they are discussed at length in Renaud 1981 and Squire 1981), two additional considerations will be given special attention here: first, the importance of the small-scale enterprises (SSE) sector and the prevalence of government policies hampering its development; second, the degree of technological choice in urban infrastructure investments and the implications of this choice for the labor-absorption capacity of urban public works, given the overall amount of resources available for such investments.

DEVELOPMENT OF SSE. The debate whether SSE in developing countries are on balance more labor intensive than large-scale firms is still going on. The recent World Bank sector policy paper on SSE (World Bank 1978a, p. 5) states unequivocally that SSE "are generally more labor intensive than larger organizations." However, another World Bank investigation dealing specifically with urban development issues and policies in India concluded that it has not been firmly established that small-scale industry is more labor intensive than large-scale industry and, in a dynamic context, large-scale enterprises appear to have been more effective in generating employment than small-scale enterprises, despite the amount of protection and encouragement enjoyed by the latter (World Bank data collected by E. Bevan Waide). A further element of uncertainty is injected by the facts that, as was argued earlier, the urban poor are not found exclusively in SSE employment and that a number of urban SSE may pay relatively high wages to their employees.[40] Furthermore, as this latter study indicates, in India especially there are important linkages and complementarities between large-scale firms and SSE because of prevailing practices of subcontracting.

Given this apparent lack of certainty regarding the effects on urban employment and on urban poverty of outright support of SSE, it would appear premature to advocate an across-the-board policy favoring SSE through government procurement policies, industrial estates, subsidized capital allocations, and the like. Two positive policy prescriptions relating to developing SSE are, however, possible. First, in the interest of increased efficiency (with possibly beneficial implications for urban employment and poverty), it is advisable to eliminate the special burdens that are placed on SSE in comparison with operations of larger scale. These strictures include a whole array of barriers, such as trade protection policies (especially quantitative restrictions) favoring large-scale enterprises (Keesing 1979), credit-rationing policies, public utility pricing,[41] and local business and property tax policies.[42] The elimination of these policies may provide as large an incentive to the efficient development of SSE in many developing countries as do the explicit policies designed to foster SSE.

The second positive policy prescription relates to the treatment of those SSE which are "not organized or conducted in a 'modern' manner; for example, traditional artisans, petty traders, and transporters in the 'informal' sector" (World Bank 1978a, p. 18). Although not without exception, it is probably true to say that these enterprises employ (or self-employ) predominantly poor people and that they tend to be relatively intensive in low-skilled labor. Besides measures that work to eliminate frequently restrictive licensing and taxing regulations (see the evidence cited above), direct measures of support should be considered, such as providing access to capital at commercial interest rates; giving access to land and regularizing land tenure;[43] providing public utility services,[44] technical assistance, and informal training; and supporting cooperatives for cheaper access to higher quality inputs and for the marketing of outputs.[45]

In the elimination of constraints as well as in the provision of outright support to these informal sector SSE, the local authorities in urban areas should be encouraged to play a much more active role than they hitherto have done in most cities.[46] Local expertise and experience are essential in determining the constraints on, as well as the needs of, informal sector enterprises in developing country cities, and often assistance to these enterprises can be provided in the context of ongoing local government programs (such as local tax and administrative reform, public utility investment and pricing, slum-improvement projects, and the like). This is the kind of approach that appears to be evolving in the World Bank's urban development projects (see World Bank 1978a, pp. 90–92) and in other efforts at comprehensive urban poverty programs in various developing countries (see Cousins 1977; USAID 1976, vol. 2, ch. 4; Friedmann and Sullivan 1974, p. 392), although even these projects have at times bypassed the local authorities and thus have missed important opportunities for improvement.

A caveat, however, should be added that comprehensive programs to assist the development of informal sector SSE require considerable investments in project design and management, as the experience of World Bank projects has shown. Furthermore, although the cooperation of local authorities may be essential in carrying out certain aspects of these programs, local governments may not always be willing or interested in cooperating because of the political dominance and opposition of entrenched interest groups. Finally, local authorities are often viewed with distrust and suspicion by slum dwellers and informal sector operators because of the authorities' history of obstructionist policies and practices and because of their functions as tax collectors. Nevertheless, it would be a mistake to neglect the many policies of local governments that tend to affect the demand for labor services of the urban poor, although in some instances it may be necessary to bypass these authorities in the actual implementation of the programs.

INVESTMENT IN URBAN PUBLIC INFRASTRUCTURE. One of the most salient features of urbanization is the large need for public infrastructure investment, particularly for water supply, waste disposal, road building, school construction, and the like. Moreover, all the existing facilities need to be operated and maintained; this requires considerable capital and labor inputs, which in turn raises the question of to what extent the demand for unskilled urban labor could be boosted by employing relatively labor-intensive techniques for the construction, operation, and maintenance of basic urban services. Information on this question is quite limited, and what exists is not very definite. A recent World Bank study of public works programs in developing countries concluded that efforts to design and implement labor-intensive public works projects in urban areas have not been successful in the past and are likely to be much more difficult to implement in urban than in rural areas (Burki and others 1976, pp. 17–19). In a somewhat different vein, World Bank experience for the developing countries of Europe, the Middle East, and North Africa indicates that investment costs per job created are quite substantial for water supply, sewerage, transport, and nonresidential construction. For other developing countries, the evidence on investment costs per job created in these sectors seems to be more favorable.

There can be little doubt that past "make-work" urban public works programs (such as "the Christmas Program" in Kingston, Jamaica, which consisted mainly of street and sidewalk cleaning; see Burki and others 1976, p. 17) hold little prospect for improvement because of low productivity and high budgetary cost. There are, however, some areas of urban public service provision where labor absorption can be significantly improved by a judicious choice of labor-intensive technologies. Such a choice of technology is often advisable on other grounds as well, such as reducing cost per service unit provided (and thus increasing the coverage of the urban population for given amounts of public resources spent) or in the interest of conserving foreign exchange. Nevertheless, consideration of the employment effects of alternative technologies in public service provision remains useful.

Examples for extremely diverging technologies have been documented for the collection and disposal of solid and sanitary wastes. Recent World Bank data (1977; compiled by Alfredo Steir-Younis) have shown that, in the case of solid waste collection and disposal, local authorities are generally in charge, and particularly in the larger cities they frequently are asked to replace poorly managed conventional waste collection and disposal techniques with modern techniques employed in the industrialized countries.[47] The former rely heavily on labor-intensive methods for picking and sorting in the recycling of usable solid wastes and for the collection of wastes from households. The latter, in contrast, tend to rely on highly capital- and foreign-exchange-intensive techniques for collection (compactor trucks) and disposal (incinerators, composters, and the like) and usually eliminate the possibility of recycling. In those few countries and cities where a constructive approach to improving and adapting conventional waste disposal techniques has been taken, both employment and labor earnings have increased. In one city in Colombia, for example, a private development corporation organized trash pickers into a self-managed, profit-sharing enterprise for trash processing, which quickly increased its employment from fifteen to sixty men and raised daily earnings substantially (USAID 1976, p. 64).

In the case of sanitary waste disposal, recent World Bank studies (Kalbermatten, Julius, and Gunnerson 1982; Kalbermatten and others 1982) have shown various low-cost alternatives to the high-cost, waterborne sanitary sewerage systems commonly found in industrialized countries. Waterborne systems have been introduced in many developing country cities, although usually on only a partial basis because of budgetary constraints. Whereas the labor intensity of the alternative technologies was not explicitly investigated in the World Bank studies, there is little doubt, given the technological difference in the nature of the investments required, that the labor intensity of the low-cost sewage disposal alternatives is considerably above that of the waterborne sewerage system.

These are two extreme cases where the choice of technology can have a considerable impact on the labor intensity of urban public service investments. In other areas the scope for increasing labor intensity through an appropriate choice of technology may be less. It should, however, be made explicitly a criterion in determining the design of urban infrastructure projects. This may in some cases require research into the alternatives available in various countries—as in the World Bank studies on sanitary waste disposal technology—or it may merely mean a systematic evaluation of alternatives available in a particular country and city. At the micro level such an evaluation would make use of the well-known techniques of economic analysis of projects (especially shadow-pricing of unskilled labor and of foreign exchange; see Squire and van der Tak 1975); at the sectoral or intersectoral level such techniques as linear programming would be used.[48]

In summary, there may be considerable scope for increasing the demand for low-skilled urban labor by policies that encourage appropriate choice of technology and scale of operations both in private and public investment. As throughout this paper, emphasis here was placed on actions that may be taken at the sectoral, city, or even project level, since these are considerations that often get only minimal attention in the discussion of urban employment and labor markets.

CITY GROWTH. Perhaps one of the most interesting phenomena of urban development in developing countries is that some cities in a particular country appear to be growing rapidly *and* doing relatively well in absorbing the growing urban labor supply while other cities within the same country appear to be doing very poorly, especially in absorbing labor. As indicated earlier, city size may be a relevant aspect in explaining such differences, but size is not the only factor, since some of the strongest contrasts may be observed between cities of comparable size. Calcutta and Bombay are such a contrasting pair of cities in India; Barranquilla and Medellin form another in Colombia.[49]

The reasons for these diverging patterns of growth and labor absorption obviously differ from country to country and from city to city. And for the most part they are likely to be beyond the control of local authorities within a city. For instance, Calcutta has been hurt by various exogenous developments. It was cut off from large parts of its natural hinterland by changes in national boundaries; it suffered from national transport price policies which undermined its national locational advantage; and it was bypassed to a certain extent in allocations of national public investments (1978 World Bank data compiled by C. I. Wallich). These and other exogenous factors seriously impeded industrial growth in the city during recent years, while migratory flows to the city continued—albeit at lower rates than in most developing country cities—because of push factors in the rural hinterland and because of the political upheavals in neighboring Bangladesh. Bombay, in contrast, did not have to contend with any of these exogenous depressing factors and has acted as a pole of attraction for new investment and job creation; this— at least in relative terms—made it an example of successful urban labor absorption in India. More generally, one may conclude that regional economic endowments and growth, national public investment patterns, and changes in the transport network are some of the more important exogenous factors explaining the differences in economic growth and labor absorption among different cities of similar size within the same country (Renaud 1981).

Besides these exogenous factors, there are also important determinants of urban growth and labor absorption endogenous to a city. In particular, the quality of management by the urban authorities may have an important effect on whether and how a city grows. In addition to influencing the labor intensity of public and private activities as was discussed in the preceding section, urban government can help or hinder the growth prospects of a city in the aggregate and thus boost or retard the growth of labor demand within the metropolitan area. Among the elements of urban management at issue here are: the provision of adequate public utilities for industry and commerce; the existence of a well-functioning urban transport system for the speedy distribution of goods and services; availability of developed land for new industrial developments; adequate public marketing facilities, both wholesale and retail; a good communications system (telephones and postal); and a public administration that minimizes efficiency losses and compliance costs for regulations and taxes.[50] While the exact quantitative effect of any one of these elements on urban growth and employment absorption is difficult to ascertain, there can be little doubt that the failure of urban management in the past in such cities as Calcutta or Barranquilla has contributed considerably to the poor performance of these cities compared with the much better performance of Bombay or Medellin, where urban management has been of much higher quality. A comprehensive approach to improving urban management across the board may therefore be required in many developing country cities to increase their absorptive capacity. Control of central city congestion (as in Singapore; Watson and Holland 1978), improved public utility services and road infrastructure at cost-covering charges,[51] a streamlined administration of local taxes and regulations, and provision of a wide variety of marketing facilities are all within the purview of urban management and do not in general require higher-level government intervention unless, as is too often the case, constraints by higher-level governments on local revenue and expenditure authority limit the local freedom of action.

Although the general area of urban administration, management, and finances is not addressed here, three pertinent managerial aspects need mention. First, the location of public facilities—such as industrial parks, public markets, transport terminals, and the like—is of utmost importance in urban areas since, as many examples have shown in the past, poor location may well result in substantial underutilization of these facilities while bottlenecks are generated elsewhere. The example of poorly located new public markets in Cartagena, Colombia, is a case in point (Linn 1975). Second, in attempting to improve urban management and administration it is important to bear in mind not only the economic interests and needs of the modern sector. If one of the prime objectives of urban employment policy is to improve the absorption of low-skilled labor, then urban management must be geared also to provide the complementary public services required by activities using such labor, and to adjust its regulatory and taxing practices to minimize the compliance cost for the informal sector. Earlier sections have indicated many areas where improvements are feasible. Third, attempts to attract new investment to a particular city by offering local tax holidays is not a good way of increasing employment in the city. The impact of such action on private investment decisions is not likely to be significant, especially where offsetting actions are taken by other cities (as, for instance, in Colombia; Bahl and

Linn, forthcoming). Indeed, by making capital cheap such action may increase capital intensity, thus reducing labor absorption. Finally, there is the obvious burden on local finances, which are usually already in poor shape.

One should be under no illusion that improvements in urban management, administration, and finance are easy. They are particularly difficult in an environment where, because of exogenous factors and past mismanagement, the urban absorptive capacity is low, as in Calcutta and Barranquilla. Nevertheless, improved urban management must be included in any program intended to increase the ability of cities to absorb their abundant labor supply.

Imperfections and Transactions Costs of the Urban Labor Market

Up to this point it has been implicitly assumed that the labor market works well in matching demands and supplies at market-clearing prices for all skill categories and for all types of activities. Market imperfections have been discussed only in markets other than the labor market. For instance, governmental controls on activities of street hawkers in central cities represent a limitation on the location decisions regarding street vending and thus are an imperfection in the land market. Failure to price urban transport correctly leads to congestion and, among other things, to increased transactions costs for the commodity markets because of the inefficiency in the transport system. Other examples could be cited. In each case removal of imperfections in markets other than the labor market was analyzed as a possible means to increase the demand for labor, particularly among the lower skill categories. This section briefly discusses market imperfections operating specifically in the urban labor market and policy steps that may be taken to reduce them.

As a first step it is necessary to review the available evidence regarding the existence of labor market imperfections. Some recent studies of urban labor earnings in developing countries have found that the standard human capital variables such as age, education, experience, sex, and the like fail to account fully for earnings differentials between different labor market segments (Mazumdar 1979; Mazumdar and Ahmed 1978; Sant'Anna, Merrick, and Mazumdar 1976). Labor market imperfections may account for some of the unexplained variance in earnings. Institutional practices such as minimum wage legislation, public employment restrictions, educational requirements unrelated to productivity criteria, ethnic and caste barriers to job access, and labor registration requirements have frequently been documented (for example, Cohen 1978, Peattie 1979, Webb and Pfeffermann 1978). Other elements of labor market imperfection that have not received as much attention relate to the lack of adequate information transmission (although the information system among low-skill and low-income groups is probably better than is generally assumed) and, more important, to commuting costs (both in time and money), which essentially act as transactions costs in the labor market.[52]

The importance of these transactions costs in employment and earnings reduction, although difficult to assess on a global basis, is vividly demonstrated by the extreme political sensitivity of increases in urban public transit fares and by the impact of commuting costs on the employment patterns of low-income households that are relocated from relatively convenient central locations to peripheral ones (as in Rio de Janeiro; see Perlman 1976).[53] The management of urban land use and of the urban transport system should therefore be geared to reduce these transactions costs to the extent feasible. One way to achieve this is to permit or even encourage industrial and residential land use patterns that minimize the length of work trips, rather than to separate industrial and residential areas by rigid zoning regulations or poorly located investments in infrastructure or industrial parks.[54] Especially for those cities that are still relatively small but are growing rapidly—as is the case for many cities in Africa and for some of the intermediate-size cities in other developing countries—there may be considerable gains reaped from land use planning, since the physical structure of these cities still permits a considerable degree of flexibility largely absent in the large metropolises. Other elements of a policy reducing the transactions costs are the control of central city congestion through appropriate charges to limit use of private automobiles (as in Singapore; Watson and Holland 1978) and the provision of a good system of arterial and neighborhood access roads supplemented by an effective public transit system.

Again, in designing these measures it is crucial to bear in mind that it is the low-skill and low-income groups that are hardest hit by the transactions costs created by poor land use and transport policies. A common planning bias, for example, is to improve city roads to keep up with rapidly increasing private automobile traffic while failing to provide pedestrian or bicycle paths or crossings, to make city roads more passable for buses, or to provide adequate neighborhood access roads in poor areas. More will be said about these and related policies in later chapters; the main point here is that urban management and planning are crucial to the working of the urban labor market.

Summary of Policy Implications

That policy actions at the city or project level have so far been emphasized should not lead one to overlook that the national government controls some of the most important policy instruments for employment creation and improved productivity in urban areas (such as trade protection, capital market policies, national public investment and taxation, education and health policies, and so forth). Nevertheless, city- and project-specific instruments are of relevance for several reasons.

First, local urban authorities and specific projects frequently play an important role in the implementation of national policies.

Second, since there are a number of actions taken at the city level that interfere with employment generation and productivity increases, and others that could be taken to foster employment and productivity, there is good reason to consider these actions. If progress is to be made in solving the general problem of urban poverty and the employment problem in particular, action must be taken on all possible fronts. This implies that concerted action is necessary at both the national and the city level regarding labor demand, labor supply, and labor market imperfections, in the form of both general and urban poverty-oriented employment policies.

Third, it is just as important to be aware of what city- and project-specific policies cannot do as it is to consider what they can do. Misplaced priorities on employment or productivity generation at the city level, in a context where the general environment is not favorable, are just as wasteful of resources as is the neglect of opportunities for improving employment and productivity where this is feasible (particularly if programs such as reform of urban management, taxation, and adminstration, and public service investment programs are already ongoing).

In conclusion, a list of commonly found policies negatively affecting urban employment in developing countries may be contrasted with a set of alternative policy measures that represent a more supportive approach to reducing urban poverty through increased employment and earnings. For the sake of clarity, these points are organized around a few major headings, but inevitably there is some overlap (with some prescriptions appearing under more than one heading and some equally appropriate under other headings). Furthermore, no claim is made here that the list is all-inclusive—merely that it captures the major aspects of city- or project-level policy. Many of the prescriptions will be refined in the more detailed analysis of urban service provision and urban management in the following chapters.

Administration, Regulation, and Taxation

Traditional policies:

- Define "informal" sector activities as negative, unproductive, or undesirable, and on this basis attempt to control them by such policies as slum eradication and restrictions on "informal" sector activities
- Employ "beggar-thy-neighbor" policies to attract private investors (especially from the modern sector) by improving the aesthetics of

the city through elimination of the informal sector or by offering local tax holidays.

Proposed policies:

- Minimize unfavorable and discriminating constraints in public administration, regulation, and taxation that inhibit the operations of SSE, in particular those in the informal sector
- Minimize private compliance costs of public administration, regulation, and taxation by reducing red tape and waiting time for public permits and tax payment procedures
- Eliminate unnecessary restrictions in local public hiring practices that are unrelated to productivity considerations, but at the same time adopt wage policies for local authorities that will attract adequately skilled personnel (especially important in smaller, noncapital cities that have difficulty attracting well-trained government personnel).

Public Service Investment

Traditional policies:

- Attempt to minimize rural-urban migration by withholding public services from urban slums
- Expect that "make-work" urban public works programs will provide a solution to the urban employment and poverty problem
- Replace conventional labor-intensive public service technologies by modern capital- and foreign-exchange-intensive techniques without careful sectoral and project-level analyses, including the shadow-pricing of labor and of foreign exhange.

Proposed policies:

- Search for labor-intensive techniques in providing urban public services (this may require research and evaluation of alternative technologies at the sectoral, national, or even international level)
- Carefully consider the location of urban infrastructure investments with an eye toward minimizing the length and costs of commuting trips; facilitating goods transport, marketing, and so forth; and providing the poor with access to service facilities such as schools, hospitals, and health and family planning centers
- Emphasize investments in distribution networks of public utilities, especially electricity, as a way to encourage SSE development.

Public Service Pricing

Traditional policies:

- Discriminate against small public utility users (this applies in particular to the usually inefficient practice of charging declining block rates for electricity)
- Fail to introduce "life-line" service rates for poor urban residents on the grounds that this would induce rural-urban migration.[55]

Proposed policies:

- Set urban service prices equal to the incremental cost of providing the services, except where external benefits from service provision are clearly substantial or where life-line tariffs to poor consumers can be applied
- Introduce charges for central city road use by private automobiles to ease congestion
- Structure service prices for the poor so as to maximize their ability to connect to the services; in particular, consider the introduction of life-line services and the replacement of lump-sum connection fees by recurrent charges.

Education, Health, Nutrition, and Population Planning

Traditional policies:

- Overinvest in education where the productivity of such investment is low (as indicated, for instance, by low social rates of return to education); this applies especially to formal primary school education in Latin America and to secondary education of the liberal arts kind in many other countries.

Proposed policies:

- Consider the potential contribution of urban local authorities to education, health, nutrition, and population planning programs
- Emphasize informal education and training and technical assistance for informal sector SSE
- Locate the physical facilities for these services so as to maximize access by the poor.

SSE

Traditional policies:

- Discriminate against SSE, especially those in the informal sector, through regulation, taxation, and administrative practices, in particular by local authorities
- Expect to solve the urban employment problem by SSE programs alone.

Proposed policies:

- Focus on informal sector activities in any attempts to stimulate SSE, since the informal sector SSE are most likely to be harmed by discriminatory public action, lack of access to capital, inputs, and markets
- Consider the potential of local authorities to assist in the provision of training, extension services, cooperative development, and the like for SSE
- Induce local authorities to consider the needs of SSE in urban service provision, particularly in the extension of electricity services, location of public markets, and improvements in land tenure security in slum areas.

Land Market

Traditional policies:

- Prevent efficient residential and industrial location decisions by inappropriate zoning regulations
- Prevent access of operators of informal SSE to favorable locations
- Introduce rent control, which tends to impede labor mobility within the city and to reduce investment in housing.

Proposed policies:

- Improve land tenure security in slum and squatter areas, since this will stimulate investment in informal sector SSE directly (as well as indirectly, by improving access to capital through enabling property owners to offer collateral to lenders)
- Act to supply adequate urban space for the poor at reasonable locations so that they can carry out SSE in their homes.

Migration

Traditional policies:

- Attempt to control migration by withholding urban services from slums and squatter areas, by not applying life-line service rates, or by restrictions on informal sector activities.

Proposed policies:

- Price urban services at incremental social cost, including the use of central city road space, since this means that private investors, in particular, will be forced to consider the full social cost of their decisions to locate in a specific city or section within a city.

Notes to Chapter 2

1. See Squire (1981), Keesing (1979), and Renaud (1981), among others.

2. Some of the case studies of urban labor markets carried out by the ILO are good examples of this type of neglect. See, for example, Lubell (1974); Joshi, Lubell, and Mouly (1976); Schaefer and Spindel (1976).

3. See Bromley (1977), Mazumdar (1976), Peattie (1974), and Perlman (1976) for critical reviews of elements of this profile; they also provide ample references to exponents of the "conventional" view.

4. See Beier and others (1975) and sources cited therein. Also see Squire (1981) and McGreevey (1980).

5. See Mazumdar (1976); Sant'Anna, Merrick, and Mazumdar (1976); Webb (1976); Webb and Pfeffermann (1979, app. A); and Peattie (1979).

6. There are other identifiable, but usually relatively small, groups of poor or very poor people in developing country cities whose characteristics vary from city to city. In Bogota, for instance, one small but highly visible and especially distressing group are the "gamines," young children typically between the ages of five and fifteen who band together in small groups separate from their families to eke out a miserable existence. Another, more common set of very poor people is found among households with female, sick, or disabled heads of household.

7. See Bromley (1977), Peattie (1979), and McGee and Yeung (1977). Entry may, however, be quite unrestricted at locations where earning opportunities are minimal.

8. "As in most Latin American cities, the street traders of Cali are closely regulated by the municipal and departmental authorities. Several hundred pages of municipal and police regulations specify in great detail where and under what conditions street trading may take place. All street traders are expected to carry identity cards and other official documents, and most of them are also expected to obtain trading licenses and health permits from the municipal authorities" (Bromley 1977, p. 6). For similar observations applying to street vending in Khartum, see International Labour Office (1976); for restrictions on hawkers in Southeast Asian cities, see McGee and Yeung (1977).

9. See the discussion of the municipal taxes and license fees for Cartagena (Colombia) in Linn (1975).

10. Bromley (1977, p. 7) states that "almost all street traders contravene official regulations in one way or another." See also International Labour Office (1976) for similar practices in Sudan.

11. For instance, the fear of official roundups limits the typical street vendor to offer only as much as he can quickly pack up and carry away when the inspector's truck appears at the streetcorner (Bromley 1977, p. 8).

12. "The implementation of this plan was reflected in much more liberal licensing policy; the enforcement of law through education, not prosecution; the provision of loans and other inducements, particularly for the *bumiputra*; and the recognition that hawking provided an important avenue for employment and entrepreneurial development" (McGee and Yeung 1977, p. 49).

13. Even lottery tickets in Bogota, which ostensibly are made available for sale by the very poor to generate employment for these groups, frequently find their way through the hands of relatively well-to-do intermediaries (Peattie 1979).

14. This point is substantiated by Peattie (1974) and by McGee and Yeung (1977) on the basis of field research.

15. One might want to argue that negative externalities are imposed by unrestrained informal sector activities, especially in terms of the "nuisance" which they generate for the (relatively few) wealthy urban dwellers. Even then, however, value judgments are inevitable, for what weight is one to give to these externalities in practice? In the typical developing country city the official views are dominated by the interests of the elite, and thus the weight given to the "nuisance" of informal sector activity is substantial. If one were to give a low weight in evaluating them, then very likely one would come to view informal sector activities, on balance, in a more positive light.

16. For instance, where there is *clear* evidence that the operations of the informal market contravene basic norms of ethics and law (rather than of aesthetics), as in the case of drug trading, smuggling, child labor, and the like.

17. A further complicaton is that the immediate losers of a more supportive public attitude toward such activities as street vending may be occupations carried out by other low-income groups, such as merchants occupying booths in the municipal markets (Bromley 1977).

18. Another implication is that job creation makes other types of target-group-oriented policies, particularly the basic needs approach, a more direct means with which to improve the welfare of the poor with relatively low "leakages" and at reasonable administrative costs.

19. For instance, estimates have been made that one primary manufacturing job in India can lead to three to four formal sector service jobs and at least the same number of jobs in the informal sector (1978 World Bank data compiled by E. Bevan Waide).

20. This argument applies especially in South Asia, but possibly to a lesser extent in Latin America.

21. See Squire (1981) for a more extensive discussion of complex labor market models.

22. This is the assumption implicit in most population projections; see "World Development Indicators," table 17 (annex to World Bank 1979a).

23. See Cuca (1979) and Squire (1981) for a more extensive discussion of family planning policies.

24. In Colombia, for instance, five out of twenty-two departmental (state) capital cities experienced net out-migration according to 1973 census figures (Linn 1979a).

25. This factor affects the demographic structure of cities and has important implications for the fertility rates in cities and for the need for public services. These considerations will be addressed later.

26. See Friedmann and Sullivan (1974) for citations of studies supporting the theory of "excessive" migration. For contrasting evidence, see Mazumdar (1979). Squire (1981) addresses this issue in greater detail.

27. Not too much should be made of these effects, given our limited knowledge of the relative strength of the determinants of private investment decisions. The point remains, however, that

improvements in the efficiency of urban economies, if anything, would tend to lead to a decentralization of economic activities and therefore of population.

28. Social and cultural factors may also determine the extent to which women, especially, and the young and old participate in the labor force. Among demographic factors, the age structure is the single most important determinant of labor force participation.

29. See Perlman (1976); Sant'Anna, Merrick, and Mazumdar (1976). The general question of transactions costs and labor market imperfections will be taken up further below.

30. See World Bank (1975a and 1980a) on the complexity of the interrelations between education, nutrition, and family planning. See also chapter 6 for a discussion of social services.

31. For example, in Colombia (Berry 1974, Peattie 1979) and India (Friedmann and Sullivan 1974).

32. The existence of unemployment also indicates, and is predicated on, the existence of labor market imperfections (Squire 1981).

33. Recent World Bank data on El Salvador substantiate this hypothesis. Mazumdar and Ahmed (1978), however, indicate that, at the lower end of the skill and wage pyramid, on-the-job experience may be more important than formal education in determining wage.

34. See Bird (1978) for a discussion of the interrelationship of national and local authorities in urban education.

35. There exists a strong two-way relation between the two; see Reutlinger and Selowsky (1976), World Bank (1975a), and chapter 6 below.

36. Water supply and waste disposal are generally the responsibility of local governments in the medium-size and large cities of developing countries. They frequently also carry out environmental health programs and are responsible for neighborhood health centers. See Bahl and Linn (forthcoming).

37. See Webb and Pfeffermann (1979) for Brazil. Other economies where, according to World Bank economists, the employment issue is less pressing (mainly because of rapid aggregate economic growth) are Algeria, Syria, and Nigeria.

38. The demand for high-skilled labor, to the extent that it is complementary with capital, may, however, be fostered by these policies. Given the usual scarcity of the required skills in developing countries, this contributes substantially to the high wages paid to high-skilled labor.

39. Aside from the above-mentioned policies, other factors may in part explain the capital intensity of much of the industrial development in developing countries: Maybe the most important is the scarcity of management skills, which tends to be highly complementary with the development of labor-intensive technologies. See also an exhaustive listing of factors in World Bank (1978a), p. 16–17.

40. These SSE are classified in World Bank (1978a, p. 18) as "small manufacturing firms that are relatively modern" and "organized nonmanufacturing firms such as those engaged in construction, repair, transportation, and trading," in contrast to "enterprises not organized or conducted in a 'modern' manner, e.g., traditional artisans, petty traders, and transporters in the 'informal' sector."

41. Especially the conventional, but usually inefficient, declining block rates for electricity, which are an area where improved public utility pricing would eliminate an unnecessary burden on SSE.

42. In Colombia, for example, the municipal industry and commerce tax frequently burdens SSE much more heavily than larger enterprises (Linn 1975). Similar examples may be found elsewhere, for property and business taxes alike (Bahl and Linn, forthcoming).

43. This provides an incentive for developing smallest-scale enterprises on residential premises (see Vernez 1973).

44. In particular, connection to the electricity network may stimulate smallest-scale enterprise. Very often slum dwellers will risk their lives to make illegal (and highly unsafe) connections to power lines to be able to run small electric appliances such as sewing machines.

45. A recent study supported by the U.S. Agency for International Development (USAID) has reviewed the experience with programs designed to assist commercial and industrial activities at the smallest scale among the urban poor in developing countries. It concluded that, if properly designed, such programs can be effective in raising income among the target groups; see Beardsley (1980) and Council for International Urban Liaison (1980).

46. This is in marked contrast to the cities of China, where the local authorities have played a major role in shaping and assisting the development of all aspects of production (Andors 1978). On a lesser scale, the Malaysian experience with support for hawkers is also a case in point (McGee and Yeung 1977, p. 49).

47. More often than not the initiative rests with the manufacturers of the modern equipment, who attempt to convince local officials of the desirability of their techniques for obviously self-serving commercial reasons.

48. For an experimental application of linear programming in the design of a public service investment strategy across cities and a number of public service sectors, making allowance for alternative technologies, see Thoss and Linn (1978).

49. For Colombia, similar contrasting experiences may also be observed for intermediate-size cities (for example, Buenaventura and Bucaramanga; Linn 1979a).

50. A particularly drastic example for high efficiency costs of urban taxation is the so-called octroi tax frequently found in the cities of the Indian subcontinent. This tax is levied on all goods entering a local jurisdiction just as an import tariff is levied at national boundaries. In some cities, such as Karachi, where more than one local government has jurisdiction over the metropolitan area, octroi taxes are levied even on goods traffic within the metropolitan area (Bahl and Linn, forthcoming).

51. Note the important contribution to urban development made in Colombia by urban transport improvements under the so-called valorization schemes in Bogota, Medellin, and Cali (Doebele, Grimes, and Linn 1979).

52. Another example of unnecessarily elevated transactions costs, which limit labor mobility within a city, occurs where rent control is prevalent. Because of resultant housing shortages and the widespread requirement of cash payments ("key money") at the beginning of a lease, many renters may be locked into existing rental arrangements.

53. General strikes, street riots, and the like are not a rarity in response to transit fare increases in many developing country cities, whereas the increases in the charges for other urban services are generally received with less hostility.

54. The Colombian efforts at developing multinodal city design through a multifunctional "cities-within-the city" program is an interesting effort in this direction. The reduced importance of the railroad and the increased use of trucks in intercity goods transport may well encourage a spontaneous decentralization of intraurban industrial location away from the conventional concentration along railway terminals to areas where land is cheaper and labor more readily available. There is some evidence that this is already happening in Bogota (Lee 1979). Rigid enforcement of outdated zoning regulations might well impede this development.

55. These tariffs are very low for small initial blocks of service consumption, but are set equal to cost of service provision for consumption levels beyond essential, life-supporting levels (see chapter 5).

3

Redistribution of Urban Incomes
through Fiscal Policy

THE PRECEDING CHAPTER considered possible policy actions to alleviate the problem of urban poverty through increases in labor income in response to increased employment and productivity. Although some of these proposed actions promise to raise the incomes of the poor, these gains are likely to be slow, with substantial improvements occurring only over long periods of time, possibly generations. The question must therefore be asked whether there exist any shortcuts that might more quickly eliminate at least the worst manifestations of urban poverty, any policies that might more rapidly raise the incomes of a large number, if not all, of the urban poor above the threshold of absolute poverty.

The most obvious alternative to a slow process of raising the labor incomes of the urban poor is to redistribute through public action the incomes earned by high-paid labor or by other assets, such as capital and land. The purpose of this chapter is to evaluate the potential of public action in achieving income redistribution in urban areas. In doing so, the assumption will be made that eradication of urban poverty cannot expect to draw on net resource transfers from rural to urban areas. Almost without exception, average urban incomes are higher than rural incomes, the number and proportion of absolute poor tend to be smaller in urban than in rural areas, and public policy, if anything, has tended to draw resources away from rural and into urban areas in many developing countries. These conditions set up a prima facie case for redistribution in favor of rural, rather than urban, areas.[1] Redistribution for alleviation of urban poverty will thus have to draw essentially on the incomes generated in urban areas themselves.[2]

This chapter is arranged in three sections. The first briefly discusses the scope for general income redistribution, and the second centers more extensively on the issue of this study—how urban poverty, in particular absolute urban poverty, may be reduced by public policy. The last section summarizes the chapter's major policy implications.

The Scope for General Income Redistribution

The objective frequently, if only implicitly, set for redistribution policy in popular and academic discussions of income inequality in developing countries is that the distribution of income be shifted on the whole toward greater equality. For instance, changes in the Gini coefficient or shifts in the Lorenz curve are common measures of the effectiveness of public tax and expenditure policies in increasing equity. Measured in this way, redistribution through public policies has not, on the available evidence, been carried very far in most developing countries.

A recent survey of thirty-two studies of tax incidence—that is, of the distribution of the tax burden across income classes—found that twenty-two studies show some progressivity in taxation in as many countries; eight studies show approximately proportional (or neutral) tax rates, mainly in Latin American countries; and two studies (of Greece and the Philippines) show the incidence of taxes to be regressive (De Wulf 1975). As De Wulf points out (p. 71), this result is perhaps somewhat more positive than might have been expected, given the generally gloomy evaluation by critics of tax systems in the developing world. Nevertheless, there can be no doubt that in most countries the tax system does little to alter the distribution of income.[3]

Serious estimation problems are encountered in the analysis of tax incidence, mainly because it is difficult to know who bears the final burden of a tax, once it is recognized that the shifting of tax burdens through factor and commodity price adjustments from the initial taxpayer to others is not only possible but in fact quite likely for many taxes (Bird and De Wulf 1973, De Wulf 1975, McLure 1975). Nevertheless, these problems appear minor when compared with the difficulties of establishing the incidence of government expenditures. The measurement of the benefits of government spending, as well as the distribution of these benefits as they are shifted from initial recipient to final beneficiary, is a very difficult area of economic analysis—especially when a wide range of government expenditures is subjected to analysis (De Wulf 1975). One therefore must proceed with extreme caution in interpreting the results of studies of the incidence of government expenditure, which on balance appear to indicate that the distribution of income is improved by government expenditures.

Analysis of studies of both tax and expenditure incidence leads one to conclude that government budgets in developing countries have on balance tended to improve the distribution of incomes in developing countries in general, and in the urban areas of developing countries in particular, but that their impact has remained slight when measured against the existing inequalities in incomes.[4] It is not difficult to determine the reasons for this limited impact. First and foremost, there is the political obstacle: the wealthy tend to dominate the political arena, and obviously they have no interest in a large-scale redistribution through the public sector. A second and related point (also made by Harberger 1977, p. 263) is one of perception of inequality, which is well stated by Bird and De Wulf in reference to Latin America (1973, pp. 676–77):

> A serious problem with the more intensive use of the tax system for redistributive purposes is that, while income in Latin America is so un-equally distributed that there are, by anyone's standards, a great many poor people, there are only a small number of rich people by relative national standards. This is not a mere play on words. The point is that the average incomes and consumption standards of those at the top of the Latin American pyramid, while much higher than those at the bottom, are in general only roughly equivalent to the average levels prevailing in the developed countries. There are, of course, some wealthy people in most countries, but it seems nevertheless true that most of the relatively rich in Latin America appear to consider themselves to be middle class, the middle class to be poor, and the poor to be virtually non-existent. The cosmopolitan perspective from which professionals and other members of this upper-income group tend to view their relative position in the world is at least a partial explanation for the apparently widespread ex-istence of this truncated perception of the national distribution of the good things of life. Combined with the political dominance of the (rel-atively) well-to-do in Latin America, this fact perhaps more than suffi-ciently explains why few efforts, and even less success, to redistribute income and wealth through the fiscal system may be noted in most countries.

Third, any serious effort to tax incomes progressively faces three major ways of attempted escape from the progressive tax bite: flight of capital and highly skilled labor from the country; evasion of taxes by subterfuge; and reduction in work effort. The importance of these avenues of escape and the degree to which they can be closed will vary from country to country, but they certainly limit the progressivity of any tax system (Harberger 1977).

Finally, the difficulties of achieving the goals of significantly increased equality in developing countries through government taxes and expenditures, when these are superimposed on a highly skewed distribution of income, are shown in table 3-1, which reports on a hypothetical exercise carried out by Harberger (1977) to demonstrate the limited redistributive potential of gov-

Table 3-1. *Gini Coefficients for Alternative Tax-Expenditure Packages*

	Basic distribution of income	
Policy package	U.S. type	Developing country type
None	0.402	0.498
Progressive tax, proportional expenditure	0.372	0.462
Proportional tax, egalitarian expenditure	0.377	0.456
Progressive tax, egalitarian expenditure	0.347	0.419

Source: Harberger (1977, p. 276).

ernment budgets. Starting with a "typical" distribution of income found in developing countries (Gini coefficient of 0.498), he superimposed combinations of alternative hypothetical tax and expenditure policies to determine their distrubutional effects. His finding was that—even under the most extreme hypotheses; that is, a highly progressive tax and an egalitarian expenditure policy whereby taxes increase more than in proportion to income, but expenditures are distributed equally across all households—the Gini coefficient is only improved to 0.419, still higher (indicating more inequality) than the without-government Gini coefficient for the United States (0.402).

Other, more drastic measures for income redistribution, in particular the redistribution of asset ownership, tend to hold greater prospects for success. In rural areas, land reform is frequently suggested as a way to share the rent of land more equally and to increase the employment and productivity of rural labor. For urban areas, no ready equivalent measure of asset redistribution appears to exist. The closest to it is probably the de facto change in urban landownership through land invasion, particularly in Latin American cities. It can hardly be said, however, that these ownership transfers represent instruments of government policy in most cities. In any case, there are no estimates available regarding the effects of urban land invasions on the distribution of urban incomes, although the direction of the change is quite unequivocal. Other examples of asset ownership transfers may be found in the case of nationalization of selected industries, transfer of enterprise ownership to worker management (in Chile and Yugoslavia, for instance), and the total socialization of all productive assets commonly found in centrally planned economies. The last two of these three approaches appear to have reduced income inequality significantly, but the first has not been as successful in achieving this goal. What is even more important is that, for two principal reasons, none of these approaches in and of itself deals with the problem of urban poverty. First, socialization of productive assets may decrease inequality by transferring the returns to these assets from the previous asset owners (the very rich) to the public sector, which then may allocate these funds in several ways, only one of which is toward redressing poverty. And even if this direction is chosen among others, there is no guarantee that such a program will actually affect the urban (rural) poor on a broad basis. For instance, if urban service standards are set very high, even a program explicitly geared to provide these services to the poor will not achieve broad coverage because of resource limitations.

If income redistribution is to be successful and equitable, one clearly needs to make the focus on poverty quite explicitly the objective of analysis and policy. Otherwise there is no assurance that studies of government tax and expenditure incidence and related measures will address the question of how and to what extent urban poverty may be eliminated by public policy. That tax policies have not significantly reduced, let alone eliminated, inequality does not mean that appropriately designed tax and expenditure policies cannot significantly reduce poverty. And that other policies (for example, nationalization) have reduced inequality does not necessarily mean that they have also extensively reduced poverty. The next section will attempt to analyze the potential of government taxation and expenditure as policy tools for the alleviation of urban poverty.

The Scope for Alleviating Urban Poverty through Fiscal Policy

The study of fiscal instruments, especially taxation and public expenditure, can be simplified and the constraints to implementation reduced by shifting the focus of redistribution policies away from the objective of leveling the skewness in the income distribution to the goal of poverty alleviation. In essence, the argument is that it is easier, analytically and practically, to evaluate how changes in selected taxes and public expenditures affect the welfare of a particular group, namely those subsisting in absolute poverty, than it is to study the impact of all taxes and all public expenditures on all income groups; that it is easier to get general political agreement on programs designed to eliminate absolute poverty than it is on a program of general redistribution; and that, if the elimination of poverty is in fact accepted as an objective having strong ethical justification, an explicit focus on poverty elimination is more likely to lead to policy prescriptions actually serving this goal than is an approach to the redistribution issue from the viewpoint of eliminating inequality. This is not to say that difficulties of analysis and implementation do not remain, yet the position taken in this section, and throughout the remainder of this volume, is closely related to, and indeed draws on the arguments supporting, the basic needs approach to development policy.[5]

The purpose in this section is not to develop global measurements of basic needs or of resources required to satisfy these needs; rather, the attempt will be made, first, to evaluate how tax policy can be adapted to reduce the tax burden placed on the urban poor and, second, how in general terms government expenditure may be expected to contribute to the alleviation of poverty and the meeting of basic needs. Measures relating to specific functional areas of government spending will be taken up in subsequent chapters.

Contribution of the Tax System to Poverty Alleviation

The following passage from Bird and De Wulf (1973, pp. 672–73) provides a good starting point for a discussion of the role of tax policy in poverty alleviation (this section also relies heavily on McLure 1975):

> Taxes cannot, of course, make poor people rich. If our main concern is with poverty as such, with the waste and misuse of human resources and the stunted opportunities of those whose incomes fall below some minimum decent standard, remedies must come primarily through the expenditure side of the budget, either by direct public provision of such services as housing, medical care, and education, or by simple transfers of income, or through employment-creating policies. If the principal aim of redistributive policy is to level up—to make the poor better off—the main role that the tax system has to play is thus the limited and essentially negative one of not making them poorer.

Basically, then, the questions relating to the role of taxation are: How can regressive taxes be amended, reduced, or eliminated to lower the tax burden on the poor? To the extent that new public revenues must be generated by increased taxation, what progressive taxes can be relied on more heavily to ensure that the burden does not fall on the poor to a significant extent? In keeping with the focus in the remainder of this volume, particular attention will be paid to those revenue instruments that are commonly within the authority of urban government, and measures suggested here are not meant to provide a panacea for the solution of the urban poverty problem. They are to be understood merely as ingredients of a comprehensive strategy to address an extremely complex problem, which cannot be solved by using only one or a small number of policy instruments.

REDUCING REGRESSIVE TAXES. The urban poor do pay taxes, and in particular taxes levied by local authorities. The first part of this proposition is verified by the first column of table 3-2. The urban poor are estimated to pay somewhere between 8 and 12 percent of their incomes in the form of taxes, which is greater than the proportion paid by the rural poor, less than that paid by the urban rich, but in general not much less than that paid by middle-income groups in urban areas. Although the urban poor are generally not reached by direct taxation such as income and wealth taxes, they contribute considerably through indirect taxes such as import duties, sales taxes, sumptuary taxes (on such luxuries as alcoholic beverages, tobacco, and gambling), and other excise taxes. It is precisely this phenomenon, coupled with the fact that local governments in urban areas often are forced to rely on indirect taxes—the only major exception is the real property tax (Linn 1980)—that explains why local government taxes often contribute quite heavily to the tax burden on the urban poor. Many studies of tax incidence neglect to consider indirect taxation by local governments because of lack of data, or

Table 3-2. *Results of Seven Tax Incidence Studies*

Country and basis of measure	Approximate tax rate			
	On urban poor[a]	At the fourth quintile	On urban rich[b]	On rural poor[a]
Brazil (1962–63)				
Income	16[d]	20+	20[d]	4.5
Colombia (1970)				
Income[c]	7.5	9	20	8
India (1963–64)	11.5	14	33	6
Gujarat (1967–68)				
Income	6	7	15	—
Expenditure[e]	6	6	11	—
Mysore (1968–69)				
Income	9	9	18	6.5
Expenditure	8.5	9.5	16	6
Lebanon (1968)				
Expenditure	8	—	20–23	—
Pakistan (1966–67)				
Income	10.5	12	22–24	5
Expenditure[e]	9.5	11	15+	4

— Not applicable.

Source: McLure (1975).

a. Urban and rural poor are roughly the 40 percent of households with the lowest incomes.

b. The urban rich are the 2 to 5 percent of households with the highest incomes.

c. Estimate is based on the assumption that the corporation income tax is borne in equal proportions by Colombian consumers, Colombian shareholders, and foreign shareholders.

d. Approximate, since the original sources do not allow much precision.

e. Indirect taxes only.

Table 3-3. *Incidence of Local Government Taxes in Bogota, Colombia, 1970*

Household income (thousands of pesos annually)	Local government tax burden (percent of income)	Share of local taxes (percent of total taxes paid)
0–12	2.4	30.0
12–24	3.4	34.0
24–36	2.8	26.4
36–60	2.8	24.8
60–174	2.4	20.2
174+	1.6	7.3

Source: Linn (1976a).

they do not show separate tax burdens for different levels of government. Figures computed for Bogota confirm this conclusion. For the lowest two income groups in Bogota, local taxes in 1970 accounted for about a third of total taxes paid; for the highest income group, the share of local taxes was less than 10 percent (see table 3-3). Tax relief for the urban poor should thus focus especially on the compostion and structure of indirect taxation at the national level and on the tax practices of local governments in urban areas.[6]

The tax burden of the urban poor can be lightened by increasing the coverage of exemptions of basic necessities from such indirect taxes as general sales taxes and import duties; reducing sumptuary taxes; and reducing or eliminating local excise and nuisance taxes, which frequently have a regressive structure. Exemptions from sales and import taxes should specifically include such items as unprocessed foodstuffs, which constitute a good portion of the urban poor's consumption. Going much beyond that will increase administrative and efficiency costs of exemptions and may well increase leakage of the exemptions to higher income groups (McLure 1975, p. 19).

Sumptuary taxes in theory can be applied mainly to items of luxury consumption, but in many countries they actually form a good portion of the urban poor's tax burden. Taxes on beer or on cheap brands of liquor, on tobacco products, on popular betting games, and on lotteries are found in many cities of the developing world. Although these taxes have the advantage of being easy to collect and have a certain ethical appeal (especially to the urban elite, since these taxes are seen as limiting vice), they are in fact highly regressive. The reason for this is that the income and price elasticities for consumption of these items are extremely low; thus the tax burden for their consumption falls mainly on the poor without, however, significantly reducing the consumption of the items concerned.[7] For example, in Bogota the local taxes on alcoholic beverages and tobacco products have accounted exclusively for the regressivity of local taxation. In recent years the local beer tax in Bogota was the one local tax whose revenues grew in real per capita terms, so that its contribution to total local tax revenues reached 50 percent, while the contribution of other local taxes, especially the property tax, dropped in relative and absolute terms (Linn 1976a).

Local excise taxes—such as selective taxes on local business and commerce and on local trade (particularly noteworthy is the octroi tax found in many cities of the Indian subcontinent)[8]—are frequently regressive. Often, however, an improved rate structure and exemption policy could go far in reducing a considerable part of the burden these taxes place on the urban poor while retaining their revenue-generating capacity (for an example of the restructuring of a local industry and commerce tax—in Cartagena, Colombia—see Linn 1975).

INCREASING PROGRESSIVE TAXES. Elimination or reduction of taxes on the poor, although it is not likely substantially to reduce public revenues, needs to be balanced by increased taxes that presumably would have to fall heavily on the higher income groups.[9] Other policies, such as reduced trade protection designed to increase labor absorption (see Keesing 1979) would be another reason for the need to increase tax revenues, quite apart from the additional need for public resources generated by an emphasis on basic needs policies.[10]

A comprehensive discussion of tax policy cannot be undertaken here. For a brief overview of potential changes designed to increase the progressivity of typical national taxes (such as personal and corporate income taxes, wealth and capital gains taxes, and death and gift taxes), the reader may want to consult McLure (1975). Substantial increases in tax burdens on the rich and middle-income groups are limited by the general constraints on tax policy mentioned earlier, and the approach has to be designed to fit the special conditions of each particular country concerned. Only a few comments are warranted here regarding some financing instruments of special relevance to urban areas and urban governments. First of all, the effort to increase public revenues in a progressive way must concentrate on those taxes and charges for which escape by the wealthy taxpayers (through evasion, brain or capital drain, or reduction in savings or work effort) can be minimized. The instruments discussed are the taxation of urban real estate and of the use and ownership of automotive vehicles and various forms of benefit-related charges for publicly provided urban services.

URBAN PROPERTY TAXATION. Beginning with the property tax, which is found to play a role in financing urban development in most developing countries (Bahl 1977, Smith 1974), it is necessary to dispel the common misconception that this tax in its basic form—that is, levied at rates proportional to the value of real estate—is regressive in incidence.[11] Recent economic analyses of the incidence of urban property taxation in developing countries have established beyond reasonable doubt that this tax in fact is likely to be quite progressive, unless statutory provisions and administrative practices counteract and possibly eliminate its inherent progressivity (Bahl and Linn, forthcoming; Linn 1977).

An extensive review of such statutory and administrative practices in urban property taxation in cities of the developing world has also shown that deviations from the basic proportional property tax are quite frequent and, depending on the country and city concerned, can either increase or reduce the progressivity of this tax (Bahl and Linn, forthcoming). Features that increase the progressivity of urban property tax are: progressively graduated tax rates or assessment ratios; exemptions or low assessment ratios for low-value properties; higher than average tax rates on vacant lots or commercial properties; lower tax rates on improvement than on site (land) value; better than average collection efforts for high-value properties. As it happens, these features in the converse (regressively graduated tax rates, low assessment ratios for high-value properties, lower taxes on vacant lots, higher rates on improvements than on site value, and lower average collection effort on high-value properties) are also quite common and tend to reduce the progressivity of the urban property tax. In addition, owner-occupied properties are quite frequently given preferential treatment over rental properties, which further reduces property tax progressivity and burdens the urban poor, who are more likely to rent.

Taking a broad overview of urban property tax administration in all of the cities and countries surveyed by Bahl and Linn (forthcoming), and assessing the distributive effect of these practices, one may conclude that in a majority of thirty-two cases the overall impact of these institutional aspects is progressive if compared with a proportional property tax. In some cities the direction of the effect of administration practices is unclear, or procedures with mutually offsetting distributive effects are being applied. That contradictory practices are in effect clearly reflects the ad hoc nature in which distributive objectives are pursued in property taxation. In these cities progressively structured tax rates and exemptions of owner-occupied properties typically coexist side by side.

This brief review of property tax incidence in developing country cities can conclude with two policy recommendations. First, in those cities where regressive property tax practices are prevalent an effort should be made to eliminate these practices, since their removal would improve revenues, efficiency, equity, and administrative ease. Furthermore, at least some of the measures that increase the progressivity of property taxes—such as higher tax rates for site value than for improvement value, higher than average rates of taxes for vacant lots, and exemption of low-value or slum properties—would very likely increase progressivity and efficiency.[12] Second, overall reliance on property taxes could probably be increased in many cities in developing countries. Average effective tax rates tend to be extremely low compared with those found in the industrialized countries (Bahl 1977), and real estate taxation, especially urban land taxation, is hard to evade if the tax is properly administered. Efficiency losses in property taxation are thus likely to be limited.

Lest it be thought that these two suggested improvements in property taxation for urban areas of the developing world are of the pie-in-the-sky variety, especially in their administrative and political feasibility, one may add that recent experiences with property tax reform in such diverging environments as Jamaica and Jakarta, Indonesia, show that progressive change is possible.[13] Of course, such changes take considerable time and effort, but they should be seen as falling within the realm of the possible, and concerted efforts can be made in many developing country cities to improve property taxation. The effect on revenues could be substantial: although for a sample of forty-seven developing economies the average contribution of property taxes to total tax revenue was only 5 percent between 1969 and 1971, it was 10 percent in Turkey, 12.5 percent in Lebanon, 14.5 percent in Taiwan, 23.8 percent in Nepal, and 27.1 percent in Singapore (Chelliah, Baas, and Kelly 1975). In the case of Jamaica, property tax revenues increased fivefold in the period from 1972 to 1976, and the contribution of property taxes to total national government tax revenues increased from 2.6 percent in 1971–72 to 5.4 percent in 1975–76 as a result of the property tax reform (Risden 1979).

One of the particularly attractive aspects of effective urban land taxation is that it can act as an instrument to appropriate for public use some of the windfall gains that urban landowners reap in the rapidly growing cities of developing countries. These windfalls are one of the major ways by which the benefits of public infrastructure provision and of the agglomeration economies of urban growth are translated into increased wealth. Particularly in cities where the ownership of land is highly concentrated, a substantial share of the benefits from urbanization accrue to a few rich people. An effective system of benefit charges for urban services that recovers at least the cost of service provision will reduce the need for general land taxation, but usually there is plenty of scope for improvements in both property taxation and benefit charges. Property taxes designed specifically to capture land value increments have been tried, but, with the exception of experience on the island of Taiwan, a general tax on land value increases does not appear to have worked successfully in either developing or industrialized economies (see Grimes 1974 and Shoup 1978).

URBAN AUTOMOTIVE TAXATION. Another area where potential improve-ments in taxation and urban development closely overlap is the area of automotive taxation. (This section draws heavily on Churchill 1972, Linn 1979b, Smith 1975, and Walters 1968.) Automobile ownership and use provide an excellent but much neglected tax base for urban governments in cities in the developing world. The number of automobiles registered in the cities in recent years has grown much faster than the city populations, and in all developing countries car ownership is heavily concentrated in the largest cities. Furthermore, the overwhelming proportion of the urban motor vehicle fleet in developing countries consists of automobiles, and these in turn are owned and operated mainly by the upper income classes. Traffic congestion and air pollution are as bad in many of the cities of the developing world as in those in the industrialized nations, and are largely due to automobile traffic and emissions. These trends, patterns, and problems are likely to become even more pronounced with the rapid expansion of urban areas and with continued increases in incomes in developing countries. (These trends and their implications are further examined in chapter 4.) In any case, ownership and use of motor vehicles are a uniquely *urban* phenomenon in developing countries, even more so than in industrialized countries. Therefore, special attention should be paid to questions of automotive taxation in the cities of the developing world.

Since the present discussion is concerned less with increasing efficiency than it is with the issue of how to raise additional public revenues in a progressive way, the main tax instruments considered here are fuel taxes, taxes on the import and sale of motor vehicles, and taxes on automobile licensing and ownership transfer, rather than on charges designed to reduce central city congestion.[14] National governments tend to rely more heavily on taxes on automobile imports and on fuel use, whereas urban local gov-ernments, if they apply automotive taxes at all, rely more heavily on annual license taxes. The use of all these taxes varies widely between countries.[15] In most cases, increased utilization of some of these taxes is a distinct pos-sibility, to judge by the experience of selected high-tax countries (for example, Colombia, Pakistan, Mexico, Egypt, and Indonesia, which have very high import duties of 200 percent or more). Each of these measures has some advantages and disadvantages in ease of collection, efficiency, and revenue capacity; all of them, however, are likely to put only slight burdens on the urban poor, even less on the rural poor. The choice among them in specific developing countries depends very much on the extent to which they are currently used, and no general prescription (beyond the one that increased reliance on automotive taxes does seem feasible for most developing countries) can be derived, except that import and sales taxes on automobiles are probably inferior in most regards to other automotive taxes.[16]

Two additional points are of particular relevance to the administration of automotive taxes. First, in most countries the bulk of automotive tax revenues is raised at the national level, while local urban governments make only very limited tax efforts in this area. There is, however, scope for increased local action on this front in many cities through the levying of differentially higher fuel and vehicle license taxes in urban areas (Linn 1979b). This is particularly the case if general trade liberalization were to lead to substantial reductions in automobile tariffs. Second, care must be taken in tax design to exempt, wherever possible, tax bases that are primarily used by low-income groups, in particular fuels destined for home use and for buses.[17] Also differentially higher rates on luxury cars, applied in some countries as import tariffs (World Bank 1975b, app.), will increase the progressivity of automotive taxes at the upper end of the income scale without, however, doing much to increase revenues or to lower tax burdens of the poor.

BENEFIT CHARGES FOR URBAN PUBLIC SERVICES. One may then turn to the possibility of increasing public revenues through a more progressive use of benefit charges in the provision of urban public services. Much will be said throughout the remainder of this volume regarding the importance of financing policies in the design and provision of such services. Here it suffices to point out that the failure to recoup urban services costs from beneficiaries in the past has frequently led to extensive subsidies, particularly to higher-income groups. The kinds of services for which subsidies are provided include public housing, public utilities, urban road space, secondary and tertiary education, and modern hospital care. These subsidies on balance favor the wealthier income groups for several reasons: because of the superior political influence of these groups in drawing service provision into their neighborhoods or in preempting the available services such as public housing; because of the concentration of urban property ownership in the hands of the affluent and the fact that the benefits from urban public services are at least partially capitalized into land value; and because the poor are not able to benefit from some public services by virtue of complementary private costs (for example, out-of-pocket expenses and loss of income when attending school or visiting modern hospitals or the expense of purchasing a private automobile). The elimination of subsidies for urban public services would in many cases provide additional public revenues mainly by drawing on the resources of the wealthier groups while at the same time increasing the efficiency of resource allocation, since cost-related prices make the service user aware of the resource cost of public service provision and thus will curtail demand for these services to efficient levels.

Improved service pricing and benefit taxation could significantly contribute to equity, efficiency, and public revenue availability. Public housing should be priced at full costs;[18] the average incremental capital and recurrent cost of public utility services should be charged to the user, subject to possible provisions of life-line rates or similar measures to permit access even for the very poor; central city roads used by private automobiles should be priced at social costs through area licensing fees or parking fees; the improvement of neighborhood streets and even major arterial roads should be financed from betterment levies (as widely practiced, for instance, in the cities of Colombia); the provision of public higher education could be financed from student loans or parent contributions, graduated by income levels; and the provision of modern health services for the wealthy ought to be financed fully through actuarially sound insurance schemes. All of these are broad prescriptions for the elimination of service subsidies benefiting mainly the rich. A closer look at many of these financing mechanisms will be taken in later chapters.

Benefit taxes such as those recommended here also have the advantage that it may be easier administratively and politically to raise public revenues where the relation of the charge to the benefit from a particular service is clearly established in the mind of the taxpayer than it would be where this relation is perceived to be quite remote, as in the case of income or wealth taxes.[19] There are, however, a few common obstacles to increased reliance on benefit taxation. Besides political clout by traditional beneficiaries of subsidized services, there is the problem that the expectation of free or subsidized provision of certain services (such as water supply, use of central city roads and neighborhood streets, public bus services, and education) may have become so ingrained in the popular mind that any efforts to start charging unsubsidized rates will generate considerable negative public reaction. In part, this may be explained by the fact that the introduction of even relatively small recurrent fees may lead to windfall losses on the part of property owners because of the capitalization of the entire stream of expected future charges into lower asset values, particularly lower land values. Another explanation is that people will feel unfairly treated by the introduction of measures designed to recover service costs from them if their neighbors have received the same service free of charge in the recent past. This does not mean that efforts to increase public revenues through benefit charges need to be entirely abandoned. Rather, these charges have to be carefully planned and implemented and may need to be introduced gradually. The experience of the World Bank in this area, especially as regards public utility charges, is that increased reliance on benefit charges is indeed a possibility in many urban areas, for rich and poor beneficiaries alike.[20]

Poverty Alleviation through Public Expenditures

The extensive discussion of alternative public revenue sources above notwithstanding, it is on the expenditure side of the public budget that the real potential for poverty alleviation and most of the problems in achieving it are encountered (Bird and De Wulf 1973, McLure 1975). It is through the provision of public services such as transport, shelter and urban infrastructure, education, and health care that developing country governments can attempt to eliminate, or at least reduce, the incidence of urban poverty. Obviously, the scope for urban poverty alleviation will vary between countries, depending among other things on the share in GNP of public expenditure relative to the income of the poor, and depending on the extent to which the poor are falling short of the absolute poverty threshold. Selowsky (1979a, p. 3) points out that "in a country where government expenditure and the income of the poorest 20 percent of the population account for 25 and 5 percent, respectively, of the gross national product, reallocating 10 percent of the fiscal budget to this group would increase its income by 50 percent." Moreover, if an increase in income of 100 percent is needed to lift the poor over the poverty threshold, then of course the reallocation of the budget must be in the order of 20 percent. Similarly, if the poorest 40 percent of the population fall below the poverty threshold and receive, say, 10 percent of GNP, then again a reallocation of 20 percent of the budget is required to lift their incomes by 50 percent. On the one hand, since the government sector tends to be relatively more important in urban than in rural areas and since the proportion of the absolute poor in urban areas is generally less than in rural areas (see chapter 1), in principle a much smaller shift in urban-oriented public expenditures is required to eliminate absolute urban poverty than is required in rural-oriented expenditures.[21] On the other hand, in the low-income countries, where a larger proportion of the population tends to live below the absolute poverty threshold, a larger effort in budget shifting may be required in both urban and rural areas, especially if the share of public spending in total GNP also tends to be smaller than in the middle-income countries.

But, for several reasons, shifting expenditures in favor of the poor is easier said than done. First, there are the political obstacles that may preclude such reorientation of public budgets, even if efficiency and equity goals could be served at the same time (see chapter 1). Second, direct transfers of current incomes from higher- to lower-income groups through the budget are not costless and in fact do not appear to occur on a large scale anywhere in the developing world. Even in the industrialized countries, a debate has been carried on for many years whether and how such transfers should be made.

Third, with direct income transfers out of the running one is left with the possibility of public intervention in the provision of goods and services to lower service costs to the poor by a fiscal dividend, subsidies, or both of these jointly. Reaping the benefits of fiscal dividends for the poor is, of course, the most attractive route, since this does not involve a conflict between the goals of efficiency and equity. (Yet the conflict between high- and low-income groups remains; see chapter 1.) Subsidies (unless based on externality arguments) are in general less attractive, since they involve losses in efficiency and public revenue. But for both policies the same question remains: How can one design a public expenditure policy that will ensure that the benefits from public expenditures actually accrue to the poor, rather than to the better-off? Capitalization of fiscal dividends and subsidies into land values, preemption by the rich of public housing ostensibly constructed for the poor, high drop-out rates of poor children from the conventional school system—these are just three of the many ways that public expenditure policy may not affect the poor when it intends to do so. Careful design of public expenditure programs is therefore the prerequisite for any policy that proposes to alleviate urban poverty. The remaining chapters will address this issue for specific areas of urban policy.

Summary of Policy Implications

The scope for general redistribution of income is limited in most countries, and in any case a reduction in the skewness of the income distribution by itself does not necessarily provide a solution to the poverty problem. To work toward such a solution, fiscal policies should explicitly address the poverty problem, both as regards the generation of public revenues and the allocation of public expenditures. In any case, the urban poverty problem will need to be solved by drawing on resources generated in urban rather than in rural areas. An urban poverty-oriented fiscal strategy must include the following tax and expenditure measures.

Tax Policy

The urban poor pay taxes, especially indirect taxes and taxes levied by local governments. Tax policy should therefore be designed to reduce this burden—for example, by exempting basic foodstuffs from indirect taxation and by reducing sumptuary taxes. The revenue loss from these measures will generally be minor.

In raising additional public revenues, emphasis should be placed on those revenue services that fall relatively lightly on the poor, in particular:

- Property taxation, which generally has a progressive incidence in developing country cities and which can be explicitly structured to increase progressivity without significant losses in efficiency, revenue potential, or administrative simplicity

- Motor vehicle taxation (especially taxes on privately owned automobiles), which provides an excellent base in urban areas for progressive taxation by national and local authorities
- Elimination of subsidies in public service provision where these tend to benefit mainly the middle- and upper-income classes, especially in subsidized public housing, public utilities, urban road space, advanced formal education, and modern health facilities.

Expenditure Policy

Public expenditure, in particular provision of public services, is the most important means through which the alleviation of urban poverty must be sought in the short and medium term, since productivity and employment opportunities for the poor can be increased only slowly. In theory, relatively small shifts in public expenditure would suffice in some countries to raise the absolute poor above the poverty threshold. In practice, it is more difficult to design expenditure programs in such a way that the poor derive most of the benefits, whether these benefits are derived from fiscal dividends or subsidies.

Notes to Chapter 3

1. For a recent general study supporting this view, see Lipton (1977); see also Cohen (1978), who states (p. 2): "In the Sahel, this [urban] bias is found in the subsidized prices of food, agricultural pricing policies, the allocation of public infrastructure and social services, and individual investment decisions in almost every sector." Although these and other studies present extensive evidence supporting the claim of an urban policy bias in many developing countries, an unequivocal proof of this proposition is out of the question. The analytical and empirical difficulties encountered in budget incidence studies (for an excellent review of such studies and their pitfalls, see De Wulf 1975) apply with equal force to studies purporting to prove urban policy biases.

2. This does not imply, however, that there should be no financial transfers from national (or state) governments to local governments in urban areas. A good portion of national government tax revenues are generated in urban areas, and some of this may have to be transferred back to urban governments if these do not have sufficient authority to raise local revenues commensurate with their expenditure responsibilities.

3. McLure (1975), for instance, finds for a subsample of tax incidence studies that much of the progressivity is explained by two factors: higher effective rates in urban areas than in rural areas and relatively heavy effective tax rates on the richest 2 to 5 percent of urban households. For the rest, taxes are more or less proportional even in countries where the overall incidence is quite progressive.

4. A thorough study of budget incidence for Malaysia, a country which has probably made greater efforts at redistribution through the government budget than most developing countries, shows that, while the incomes of the poorest income decile are raised by about 50 percent and those of the richest 5 percent drop by 9 percent as a result of government taxation and ex-

penditure, the incomes of the latter group remain some eighteen times as large as those of the former (Meerman 1977, p. 46).

5. See Streeten and Burki (1978) for a summary statement regarding the "basic needs" approach. The present approach does not, however, exclude the possibility that decisionmakers may want to pursue a general goal of improving incomes for the poor, rather than merely meeting selected needs defined as "basic."

6. This focus is much less relevant in discussions of rural poverty, since the rural poor tend to pay lower taxes in general and fewer local government taxes in particular.

7. See McLure and Thirsk (1980) for an eloquent indictment of sumptuary taxes in developing countries. McLure (1975) also points out that governmental concern for the negative externalities generated by gambling and alcohol and tobacco consumption is contradicted by the frequent support of lotteries and of state liquor monopolies, and by the failure to ban advertising for alcohol or tobacco products or to advertise against them.

8. As mentioned earlier, this tax is levied on all commodities entering a local jurisdiction. In Karachi and three Indian cities surveyed in a recent study (Linn 1980), octroi revenues were found to contribute some 40 percent of locally raised taxes.

9. To postulate an extreme case, assume that all taxes on the poor (the lowest 40 percent of the population in the income distribution) are eliminated from a tax structure that initially had a proportional incidence. In this case, tax revenues will drop by less than 12 percent in countries with high income inequality (for example, in almost half the developing countries surveyed by Ahluwalia 1974), by 12 to 17 percent in countries with moderate inequality, and by 17 to 20 percent in countries with low inequality (Ahluwalia 1974, p. 8). Note that the elimination of all import taxes in developing countries would reduce their tax revenues by an average of about 25 percent (Chelliah, Baas, and Kelly 1975, p. 1).

10. Obviously, mineral-exporting countries need to worry less about their ability to raise tax revenues in a nonregressive way, since they can tap the fiscal benefits of their mineral resources and shift the tax burden abroad.

11. For expressions of such a view see U.S. Department of Housing and Urban Development (1973), Robson and Regan (1972), Hauck Walsh (1969), United Nations (1970).

12. Higher than average taxation of luxury housing is advocated by McLure (1975), but is not found in any of the cities surveyed above. To the extent that luxury housing represents an identifiable category of real estate—this depends on assessment practices, but would clearly be possible in some countries, such as Colombia—such a measure would indeed be a further way to increase the progressivity of property taxation.

13. For the Jamaican case, see Risden (1979) and Bougeon-Maassen and Linn (1975); for the case of Jakarta, see Linn, Smith, and Wignjowijoto (1976). Recent developments in Jakarta indicate even more far-reaching changes than described in this report.

14. These charges, in particular parking fees and area license fees, are discussed in the next chapter. Their incidence is certainly progressive, at least in the sense that they are not likely to burden the urban poor; however, they generally yield only limited increases in public revenues net of administration costs (Linn 1979b).

15. See World Bank (1975b, annex 2) for comparative information on import taxes on cars, Smith (1975) for cross-country information regarding national taxes on fuel and automobile ownership, and Linn (1979b) for comparative information regarding the automotive taxes levied by local governments in selected developing country cities.

16. Walters (1968) argues that in general fuel taxes are too high in developing countries in that they are likely to engender efficiency losses except in congested urban traffic. He therefore appears to favor annual license taxes related to vehicle value as a means of raising fiscal resources. Smith (1975) views the efficiency losses of high fuel taxes as less serious, although he too supports annual license fees for revenue purposes.

17. The local taxes on buses in Indian, Korean, and Colombian municipalities are not defensible on grounds of equity, efficiency, or revenue generation (Linn 1979b).

18. Public housing for civil servants, however, provides an added complication: to the extent that the elimination of subsidized housing for civil servants reduces their real wages below the level at which adequately skilled professionals can be attracted to government civil service, wages may have to be increased. Yet this would appear to be a preferable approach, since it provides a clearer and more flexible salary structure for public employees.

19. In many industrialized countries, efforts are made to increase the reliance on benefit taxes and user charges in a reversal of a long trend toward reliance on general tax financing; see Bird (1976).

20. See Shipman (1967) for a discussion of changes that have taken place during the 1960s in Latin American attitudes toward financing of water supply services through user charges.

21. This statement refers only to the relative scope for urban versus rural poverty alleviation, not to the relative importance of the two goals.

4

Urban Transport

THE IMPORTANCE OF THE TRANSPORT SECTOR in urban development is multi-dimensional. The basic function of urban transport is to link residence and employment, producers and users of goods and services (both intermediate and final). Urban transport complements a large number of other urban public services because the accessibility of an urban neighborhood determines to a considerable extent whether, or at least how easily, solid waste is collected; water, sewerage, drainage, and electricity networks are provided and maintained; police and fire protection is made available; and schools and health care are within reach of urban dwellers. Furthermore, since the transport system has an important effect on a city's physical extension and population density, and population density in turn directly affects the cost of infrastructure provision, urban transport policy may have a considerable impact on the cost of other urban services.

The urban transport sector is important in other respects. It provides employment for a significant although varying proportion of the urban population. An extreme and probably somewhat biased estimate of the employment effects of a particular form of urban transport was recorded (1975 World Bank data) in Manila, where about 10 percent of the labor force is supposedly directly or indirectly involved in the provision of "jeepney" (communal taxi) services. Urban transport also places a considerable financial burden on the public authorities in urban areas; although the proportions vary, it is not unusual for urban governments to spend between 15 and 25 percent of their annual budgets on transport-related investment and operating activities (Bahl and Linn, forthcoming). Total public investments programmed for the transport sectors in Bombay and Calcutta for the period 1972–78 accounted, respectively, for 26 and 48 percent of total planned investment (1973 World Bank data).

For the urban poor, transport facilities are particularly important because by definition the poor are at the margin of subsistence and are especially sensitive to disruptions in their earnings brought about by poor transport policies, be it with respect to their access to employment or services or to their carrying out small-scale commercial and trading activities. Improved access to transport for poor neighborhoods can improve the employment prospects of the poor, reduce the money and time spent on getting to jobs, reduce the costs of inputs for their small-scale enterprise activities, and increase access to markets for their products. It also facilitates the provision of and access to all the other public services in poor areas. Finally, the transport sector itself provides the poor with employment opportunities that are not negligible (see table 2-2, above) and that can be increased or reduced by urban transport policies.[1]

Given the important role the transport system plays in urban development in general, and in the improvement of living conditions of the poor in particular, the fact that the system fails to play this role efficiently and equitably in most large cities in the developing world acquires special urgency. The following excerpt, from the report of a 1975 World Bank mission to Manila, speaks for many, if not all, of the large developing country cities:

> Metropolitan Manila's growth has far outstripped the capacity of its transportation infrastructure, both the road network and mass transportation facilities. Rapidly increasing travel demands have been accommodated by a transport system whose nature has changed little since the turn of the century. As a result, Manila is almost entirely dependent on road-based transport, road space is inadequate, and severe traffic congestion has become the normal condition. Perhaps an even more important problem is the absence of any plan to help the transport system conform to the demands generated by the emerging distribution of metropolitan employment and residence locations.
>
> Proposed solutions to Manila's transport problems range from networks of high standard roads, to subways and elevated magnetic levitation systems for public transport, to improved traffic control. Some of these options have been studied extensively and others are simply ideas, but in any case little has been accomplished in the way of investment or management improvement to either expand the system or improve its operation.

The various elements that contribute to the chaos of urban transport in most cities of the developing world have been documented (World Bank 1975b). They include a high degree of congestion and pollution in central cities (despite generally low levels of motorization); inadequacy of public transport and of paved urban road space; limited public resources; and poor management of the transport sector. Urban transport problems and misguided policies are, of course, not unique to the developing world; they are also prevalent in the cities of the industrialized countries. There are, however, two differences worth noting. First, at the low levels of incomes and resources under which developing countries have to operate, any major mistake, or any forgone opportunity to improve significantly the efficiency and equity of resource allocation, must weigh far more heavily than in the advanced countries. In the latter, such an event is troublesome but can be absorbed relatively easily given the generally high levels of urban incomes. Second, the degree of motorization, in particular the extent of private car ownership and use, is still quite low in most developing countries, although it is increasing at a rapid rate. Since many, if not most, urban transport problems are related directly to the use of the private automobile, developing country cities still have a chance to avoid the mistakes made in many of the industrialized countries in developing inefficient urban forms. Policy action, however, must be swift if this chance is not to be lost. It is encouraging that in some developing country cities conventional transport policies are being replaced by more efficient and equitable approaches.

One of the prerequisites for appropriate policy to deal with the urban transport problem in developing country cities is the realization that transport is only a means to an end, which is access and communication. These goals can be fostered not only by direct action in the transport sector but also by appropriate land use policy. Of particular importance are the decentralization of employment opportunities away from congested centers within metropolitan areas and the location of public service facilities close to intended consumers, especially in the case of public administration, health, and education facilities. Although the relations between urban land use and the transport system are extremely complex, and appropriate alternatives to traditional urban transport practices and investments undocumented over the long term, these areas cannot be ignored by planners if an enlightened urban transport policy for the developing world is to be achieved.

This chapter proceeds very much in this vein. While much of urban transport is subject to uncertainty, there exists for many policy areas evidence pointing clearly toward certain preferred actions that can be strongly supported and vigorously pursued.

The remainder of this chapter falls into two sections: the first documents some of the major trends and determinants of urban transportation in developing countries; the second reviews the transport problems faced by the urban poor in developing country cities and discusses the various policies that must be pursued to reduce these problems.

Urban Transport in Developing Countries: Trends, Determinants, and Policies

The rapid growth of cities in developing countries has been accompanied by an increased need for urban transport. Unlike small cities or towns, where it is possible to reach virtually every point on foot or by bicycle within reasonable time, large cities require extensive, motorized transport systems to permit the movement of people and goods between various locations. Indeed, the rapid rate of transport motorization attendant on rapid urbanization and income growth has led to a situation where "two kinds of population explosions have been worrying the authorities in many parts of the world during recent times—of people and of cars" (Zahavi 1976, p. 1). As the comparison of population growth rates with the rates of growth of automobile ownership for selected cities in developing and developed countries in table 4-1 shows,[2] the growth in the number of automobiles has universally outstripped the growth in population. Urban authorities should thus perhaps worry more about the former, especially since the ownership and use of motor vehicles—particularly of the private automobile—is very costly in public and private resource requirements and is likely to be more easily controlled by appropriate policy actions than is the rate of urban population growth.

This section provides an overview of the most important trends in urban transport patterns in developing country cities and of the available evidence regarding the variables (such as city size, population density, transport modal split, urban form and land use patterns, and pricing, regulation, and other institutional determinants) affecting the demand for and the cost of urban transport.

Transport Demand

Research in cities of developing and developed countries has investigated the relation between transport demand and city size, density, and motorization (Zahavi 1976, pp. 76–77). Larger city size and lower population density each tend to be associated with increased trip length; to the extent that city growth tends to be associated with declining average population density (see Ingram and Carroll 1979 for Latin American data), the effects of density and size on trip length are mutually reinforcing. If travel times are to be kept within bounds, higher speeds are required for longer trips, and higher speeds in turn require more road space per vehicle. Higher motor vehicle populations tend to compound the problem, since automobiles require more road space per passenger than do other forms of motorized transport.

City size thus is a crucial variable in determining travel length, speed, and the need for transport infrastructure investment. Since city size is to a large degree beyond the influence of policy (Renaud 1981), however, and is almost certainly beyond the policy domain of urban government in a particular city, the question of what determines the other major variables—population density and motorization—becomes important.

Many factors determine the average density of cities and changes in density over time: among others, the provision and pricing of urban services (including that of urban transport), the extent of motorization, land use policies such as zoning, differential land taxation, and employment location decisions by private and public enterprises. Income is also an important and pervasive variable, since higher incomes tend to be associated with greater demand for residential land and permit more costly urban service networks because of a lower resource constraint on public and private decisionmakers. In any case, density changes are likely to be slow and intricately involved with the type of urban transport network that is developed over time, in particular with the extent of motorization.

The degree of motorization is associated with the level of income of a country and a city.[3] From table 4-1 it is found that there exists quite a strong relation between average per capita income in developing country cities and the number of automobiles per thousand population (the correlation coefficient is 0.61).[4] Of greater importance for an understanding of transport demand, however, is the information on the transport modes used in urban travel, although there is, of course, likely to be a close relation between vehicle ownership and use.

Unfortunately, data on the modal split of urban trips by the entire range of transport modes, including walking and cycling, are very scarce (Zahavi 1976, p. ix). There is little doubt, however, that as incomes increase the proportion of nonmotorized trips in total travel tends to decline. According to recent estimates, walking trips have accounted for two-thirds of total trips in large African cities such as Kinshasa and Dar es Salaam (World Bank 1975b, p. 19); walking and cycling trips accounted for 60 percent of total trips (40 percent of work-related trips) in Karachi (USAID 1976, p. 159); and in Madras "a third of vehicles entering the central business district each day are cycles, as are more than 25 percent of vehicles passing a cordon some 10 miles out" (World Bank 1975b, p. 19). In contrast, in Kingston only 16 percent of all work trips (25 percent of school trips) are made on foot, and less than 1 percent on bicycle (Jamaica Ministry of Finance and Planning 1978, p. 2.12).[5] Despite the fact that on balance nonmotorized trips tend to decline in importance with rising income and motorization (and, very probably, with city size), the considerable variations between cities of roughly comparable conditions are quite surprising (World Bank 1975b, p. 20). These variations indicate that neither income nor motorization levels provide a sufficient explanation for differences in the share of nonmotorized trips in total travel in developing country cities.

Turning then to an analysis of the data on the modal split of motorized trips in developing country cities (table 4-1), one finds that the picture is similarly complex. Looking first at the relation between car ownership and the share of automobile trips in total motorized trips in the table, one finds a relatively low correlation coefficient (0.45). Furthermore, there is virtually

Table 4-1. *Transport Data for Selected Cities*

City	Population (thousands) (1970) (1)	Rate of growth of population (percent) (1960–70) (2)	Income per capita (U.S. dollars) (1970) (3)	Number of automobiles per thousand population (1970) (4)	Rate of growth of automobiles (percent) (1960–70) (5)
Calcutta	7,402	2.2	270	13.0	7.2
Bombay	5,792	3.7	390	13.5	8.2
Madras	3,438	4.5	180	7.9	5.8
Seoul	5,536	8.5	440	6.3	22.0
Jakarta	4,312	5.3	325	18.0	8.8
Hong Kong	3,350	2.9	850	26.2	7.1
Karachi	3,460	5.6	360	10.4	(0.6)
Tehran	3,600	7.0	950	44.4	(15.4)
Bangkok	3,090	6.2	525	49.7	12.0
Singapore	2,110	2.6	1,100	73.0	6.7
Kuala Lumpur	755	6.5	660	51.9	11.3
Mexico City	8,600	5.8	1,275	78.3	10.5
Buenos Aires	8,400	2.4	1,800	73.9	(12.1)
Sao Paulo	8,400	6.4	785	62.3	n.a.
Bogota	2,551	7.3	760	22.0	n.a.
Caracas	2,277	5.4	1,600	91.0	8.3
San Jose	435	5.4	430	47.9	10.9
Cairo	6,500	5.7	275	n.a.	n.a.
Istanbul	2,800	6.0	810	21.0	12.2
Casablanca	1,505	4.5	820	72.9	(6.1)
Lagos	1,448	7.9	555	22.8	15.5
Kinshasa	1,134	12.1	660	n.a.	n.a.
Tunis	746	2.5	500	57.6	6.0
Beirut	600	2.9	1,000	153.0	9.1
Nairobi	567	8.1	495	52.7	(6.8)
Abidjan	424	11.0	500	75.5	(12.7)
Dar es Salaam	350	9.0	710	33.0	n.a.
Lusaka	225	3.1	660	45.7	n.a.
Tokyo	14,900	3.4	2,775	83.3	16.0
London	10,547	−0.7	2,550	222.0	5.2
Paris	8,448	1.3	3,530	248.0	6.5
Athens	2,416	3.0	n.a.	60.8	12.8
Washington, D.C.	757	−0.1	5,390	316.0	2.0

n.a. Not available.   — Not applicable.

Notes: Because of the variety of sources, differences of definition, and general weaknesses of collection, the data, though indicating orders of magnitude, have only limited comparability. Caution is accordingly required in their use. The data in the table were obtained from several publications indicated below, supplemented by information in various urban and transport studies available in the World Bank. Information was also collected by World Bank missions and from government authorities. Since the sources and methods of data collection are extremely diverse, the table indicates only in rough measure conditions of urbanization and motorization. Data for columns 1, 3, 4, 6, and 7 are for 1970, except in the case of a few cities for which data for 1969 or 1971 had to be used. Rates of growth in columns 2 and 5 are for 1960–70, except for

| Number of buses per thousand population (1970) (6) | Number of commercial vehicles per thousand population (1970) (7) | Import duty on economy cars (percent) (Oct. 1974) (8) | Import duty on luxury cars (percent) (Oct. 1974) (9) | Price of regular grade gasoline per U.S. gallon (US. dollars) (Oct. 1974) (10) | Modal split of motorized trips (percent) | | | Bus fare for a three-mile trip (U.S. cents) (Oct. 1974) (14) |
					Automobiles (11)	Buses (12)	Other motorized (13)	
0.3	4.0	150	150	1.76	8	34	58[a]	3
0.3	4.5	150	150	1.76	11	41	48[b]	3
0.6	1.9	150	150	1.76	—[c]	54	46[d]	3
0.9	3.5	100	150	1.65	8	89	3[e]	n.a.
1.1	4.3	200	200	0.44	29	49	22[f]	4
2.1	7.0	n.a.	n.a.	1.10	22	55	23[g]	4–10
0.3	n.a.	300	150	0.89	16	63	21[d]	1
1.0	6.8	30	62	0.35	37	42	21[e]	3–8
1.2	16.3	80	80	0.50	29	59	12[e]	5
1.3	17.9	25	25	0.98	24	43	33[h]	6.5
1.0	21.8	35	60	1.40	47	35	18[e]	5
1.3	9.0	212	212	0.45	19	65	16[a]	n.a.
1.6	25.6	140	140	1.29	17	60	23[h]	n.a.
1.3	10.6	70	105	1.30	26	60	14[i]	n.a.
1.4	25.0	350	350	0.10	17	71	12[h]	2.5
0.6	27.3	135	135	0.13	46	35	19[a]	n.a.
1.0	34.0	100	100	0.98	23	74	3[j]	4
0.3	n.a.	100	200	n.a.	n.a.	n.a.	n.a.	2
0.2	13.1	25	25	0.80	57	28	15[i]	10
0.4	26.1	120	120	1.46	n.a.	n.a.	n.a.	10–20
1.0	8.3	75	150	0.52	12	n.a.	88[g]	n.a.
0.4	n.a.	20	20	1.52	33	58	9[e]	6
0.5	12.1	33	33	1.50	15	75	10[f]	1.5
2.3	17.3	32	32	0.54	60	10	30[e]	6
1.5	40.6	40	100	1.12	72	28	n.a.[e]	10
1.7	35.4	58	58	1.31	40	47	13[j]	5
0.6	17.3	75	150	n.a.	7	40	53[i]	3.5
1.1	22.1	10	10	n.a.	66	7	27[h]	11
1.3	134.5	40	40	1.46	35	8	57[h]	25
0.6	22.0	15.4	15.4	1.29	59	24	17[d]	25
0.4	44.4	11	11	1.40	36	21	43[g]	30
2.5	18.2	25	25	2.15	n.a.	n.a.	n.a.	10
2.9	24.1	3	3	0.55	68	32	n.a.[e]	40

a few cities where growth rates were available for a shorter period only. Growth rates in parentheses are for the country and not the city. For columns 8 and 9, a Toyota Corona was used to represent an economy car and a Mercedes-Benz 280 a luxury car. In columns 11 and 13, the data are for different years (see footnotes), depending on the most recent traffic survey available to the Bank.

Source: World Bank (1975b), annex 2.

a. Figures for 1966; b. Figures for 1968; c. Included in "Other Motorized;" d. Figures for 1971; e. Figures for 1970; f. Figures for 1972; g. Figures for 1965; h. Figures for 1969; i. Figures for 1967; j. Figures for 1973.

no correlation between income and automobile trip share (correlation coefficient of 0.13). Thus, the relation between automobile use and income—
at least for average income levels across cities—appears more remote than
might have been expected. The correlation coefficients between motorization
(defined as the number of automobiles per thousand population) and income
levels on the one hand and the share of bus trips in total motorized travel
on the other are found to be negative, as might have been expected, but
again they are quite low (-0.34 and -0.12, respectively, for motorization
and income).

These empirical findings indicate that motorization is positively related to
income, automobile use is positively related to motorization, and bus use is
negatively related to motorization, but that these relations are weak. There
are clearly other intervening variables that determine automobile ownership
and use and that may exert as strong an influence as do income and motorization. These variables include the distribution of income; the availability,
quality, and cost to the user of alternative modes of transport; and the pattern
of urban land use. Unfortunately, no studies appear to be available that
determine the quantitative contribution of these variables to the urban transport patterns found in the developing world, although the direction of impact
is clear in most cases. What is important for the present analysis, however,
is that most of the intervening variables cited above can be influenced by
policy action, particularly the availability, quality, and cost of alternative
transport modes.

For instance, it is likely that the high taxes on automobiles and gasoline
in Korea have kept automobile ownership and use at a low level relative to
the average per capita income in that city (table 4-1; see also Beesley and
others 1979). Similarly, the extreme high import taxes on automobiles in
Bogota have kept motorization in automobile use relatively low (table 4-1).
In Singapore, a scheme to limit car use in the central business district has
led to a drastic reduction in automobile traffic in the central city and a switch
to public transport modes and to car pooling (Watson and Holland 1978).

Case studies of transport in developing country cities have also indicated
that the demand for urban transport has been shaped by other factors such
as the availability (or nonavailability) of an efficient bus service or of alternative modes of motorized transport including trains, subways, minibuses,
taxis, and an assorted set of nonconventional modes (including jeepneys in
Manila and "dolmuses" in Turkey). Also, policies to reduce employment
concentration in central city locations have been tried, although with varying
degrees of success.[6] The Bombay Twin City project has been slow to decentralize employment from central Bombay. Some efforts to move wholesale
markets, public administration facilities, and industrial parks out of the congested city centers to locations closer to residential areas have been made in

Singapore and Hong Kong (Grimes 1976) and in Bombay, Bogota, and Salvador (Brazil) (World Bank data), to name only a few examples. There is little evidence on the quantitative effects these land use policies have had on transport patterns, but in some cases significant shifts in transport patterns have evidently occurred (for example, the relocation of the national and local government administration out of the congested central business district in Bogota).[7]

Thus the scope for urban transport policy is significant, and its importance is overriding. This will become more evident in considerations of the characteristics of transport supply, in particular the costs of alternative modes of urban transport.

Transport Cost

The unit cost of urban transport varies primarily with the transport mode selected, since each mode has different associated capital, operating, and maintenance costs.[8] Table 4-2 summarizes estimates of differential transport costs according to the mode selected: walking, cycling, private automobile, taxi, minibus, bus, subway, and urban commuter railway.[9] Of particular interest is the last column, which indicates the total cost in person-miles for each mode.

Walking is clearly the cheapest travel mode (although the cost estimates in table 4-2 do not account for the opportunity cost of time), comparable only to bicycling. Next in line in unit cost are buses and urban railways. Minibuses are somewhat more costly than buses according to the table, but the reverse cost pattern frequently prevails, particularly where efficiently run private minibus operations run side by side with inefficiently operated public bus companies (as, for instance, in Istanbul, Kuala Lumpur, and Manila; see Walters 1979a, b). Subways and taxis are more costly yet,[10] and for cars there is a quantum leap in costs, almost four times the cost of a taxi, some eight times the cost of a bus, and fifty-seven times the cost of a bicycle trip.

While these figures are only illustrative, they are confirmed by common observations of the relative cost effectiveness of alternative transport modes. In Bombay, for example, it has been observed that buses account for two-thirds of all daily passenger trips but only for 10 percent of daily vehicle trips, whereas cars account for only 18 percent of passenger trips but 40 percent of vehicle trips (1976 World Bank data). In Karachi, buses contribute 55 percent of road passenger miles but use only 17 percent of road passenger space; for cars, the respective figures are 44 percent and 83 percent (USAID 1976). Table 4-3 reflects essentially the same lopsided picture for Manila.

The fundamental factor at work is, of course, that the private automobile, especially when carrying only one person, takes roughly nine times more road

Table 4-2. Illustrative Costs of Urban Travel by Different Modes

Mode	Speed (miles per hour)	Persons per foot-width per hour	Track capital costs (U.S. cents per mile)		Track maintenance costs (U.S. cents per mile)		Vehicle operating costs (U.S. cents per mile)		Total cost per person (U.S. cents per mile)
			Per hour	Per person	Per vehicle	Per person	Per vehicle	Per person	
Footway, 4 feet wide	2.1	1,100	2	0	0	0	0	0	...
Bicycle track, 4 feet wide	8.0	450	50	0	0.3	0.3	0	0	0.3
Urban street, 24 feet wide, mixed traffic									
Car with driver only	15.0	29	120	4.1	0.4	0.4	13.0	13.0	17.5
	10.0	51	120	2.4	0.4	0.4	14.6	14.6	17.4
Taxi with 4 passengers	12.0	120	120	1.0	0.4	0.1	13.6	3.4	4.5
	8.6	200	120	0.6	0.4	0.1	15.4	3.8	4.5
Minibus with 10 passengers	10.0	150	120	0.8	0.6	0.1	20.0	2.0	2.9
	7.5	250	120	0.5	0.6	0.1	24.0	2.4	3.0
Bus with 30 passengers	8.6	300	120	0.4	1.0	0	50.0	1.7	2.1
	6.7	500	120	0.2	1.0	0	60.0	2.0	2.2

96

Urban street, 44 feet wide, mixed traffic									
Car with driver only	15.0	39	120	3.1	0.4	0.4	13.0	13.0	16.5
	10.0	55	120	2.2	0.4	0.4	14.6	14.6	17.2
Taxi with 4 passengers	12.0	160	120	0.8	0.4	0.1	13.6	3.4	4.3
	8.6	220	120	0.5	0.4	0.1	15.4	3.8	4.4
Minibus with 10 passengers	10.0	190	120	0.6	0.6	0.1	20.0	2.0	2.7
	7.5	280	120	0.4	0.6	0.1	24.0	2.4	2.9
Bus with 30 passengers	8.6	410	120	0.3	1.0	0	50.0	1.7	2.0
	6.7	550	120	0.2	1.0	0	60.0	2.0	2.2
Urban expressway (capacity per foot-width is independent of width)									
Car with driver only	40.0	180	900	5.0	0.4	0.4	11.0	11.0	16.4
Taxi with 4 passengers	40.0	720	900	1.2	0.4	0.1	11.2	2.8	4.1
Minibus with 10 passengers	40.0	1,200	900	0.8	0.6	0.1	17.0	1.7	2.6
Bus with 40 passengers	40.0	2,000	900	0.4	1.0	0	43.0	1.1	1.5
Subway (22,500 passengers per hour)	21.0	1,700	4,400	2.6	43.0	0.7	37.0	0.6	3.9
Urban railway (22,500 passengers per hour)	30.0	1,700	1,600	0.9	43.0	0.7	37.0	0.6	2.2

… Negligible.
Note: Detailed definitions and calculations of the cost items are given in the source.
Source: World Bank (1975b), annex 5.

Table 4-3. *Daily Person and Vehicle Trips, by Mode,*
in Metropolitan Manila, 1971

Mode	Person trips (percent)	Vehicle trips (percent)	Average number of daily passengers (assumed)
Cars	25.1	40.8	3[a]
Jeepneys[b]	46.1	28.1	8
Buses	16.4	2.0	40
Taxis	5.4	13.2	2
Trucks	5.7	13.8	2
Others	1.3	2.0	3
Total	100.0	100.0	—

— Not applicable.
Note: Trips were unlinked (that is, did not involve different modes).
Source: World Bank data.
a. Includes driver (all other figures in the column exclude driver).
b. Communal taxis operating in Manila.

space per passenger than does a bus (World Bank 1975b, p. 26). Cars thus require much heavier investments in and maintenance of roads than do buses.

This aspect takes on added importance when the central problem of urban transport—congestion—is considered. Traffic congestion, and its attendant air and noise pollution, is as bad, or worse, in many of the cities of developing countries as it is in cities of the industrialized nations.[11] And, although it may be argued that higher congestion and pollution levels than would be accepted in cities of the developed world are acceptable in developing country cities (because travel time and environmental quality are likely to be valued less at lower income levels than at high income levels; World Bank 1975b, p. 27) it is quite possible that the actual levels of congestion and pollution observed in most of the large developing country cities are beyond the optimal levels. More important, they are likely to get worse in the years ahead.

Although there are a number of reasons for the severe central city congestion observed in many developing country cities—including the low proportion of urban space devoted to roads, the mixture of traffic, poor traffic management, urban land use patterns, topographical constraints, and the prevalence of through traffic that is channeled through the city center—there can be little doubt that the use of the private automobile is a major cause of this congestion, even where the extent of motorization is still quite low (for instance, in Karachi, Bombay, and Manila).[12]

The effects of congestion on increased vehicle operating costs and reduced travel speed (and thus loss of time) have been well documented. For Central

American cities in early 1970, Churchill has estimated that, under reasonable assumptions regarding the money value of time and of travel demand elasticities, the congestion cost falls in the range of 8 to 11 U.S. cents per person-mile for an automobile whose speed is reduced to 9.3 miles per hour because of congestion. Where speed is only 7.5 miles per hour, the money equivalent of the loss in time is approximately 14 to 19 U.S. cents per person-mile (Churchill 1972, p. 131).[13]

Two further points should be made. First, most of the costs imposed by the additional vehicle using an urban roadway are external to the operator in that the other road users bear most of the additional operating costs and loss in time. The private cost of operating a vehicle on congested urban streets therefore diverges from the social cost, and inefficient use of urban streets is therefore the rule. One of the objectives of urban transport policy should be to reduce this discrepancy between private and social cost (for instance, by charging road users the marginal social cost of operating their vehicles). The second point is that bus and commercial vehicles are more seriously affected by congestion than are automobiles because of the importance of labor costs in total operating costs, the lesser degree of flexibility in timing and road choice, and the importance of losses through uncertainty in bus schedules and delivery times (World Bank 1975b, pp. 27–29).

Besides choice of transport mode and level of congestion, a number of other factors influence the unit cost of urban transport. Among these are topography, city size and density, track and vehicle design, regulations governing entry and operations of transport agents, and the quality of management, particularly when urban transport is the responsibility of the public sector. The topographical constraints are usually immutable and affect transport costs in roughly predictable fashion. The cost of urban road provision tends to increase with city size because of higher unit costs of land (and possibly labor) in larger cities. Low-density development requires a more extensive road network per residence than does high-density development. For example, a recent modeling exercise for a stylized but representative intermediate-size city in Korea indicated that for the period 1975–85 the incremental capital cost of urban transport for a development pattern with dispersed land use exceeds the capital costs for one with concentrated (high-density) land use by some 50 percent. The difference in recurrent (daily) cost was only 2 percent (Beesley and others 1979, p. 72).

Changes in track and vehicle design can also contribute to cost savings, although the scope is probably limited as long as these changes do not change the relative operating characteristics of different transport modes or as long as the scale of a project is not affected. The possibilities of cost-saving devices are illustrated by the following report by a recent appraisal mission for a World Bank urban transport project in Brazil:

Attempts were made to reduce the scale of any project element whose design was based on unjustified expectations regarding future growth, either of the urban area or of traffic. This approach resulted in important project modifications and cost savings. In Curitiba, the selection of a very low-cost paving technique cut costs by 80 percent on half of the feeder road program. In Salvador, a poor area bus penetration road was cut from the proposed four lanes to two. Overall, cost savings resulting from reducing the standards of proposed project elements were of the order of US$6.3 million in Salvador, US$32.0 million in Curitiba, and US$5.8 million in Recife—a total saving of US$44.1 million (about 15 percent of total project cost).

The cost impact of institutional and managerial constraints in the transport sector are much more difficult, if not impossible, to quantify than are the factors so far described. This does not mean, however, that these elements are of lesser importance. For instance, when 40 percent of the buses run by the national bus company in Tunis during 1972 experienced daily break-downs, the costs to the bus enterprise and the riding public were certainly considerable (1973 World Bank data). Or, as has recently been the case in Recife, Brazil, when the public bus company can restrict entry by private competitors, thus limiting the availability of bus service throughout the city, because the company itself is financially unable to extend services beyond the present scope, considerable costs are incurred by those individuals who have to walk, take a taxi, or even buy a car to get to their places of em-ployment.[14] Restrictions on entry by operators of private buses or other means of transport are quite frequent in developing country cities, particularly where publicly run bus companies exist. What is more, these public enterprises are frequently managed rather poorly and may encourage wage and benefit scales for their employees that are far above those of competitors in the private sector.[15]

The Urban Transport System

Costs alone do not determine the optimal choice of travel mode or of urban transport policy. Benefits also have to be considered, and it is clear that under many circumstances an automobile conveys much higher benefits to the user than does a bus, bicycling, or walking. Circumstances do vary, however, and they vary in particular with transport conditions and transport policy. For instance, in a highly congested central city a bicycle, or even walking, may provide more mobility than does an automobile stuck in a traffic jam and requiring a place to park. Also, a bus on an exclusive bus lane may provide far faster access to employment than does an automobile on a congested limited-access expressway. The efficiency of an urban transport system thus depends a great deal on the conditions under which the system operates. Since these conditions appear to vary quite systematically with city size, the following paragraphs will briefly outline some of the changing circumstances under which the transport system operates as the city grows, in particular the changing relative costs and benefits of alternative travel modes and related policies. Of course, the analysis must be rather broad, given the large number of factors influencing demand and supply conditions of urban transport. Policy prescriptions are similarly sketched in very general terms. They will be treated in greater detail in the following section.

For small cities and towns in developing countries (with less than, say, 100,000 inhabitants), trip length tends to be quite short, between relatively proximate employment and residential locations.[16] Nonmotorized transport can provide sufficient mobility for most people; motorized transport is chosen mainly for its convenience by the higher-income groups or for commercial transport, although minibuses may provide a useful mode of transport to all but the poorest in the smaller towns of middle-income countries. These private choices of travel mode generally do not lead to major conflicts in the use of available road space, and public investments in urban transport facilities remain quite low. Some minor efforts of traffic management may be required—for instance, traffic lights at the few busy intersections and limits on parking in the central square or on main streets to avoid unnecessary tieups. In many cases, poorly managed through traffic may pose the major problem to urban transport in these towns, and it therefore may deserve special attention and remedies (as in Southeast Asia; see Mitsui Consulting Co. 1977). In any case urban transport probably does not in general require extensive policy intervention in small cities or towns.

For intermediate-size cities (100,000 to 500,000 inhabitants) average trip length begins to reach a level at which motorized transport takes on increased importance, especially if economic activity is highly concentrated or if incomes are relatively high and permit a high degree of car ownership and the provision of motorized public transport for the major corridors. San Jose (Costa Rica), Cartagena (Colombia), Dar es Salaam (Tanzania), and Lusaka (Zambia) fall into this general category (see table 4-1). In those cities, traffic management becomes a problem, particularly in the congested city centers and around markets and intercity transport terminals. Much of the problem is caused by the fact that the street network of the old city centers is not adapted to high-density motorized traffic and by the generally unconstrained driving and parking of private motor vehicles on these streets. Nevertheless, work trips are still not significantly affected by these problems, since all employment opportunities remain accessible within reasonable time from virtually all locations in the city. This, however, does not mean that there is no scope for a conscious urban transport policy. Greater needs for transport infrastructure arise in these cities than in small towns; traffic management can be improved, particularly in the central areas;[17] and public transport, particularly buses, becomes an area of official intervention. More important, however, is the fact that many of the cities falling into this size class— particularly in Latin America, Africa, and East Asia—are growing rapidly and will in a decade or less fall into the next larger size grouping, where urban transport becomes a major problem for city management unless steps have been taken early to ensure an appropriate urban transport pattern.[18] The most important aspect here is the encouragement of a land use pattern that reduces the need for lengthy commuting trips by encouraging a balanced spread of employment opportunities as the city grows. This is, of course, easier said than done. What can certainly be avoided, however, is the kind of policy that actively encourages the spatial segregation of economic activities and residential location.[19]

For large cities (half a million to 2 million inhabitants), the average length of trips increases to the point where walking is no longer an option for many commuters, especially when employment opportunities are highly concentrated. Congestion and pollution take on more serious and widespread proportions, particularly since car ownership and use is likely to be higher in larger than in smaller cities, at least within the same country. Cities of this size tend to be mononuclear, in that most employment opportunities are concentrated in one major cluster or along an axis (often extending from the city center along the railway line). Cities with more than 2 million inhabitants are often characterized by the emergence of multinuclear employment concentrations. This may occur because of spontaneous decentralization of economic activities, such as has been observed for Bogota and Manila (World Bank data and Lee 1979); because of the incorporation of previously independent urban settlements into the metropolitan area of a large and growing city—as in the case of Cali (Colombia) and, at a somewhat lesser scale, as in Kingston (Jamaica);[20] or because of government policies to decentralize metropolitan employment, such as the "cities within the city" program in Colombia or the Twin City development in Bombay.

In any case, the transport problems of large cities have generally reached the scale where only fairly drastic policy action is likely to cut what seems a Gordian knot. In virtually all these cities, significant limitations on the use of automobiles in congested central areas are required. This is particularly important in high-income countries and cities with high and rapidly increasing levels of motor vehicle ownership. The means to achieve this goal are varied and must be combined for greatest effect. They include taxation of automobile ownership, area license schemes and parking fees in the most congested locations, and improvements in mass transit facilities, including intermediate motorized transit modes such as minibuses, jitneys, and the like.

In most large cities the improvements in mass transit facilities will probably be reserved for buses (or, when already in existence, for improved surface rail transport, as in Tunis or Bombay).[21] Buses have a high degree of operational flexibility, do not require separate rights of way (or where they do, this can be provided with relative ease on the basis of existing streets), and may need only a minimal involvement of scarce governmental administration and financial resources (since bus systems have been shown to be operated successfully by the private sector in a number of developing country cities; Roth 1973). The speed, effectiveness, and convenience of bus systems can be significantly improved by provision of reserved bus lanes, preferred treatment at intersections, and improved terminal and loading area conditions, not to mention improvements in the vehicle fleet and its maintenance.

The scope for rapid transit facilities, and especially for subways, is likely to be limited, since

> The cost of subway construction is very high; only in large cities exceeding two million population with very high densities providing large traffic volumes over many hours a day and favorable tunneling conditions do subways appear a feasible solution. Even then, the costs may only be affordable in the richer developing countries, and fares are likely to be too high for the poorer strata of society. Where a subway is feasible, account must be taken of the need to reorient the whole public transport system so that bus routes and subways complement each other (World Bank 1975b, p. 86).

Brazil, a developing country with a significant experience in subway construction and operation, appears recently to have emphasized the development of urban bus transit rather than continue its past concentration on subways (1978 World Bank data).

Finally, even in large cities increased attention should be given to nonmotorized traffic such as walking, bicycling, and other forms of traditional transport. This is especially true for cities of the low-income countries, where these travel modes still account for sizable shares of urban transport. Pedestrian malls, widened sidewalks and pedestrian overpasses, low-income neighborhood walkways, and bicycle paths are among the possible policy instruments to achieve a more effective system of nonmotorized transport.

Lest this discussion appear too removed from reality to provide practical solutions, a brief account of the experience in Singapore may be useful. Singapore is a city that reached 2.5 million inhabitants in the mid-1970s and has a relatively high income and motorization level (table 4-1). The government has pursued what is a unique example of a comprehensive, efficient, and effective urban transport policy (Watson and Holland 1978). The primary elements of this policy are (1) a scheme to relieve central city congestion by the combination of area licensing for private automobiles and graduated parking fees, (2) control of motor vehicle ownership and use by various tax measures, (3) an improved mass transit system largely based on buses, (4) various improvements in traffic management, and (5) a long-term policy of locating employment opportunities close to new housing developments, and vice versa (on this last policy, see Grimes 1976, p. 106). The effects of the congestion-relief program have been well documented and include increased travel speeds for passenger and goods traffic in the center of the city, a significant shift from the use of single-occupant cars to the use of buses and car pools, and reduced pollution levels (Watson and Holland 1978). Singapore is, of course, exceptional in a number of respects: it is a city-state with a strong and dynamic metropolitan government, a highly qualified staff, and a strong political commitment and popular support for dealing with the rising congestion and environmental deterioration in the city. Nevertheless, the example is worth careful study and replication to the extent feasible. The various practical aspects that helped to make the policy work (Watson and Holland 1978, Linn 1979a) are particularly noteworthy: adequate study and preparation, including an extensive publicity campaign; simplicity of regulation and flexibility in implementation; preexistence of an effective vehicle registration system;[22] a clear commitment to the enforcement of the scheme; and unfettered authority by the metropolitan government to plan and implement a comprehensive strategy for urban transport policy.

At the conclusion of this section, attention should be drawn to the fact that so far consideration has been given only to the efficiency of the urban transport system. There are, however, other common government objectives that can be served by the rationalization of urban transport in developing countries. Most of these go beyond the scope of the present volume and will therefore be listed only briefly:

- Energy conservation: Private automobiles are relatively energy intensive and probably account for a significant share of the increase in gasoline consumption in many developing countries. Lack of adequate data prevents a careful analysis of this problem, but the recent policy switch to an emphasis of bus mass transit as the answer to the urban transport problem in Brazil has been motivated substantially by the objective of energy conservation (1978 World Bank data).

- Foreign exchange saving: Except for the few countries with a substantial local capacity to produce cars, an unchecked process of motorization is very costly in foreign exchange. The same holds for high-technology mass-transit systems.[23]

- Public resource saving: The potential for savings in public resources by shifts in modal patterns of urban transport and by judicious project design has been discussed extensively in this section.

- Employment generation: Little is known on the employment effects of alternative urban transport strategies, but on balance it would appear that deemphasizing automobile ownership and use in favor of public transport, especially if the public transport does not involve high-technology rapid transit facilities, will increase employment.[24]
- Regional balance: One major reason for pursuing regional decentralization policies is the concern with inefficiency of the largest cities. To the extent that urban transport policy can reduce this inefficiency, the need for regional decentralization is reduced, while at the same time the elimination of effective subsidies to some urban transport users—by pricing urban transport services at full social costs—will make the large city less attractive to these users.
- Equity: Current urban transport policy in many developing countries benefits the wealthy groups, particularly those owning automobiles, while it fails to respond to the needs of the urban poor. Most of the transport policies suggested in this section on the grounds of efficiency would also improve the welfare of the urban poor; this topic is the subject of the next section.

Transport and the Urban Poor

The preceding section has outlined urban transport strategies designed to increase the efficiency of urban development. Scant attention has thus far been paid to how these policies will affect the urban poor or to how policies can be designed to maximize benefits that the poor can derive from efficient urban transport. A brief review of the role transport plays in the lives of the urban poor will help in the subsequent policy analysis.

Household expenditure surveys indicate that the urban poor tend to devote on average somewhere between 1 and 10 percent of their incomes to transport.[25] These expenditure data further suggest that in cities of low-income countries a significantly smaller percentage of incomes is spent on transport by urban dwellers, including the poor; for selected Indian cities, for example, the transport share in total household spending does not exceed 2 percent until fairly high up in the income scale. In contrast, in Korean cities low-income households spend up to 5 percent on transport. Finally, the data for Peru (Thomas 1978) indicate that the transport expenditure share is highest in the metropolitan area of Lima (between 6 and 7 percent for the lower-income half of the population), lower in the urban areas along the Pacific Coast (between 4 and 5 percent for the lower-income half of the population), and virtually insignificant in the rural regions of the Peruvian Sierra. These data reflect the effects of city size on transport needs and of rising incomes on the willingness and ability to pay for more transport.

It is important, however, not to view expenditure on transport in isolation. What is actually demanded (or needed) by the poor is *access* to employment opportunities and services. Access can be obtained either by residing close to employment or services, which requires little travel, or by residing farther away, which requires more travel. In the first case, what is saved in transport costs is usually lost in higher rents, and the reverse is true in the second case. Indeed, higher central city land and rental values are in large part a reflection of the superior access of these locations at lower transport costs compared with peripheral locations. This is where city size is an important factor: the larger the city, the greater the scarcity value of central urban land and the more difficult and costly the provision of transport to central locations—thus the higher land costs (rents). The poor have essentially three options to adjust to this effect of city growth. First, they can settle at the periphery where land costs remain low, but then they lose either because of higher transport costs or reduced labor earnings from the loss of jobs, particularly for secondary income earners. Second, they can remain (or settle) at relatively central locations and pay higher rents per household at unchanged densities. Or, third, they can accept higher densities, lower quality of shelter or public utilities, greater insecurity of tenure, or all of these combined, so that transport costs and rental payments combined can be reduced to a level that will leave enough for the other necessities of life.[26]

An improved urban transport system is therefore not the only means to improve access to employment and services for the poor; providing cheap land close to employment opportunities (or vice versa) may be just as important. In fact, for the poorest groups, who usually can only afford to walk, improvements in most forms of urban transport will not be of much help, except to the extent that a generally improved transport system may reduce the scarcity value—and rents—of centrally located land relative to more peripheral locations.[27] The importance of this trickle-down effect depends on the extent to which the transport system is improved.[28] Minor improvements obviously will not significantly affect land costs or rents throughout the urban area, although they may have significant effects on land values in the vicinity of the project being executed.

For those low-income households that can afford bus transport—which may include those in the poorest 20 percent of households in cities of the middle-income countries, but will include only a few in even the poorest 40 percent in cities of low-income countries—an improvement in the bus system will lead to some improvements in their living condition, although the extent to which this is the case will vary depending on a number of circumstances. The improvements may involve a reduction in travel times or costs, the opening up of new employment opportunities, or the opportunity to locate on cheaper land previously inaccessible because of lack of transport. In addition, however, some of the benefits may be shared by others, among them the landowners whose land value increases with improved accessibility, transport service operators, employers, renters elsewhere in the city, and consumers of the products that are produced by the activities made possible by improved accessibility (on these issues, see Gomez-Ibanez 1975, p. 199). Under most circumstances it is very difficult, if not impossible, to determine precisely the incidence of urban transport service provisions. As long as product markets are reasonably competitive on a national scale and urban transport service operators are competitively organized, much of the benefit of improved transport is likely to go to landowners and transport users. To ensure the beneficial effects on poverty from improvements in urban bus transport, it is insufficient to attempt to channel the resources in such a way that relatively poor users are affected by the provision of transport; consideration must also be given to the extent to which landownership is distributed in the neighborhoods most directly benefiting from the improvements. Improved transport access for neighborhoods where the poor predominantly rent and the land is largely owned by rich individuals will involve some leakage of benefits to the rich. In contrast, transport improvements in areas where the poor are effectively in possession of the land—even if they do not legally own it—will channel many of the benefits directly to the poor. The distribution of landownership is thus an important aspect in determining the incidence of benefits from transport projects, particularly where these affect relatively well-defined areas.[29]

More expensive modes of urban transport, especially subways and automobiles, are likely to be beyond the reach of the poor in most of the developing countries, but especially in low-income Asia and Africa.[30] What is more, the heavy investments required to provide transport facilities for these modes reduce the availability of funds for improving the transport system in ways that directly reach the poor. This is the case for automobile use in the developing countries:

> Comfort, convenience and speed of total (automobile) trips are so much greater than for other modes as to represent a quantum difference. The independence and liberty of movement they provide represent an emancipation for many owners; hence, their great appeal and the tenacity with which their use is defended. However, in terms of road space and total costs to the community their benefits are provided at very high cost. In developing countries, so long as resources available for infrastructure are so limited, the benefits of the few in automobiles using roads at peak hours are inevitably accompanied by intensified difficulties for many traveling by public transport, walking or cycling (World Bank 1975b, p. 87).

The common response to increased congestion caused by the growing numbers of automobiles—that is, investment in more and costlier roads to serve these cars and the failure to price automobile use at social costs—has meant that high-income automobile owners have derived not only the benefits of the fiscal dividend provided to them by these investments but also the benefits of implicit subsidies, since they do not bear the full marginal social costs of automobile operation. At the same time, this urban transport policy has withheld from the remainder of the urban population the benefits of the fiscal dividend derived from public investment in urban transport. Moreover, those who do not use automobiles have suffered welfare losses from the external costs (congestion and pollution) generated by those who do. Indeed, it is not uncommon that those transport modes which are relatively efficient *and* benefit the poor urban groups are labeled nuisances and are blamed for the ills of the urban transport systems in developing country cities.[31] Given this definition of the problem, it should come as no surprise that urban transport policies are frequently quite misguided.

An urban transport policy that is concerned with efficiency and poverty alleviation should therefore attempt to eliminate the subsidies for automobile users and shift the benefits of the fiscal dividend to other urban transport users by a combination of investment, pricing, and regulatory policies (briefly summarized in the remainder of this section).

Summary of Policy Implications

For each of the major areas of policy action—investment, pricing, and regulation—the proposed policies can be contrasted with those commonly found in the cities of developing countries. The differences are significant, and the changes in policy perceptions required are extensive. Such changes obviously cannot be expected to happen overnight; they have to be carefully argued and motivated on the grounds that they convey a wide range of benefits in line with many of the common goals of government policy. Some of the changes are already occurring in some countries and cities, but much remains to be done in the majority of developing country cities to come to grips with the deterioration of urban transport systems.[32] In particular, since the urban transport sector represents a highly interconnected system of competing and complementary activities, it is important to design a comprehensive strategy covering as many as possible of the policy actions listed below.

Many of the proposed policies involve constraints on ownership and use of private automobiles. Implementation of such policies is likely to encounter considerable opposition because automobile ownership and use are common popular aspirations, not only as a means of transport to and from work, but also as a means of greater general mobility and independence and as status symbols. The control of automobile ownership and use therefore requires concerted policy actions at all levels of government that combine the use of such instruments as import tariffs, annual vehicle fees, and gasoline pricing at the national level with appropriate investment, pricing, and regulatory actions at the regional and city levels.

Investment

Traditional investment policies have involved:

- Highway construction to meet the needs of the private automobile explosion
- High-technology rapid transit in a few cities (for example, Mexico City, Buenos Aires, Sao Paulo)
- Neglect of bus, commuter train, bicycling, and walking facilities
- Neglect of access roads for low-income neighborhoods, shutting them off from access to many complementary services
- Encouragement of segregated land use, including the relocation of slum dwellers to peripheral locations (as in Abidjan, Manila, and Rio de Janeiro).

Proposed investment policies include:

- Reduced emphasis on general-purpose arterial road construction mainly benefiting automobiles
- Extremely cautious evaluation of any plans for modern-technology, rapid-transit investment, especially for subways; only for the largest cities in the most advanced countries might these options be desirable for the efficiency of the urban transport system or for benefiting the urban poor
- Emphasis on improved existing mass-transit facilities, especially buses and minibuses; this would involve improving the stock of vehicles and providing good repair facilities; reserved bus lanes and preferential treatment of public transport at intersections; bus loading bays, shelters, and terminals
- Neighborhood street-paving programs, especially in the poorer neighborhoods; this should especially involve bus penetration routes that can also provide access to other service vehicles (fire engines, public utility maintenance vehicles, garbage trucks, and the like)
- Support for bicycle and pedestrian traffic, including construction of bicycle paths, sidewalks and footpaths, pedestrian bridges to permit crossing of busy arterial roads, and pedestrian malls in central city areas

- Reduction of standards in road construction and other publicly provided transport facilities wherever this does not significantly reduce the benefits derived by poor users[33]
- Efforts to decentralize employment location close to low-income residential neighborhoods, such as "flatted factories" in Singapore and Hong Kong (Grimes 1976, p. 106), public administration facilities in Bombay and Bogota, and other examples previously cited. Decentralized employment location, although it reduces congestion in the city centers, may also increase the need for public and private transport to and from peripheral areas, which can be quite costly. Employment decentralization is therefore not a panacea for solving urban transport problems.

Investment policies such as these can provide considerable benefits to the poor. For a recent World Bank transport project in three Brazilian cities, it was estimated that the percentage of the investment expected to generate benefits for the poor was 87 percent for Salvador, 69 percent for Curitiba, 64 percent for Recife (1978 World Bank data). Although these estimates are very rough and do not necessarily reflect the final incidence of benefits, they provide orders of magnitude of what is considered achievable with careful urban project design.

The relative emphasis on the different components of the proposed investment strategy will vary between countries and cities and depends mainly on income levels. In the wealthier cities, particularly in the middle-income countries, an emphasis on urban bus services (and rail service, where already existing) is quite appropriate. But in the cities of the low-income countries, especially the poorer ones, an emphasis on improved bicycle and pedestrian traffic, coupled with a well-focused decentralization of employment opportunities, would be most appropriate.[34]

Pricing

Traditional pricing policies have included:

- Underpricing of private automobile use in congested and polluted central city areas. Indeed, in some cities (for example, in Cali, Colombia) central city parking facilities are expressly subsidized by local tax exemptions (Linn 1979b).
- Subsidized urban bus and train services. Examples abound; they include Bogota, Bombay, Istanbul, and Tunis (World Bank project data 1972–76); Buenos Aires, Calcutta, and Caracas (Roth 1973). A particular problem is the failure to change fares regularly in line with rising costs or to vary fares with distance traveled (for example, in

Bogota—Linn 1976*b*—and in Korean cities—Beesley and others 1979).[35]

- Taxation of public transport vehicles by national and local governments, in particular buses. An extreme example for this practice until recently existed in Kuala Lumpur, where a bus seat tax accounted for more than 10 percent of annual expenditures of the city's bus companies (World Bank data; other examples are found in Korean, Indian, and Colombian cities—see Linn 1979*b*).

Proposed pricing policies include:

- Congestion pricing for private automobiles, following in essence the example of Singapore by applying a combination of time- and area-specific license charges and central city parking fees, including not only on-street and public off-street parking but also private off-street parking facilities. Any tax advantages given to private parking facilities should be eliminated.

- Taxation of automobile use and ownership that is not area- or time-specific (fuel taxes, import taxes, general license fees, and so forth) is a second-best answer to the urban congestion problem. It does, however, serve other policy objectives, particularly since it raises public revenues in a progressive fashion; it is also possible to apply somewhat higher general taxes on automobile use and ownership in large cities than in smaller towns or rural areas (see Linn 1979 for a discussion of automotive taxation in developing country cities).

- Public transport vehicles, and in particular buses, should not be taxed, at least as long as automobile use is effectively subsidized by the failure to levy congestion charges. The taxation of bicycles and other non-motorized vehicles should also be subjected to careful review.[36]

- Cost recovery of public road investments through betterment charges. The feasibility of this taxation scheme has been demonstrated at least in the case of Colombia, where the so-called valorization charges have financed substantial portions of the urban infrastructure investment, especially road construction in the large cities.[37] This tax scheme was particularly successful in providing improved streets in poorer neighborhoods while it recovered at least part of the costs and thus facilitated replicability of the program.[38]

- Careful evaluation of bus fares with a view to eliminating widespread subsidization, introducing distance-graduated tariffs, and allowing flexibility over time in making more frequent, but less drastic adjustments to keep fares in line with costs during inflationary periods.[39]

The difficulty of implementing the recommended changes in pricing policies must, however, be explicitly recognized. Urban transport pricing policies, in particular the imposition of congestion charges and elimination of public transport subsidies, are highly visible policy measures that have a wide range of effects, both positive and negative, on many urban dwellers. These effects are reinforced by the fact that substantial losses (as well as gains) may be sustained in the short term as a result of capitalization of higher charges into the value of fixed assets (especially land). Optimal employment and residential patterns may change rather swiftly as a result of significant changes in transport prices, whereas firms as well as individuals tend to be locked into their existing locations at least over the short term and may face considerable transactions costs in relocation. Because of all these factors, transport pricing policy is very much in the political arena, and drastic changes may fail to be implemented because of well-orchestrated lobbying efforts or because of disruptive popular reactions such as strikes, street violence, and the like. The only way to deal with these problems is by combining changes in pricing policies with other urban transport policies. The scope and quality of mass-transit services especially should be improved—by a well-focused publicity campaign linking the costs of a new transport pricing scheme directly to the benefits derived from improved services and, if necessary, by gradually phasing in the pricing changes, thus permitting individuals to minimize the transition costs that inevitably arise.

A particularly troublesome and recurring problem in transport pricing is the question of subsidies for mass transit. The case for subsidies of mass transit on grounds of efficiency is based on the view that the absence of congestion charges heavily favors the use of the private automobile. It is well known, however, that mass-transit subsidies are distinctly a second-best alternative to congestion pricing (Churchill 1972, Gomez-Ibanez 1975, Roth 1973, Walters 1968, World Bank 1975b). What is more important, particularly in developing countries, is that the public resource shortage generally does not permit large-scale subsidization, with the result that subsidized transport systems are underfinanced, tend to become decapitalized, and thus suffer a lower scope and quality of service.[40] Once this happens, it becomes very difficult to raise fares, not only because those benefiting from the subsidies will object to the loss of a "free ride," but also because in the eyes of the user the quality of service is so low as not to deserve higher payments. An additional problem arises from the fact that mass-transit subsidies often take the form of heavy subsidization of capital costs. This tends to favor capital-intensive mass-transport solutions (subways, stage buses) over more labor-intensive options (minibuses), especially when such subsidies go hand in hand with the high labor costs of unionized public transport employees (Walters 1979b).

The argument for subsidized bus rides on grounds of equity, which holds that low-income groups ought to receive income supplements through subsidized transport, also has important limitations. First, there is the question of direct incidence of subsidies: as discussed earlier, a substantial portion of subsidies may leak to wealthy landowners, transport operators, employers, or to the general consumer. The poor, especially in low-income countries, frequently cannot afford to pay even for subsidized mass transit and thus do not benefit from subsidies. Furthermore, and especially in the case of subways, many middle- and higher-income groups also use mass-transit facilities (Zahavi 1976), thus further reducing the effects on poverty of mass-transit subsidies. Second, the impact of subsidies on the scope and quality of service tends to cut the benefits that a subsidized mass-transit system can convey to the urban poor. Those excluded from the service because of decapitalization suffer doubly—they lose not only the subsidy but also the fiscal dividend of mass transit. The strength of these equity-related arguments against subsidies depends, however, on several factors, most important among them the level of income in the country or city. In middle-income countries, all except the very poorest groups can afford some form of mass transit at reasonably small subsidies, and general tax resources may be more readily available to maintain a widely spread service network (especially for bus service; see the Brazilian examples cited earlier). Subsidies thus may well reach down quite far in the income distribution without overly deleterious effects on the efficiency of the transport system. In the low-income countries and cities, however, a large proportion of the poor cannot afford even subsidized transport. Furthermore, financial resources tend to be very scarce, and thus the mass-transit system is bound to suffer. The net effects are that subsidies do not reach the poor and that the mass-transit system loses passengers at both ends of the income scale because of declining services. At the high end of the income scale people switch to automobiles, congestion increases, and the efficiency of the transport system is lowered; at the lower end of the income scale people drop out of mass transit (or are never served in the first place) because services in old, established city neighborhoods have to be cut or because in newly established areas they are not provided.

Regulation

Traditional regulatory practices have included:

- Restriction on entry for privately operated transit modes such as buses, minibuses, jitneys, rickshas, or bekjas[41]
- Regulation of routes, timetables, and safety of mass-transit vehicles, but these are usually poorly enforced
- Control of fares on privately operated transit modes at levels that do not permit maintenance of vehicles, bus routes, and service quality
- No significant controls on the operation of the private automobile in

congested city areas and no significant controls that would favor the operation of mass-transit modes or nonmotorized transport.

Proposed policies include:

- Limiting the operation of private automobiles in busy, congested areas and imposing total daytime bans on parking rather than charges (Churchill 1972)
- Giving other traffic modes preferred treatment by providing reserved lanes for buses and jitneys and by restricting certain streets or areas for exclusive use of nonmotorized traffic (as has been done in some Brazilian cities and in several Western European and American cities and towns)
- A review of all regulatory practices affecting the entry and operation of buses, jitneys, and the like, with the goal of easing constraints on entry, and a stricter enforcement of safety and operating regulations (Roth 1973)[42]
- A review of fare regulations for private mass-transit services, with the objective of providing the operators with incentives to expand their services in line with the growth of a city.[43] The justifications for such a policy parallel those put forward earlier in the discussion of mass-transit subsidies.

Complementary Policies

There are additional policy measures that do not fall squarely under the three subheadings of investment, pricing, and regulation, but that must be considered in the pursuit of an urban strategy designed to improve the whole system's efficiency and its services to the poor. The more commonly proposed measures are briefly listed below.[44]

- Staggered working hours, which may help relieve high peaks of congestion and public transport use and thus reduce the need for costly investment in peak-related capacity; higher peak fares for mass transit can work in the same direction. The effect of these measures, however, is not likely to be very large, especially if the urban transport system operates under conditions of excess demand for much of the day anyhow, as is often the case in developing country cities (World Bank 1975b).
- Fringe parking and shuttle-buses, which may be useful complements to a policy of controls on automobile use in central cities. In Salvador, Brazil, such a scheme was very successful (World Bank 1975b), but it had little effect in Singapore (Watson and Holland 1978).
- Nationalization of mass-transit facilities, especially of urban bus services, is not likely to improve service provision in most circumstances (Roth 1973,

World Bank 1975*b*). Although there are a few examples of successful public urban bus companies (in Bombay and Jakarta, for instance), the overwhelming experience appears to be that private operators can provide bus service cheaply and efficiently, even under the most adverse of circumstances (many of which result from public actions such as taxation and fare regulation); Kuala Lumpur is a good example in point.

• Improved credit facilities for the purchase of public transport vehicles, including nonmotorized vehicles such as rickshas and bekjas.[45]

• Support for nonmotorized transport, including pedestrian traffic and human-powered vehicles. Examples of successful separation of slow-moving nonmotorized from fast motorized traffic may be found in selected intermediate-size cities in Southeast Asia (Mitsui Consulting Co. 1977, p. 10).

• Improved management, accounting, automobile registration, and enforcement of regulations, which are essential elements in an effort to rationalize urban transport and to ensure that improved services are provided to the poor.[46] This will often require increased staff training for the public authorities in charge of managing urban transport, some investment in complementary capital items (such as tow trucks, communications equipment, and the like), and some increases in staffing. The apparent success of a city such as Jakarta in many of these areas (especially vehicle registration, vehicle tax collection, and management of a public bus company; see Linn 1979*b*) would tend to indicate that improvements should be feasible in many other cities, too.

• Comprehensive urban transport sector planning and administration and its integration into overall urban land use planning and implementation. These measures are essential; the systems nature of urban transport requires a comprehensive approach relating to all major modes and policy instruments. The fragmentation of responsibility of the transport sector among many public institutions, which prevails in most developing country cities, often prevents comprehensive action. The successful design and implementation of a comprehensive urban transport policy in Singapore must be attributed in no small measure to the relatively clear assignment of public responsibility for urban transport in that city. Finally, the need to put transport planning and policy in the context of wider land use planning considerations derives from the close complementary relation that urban transport has with residential, employment, and public service location decisions. Public policy planning in these areas should always consider the implications for the transport system; similarly, urban transport strategy must explicitly deal with its relation to, and effects on, public and private decisions regarding residential, employment, and service location.

Notes to Chapter 4

1. Most notable on the negative end of the spectrum are policies banning *bekjas* (cycle-powered taxis) in Jakarta (World Bank 1975b, p. 40), and on the positive end the encouragement of similar vehicles in Hyderabad through appropriate credit policies (Cousins 1977).

2. The data in this table are subject to a fairly wide margin of error due to the difficulties of measurement and the variety of sources.

3. Zahavi (1976) has shown that this holds for countries and cities, whether or not one considers only developing countries, or developing countries and developed countries jointly.

4. For the cities of the middle-income countries, the mean rate of automobile ownership is 54.4 per thousand (standard deviation: 35.2); for the cities of the low-income countries it is 23.0 (standard deviation: 18.3).

5. The same study for Kingston also showed, however, that a slight *increase* has taken place in recent years in the share of walking trips, which is attributed to the increased spreading of employment opportunities especially in the low-income areas of the city.

6. The degree of employment concentration tends to be high in developing country cities. For instance, in large Brazilian cities up to 60 percent of daily trip destinations are in the city center, and in Tunis 70 percent of metropolitan area jobs are located in the congested central business district (World Bank project data).

7. Ward (1976) cites evidence for London and Paris, where satellite towns have led to considerable local employment generation, with the result that the number of center-periphery work trips is relatively low.

8. No attempt has been made to update existing estimates of transport cost surveys. In most cases, therefore, cost figures reflect price levels of the early 1970s. General price inflation certainly has raised all absolute costs, and changes in relative prices, especially for petroleum products, may have changed relative costs. But the changes in relative costs alone are not likely to have reversed the ranking of transport modes according to costs.

9. The report from which this table is taken emphasizes that these cost figures are merely illustrative and will vary from city to city, and even among locations within a city (World Bank 1975b, p. 72).

10. These figures do not, however, adequately reflect one of the major problems associated with construction of rapid mass-transit facilities: "The minimum capacity of any separate right-of-way established for public transport is very large, while costs of construction are inevitably high. Construction costs of metros, for instance, typically average in excess of $10 million a lane-mile and are much higher than this where tunneling conditions are difficult" (World Bank 1975b, p. 29). Given the capital scarcity in many of the developing countries, a subway in particular is likely to be very costly in terms of alternative investment opportunities forgone. The load factor assumed in table 4-2 is also very high for metros and urban railways and may not be realized in actual fact.

11. See Churchill (1972, p. 116). Garza and Schteingart (1978, p. 75) describe the impact of pollution in Mexico City as follows: "Mexico City is one of the most polluted cities in the world. . . . Approximately 60 percent of the air pollution is due to the use of motor vehicles, which annually consume 3 million cubic meters of gasoline and 400,000 cubic meters of diesel fuel. This has produced a notable increase in chronic respiratory and cardiovascular disease among the city's inhabitants." For the link between motor vehicle use and air pollution in Manila, see Viloria and Associates (1977).

12. See World Bank (1975b, p. 21). Topographical constraints are frequent in the large cities

of developing countries, as exemplified by Abidjan, Bombay, Manila, La Paz, and Salvador and Recife (both in Brazil). The importance of through traffic in adding to central city congestion has been identified in World Bank reports on Abidjan, Tunis, Manila, and a number of Brazilian cities.

13. The measure of congestion cost used here is one that reflects the toll required to produce optimal travel speeds. See also Walters (1968) for estimates of congestion costs.

14. Loss of employment or the need to pay higher rents at locations closer to employment are other possible costs.

15. See Roth (1973) and Walters (1979b) for examples. Of course there are exceptions. For instance, the public transport facilities in Bombay and the city bus company in Jakarta were well run during the 1970s (World Bank data and Linn, Smith, and Wignjowijoto 1976).

16. The ranges of city size given in this and the following paragraphs are mere orders of magnitude; obviously no hard and fast lines can be drawn. See also Grimes (1976, p. 47) for a similar size grouping.

17. For example, by restraints on parking, by reserving certain streets for exclusive use of public transport or of pedestrians, and so forth. Many European towns falling into this size category (for example, Munster, Germany, with 350,000 inhabitants) have in recent years taken such steps with considerable success.

18. Abidjan, Ivory Coast, for instance, grew from a population of 340,000 in 1965 to 1,000,000 in 1975 (these are approximate figures, since reliable population data for this city are lacking).

19. This appears to have been the case, for instance, in Abidjan during much of its recent growth (1976 World Bank data).

20. In Cali, the industrial town of Yumbo has effectively been incorporated into the metropolitan area; in Kingston, the previously separate urban area of Spanish Town has now become officially part of the Kingston metropolitan region.

21. There may also be some scope for improving light surface rail transport, especially tramways; see USAID (1976) for a discussion of this option.

22. A good motor vehicle registration and licensing system is crucial to the success of a scheme to tax motor vehicle ownership or use, but it is also essential for the purpose of identifying and prosecuting traffic offenders and for curbing motor vehicle theft, which in some developing country cities (for example, Bogota) has reached epidemic proportions. In this respect motor vehicle taxation is quite similar to real estate taxation, for which the existence of a good physical cadastre is essential. The cadastre in turn serves other important purposes besides property taxation.

23. For some indicative values of the foreign exchange content of alternative urban transport modes, see USAID (1976, p. 158).

24. This conclusion is subject to qualifications in countries that have already developed a substantial domestic automobile industry. These are mainly among the most advanced of the developing countries.

25. See Grimes (1975, p. 68) for data on Bogota, Hong Kong, and selected Indian and Korean cities. See also Thomas (1978, p. 26) for data on Peruvian cities.

26. The extreme case is found in the large cities of the low-income countries: "People who sleep in the downtown streets of Karachi, Calcutta, and other cities of South Asia often do so not because they cannot find shacks on the periphery, but because they cannot afford the cost in money or time for daily travel to their homes. Many have dwellings on the city outskirts and visit their families once a week" (Grimes 1976, p. 27).

27. "The cheapest form of mass transit is the urban bus—approximately 2 U.S. cents per passenger per mile under conditions found in many developing countries. A ten-mile, roundtrip commute to work would cost 20 U.S. cents per day, 5 percent of income where the daily wage

is US$4.00 and 20 percent where the daily wage is US$1.00" (Beier and others 1975, p. 63). Clearly, few low-income earners can afford to spend 20 percent of their incomes on transport, unless they pay no rent (for example, because they are squatters on rent-free land).

28. There is some, albeit highly conjectural, evidence that the extensive road construction program in Bogota (which was financed mainly by betterment levies), combined with a well-functioning bus system and a relatively low density of private automobile traffic, has kept down the rate of growth of land values in that city compared with other cities in developing countries (Doebele, Grimes, and Linn 1979).

29. Quantitative estimates of the distribution of urban transport investments between transport users and landowners do not appear to exist. However, the valorization scheme in Colombian cities, which successfully recovers much of the costs of urban road construction in these cities by charges on landowners in areas adjacent to road improvement projects, would indicate that a substantial portion of the benefit from such investments is in fact reaped by the landowners. If this were not the case, it would obviously be much more difficult to make this financing scheme work.

30. "To judge by the recent experience in Mexico City and preliminary estimates elsewhere, fares will need substantially to exceed 10 cents for an average trip of two or three miles if full costs are to be covered—even where very high-density traffic is encountered" (World Bank 1975b, p. 84). Thus, unless high subsidies are offered to subway users, the low-income groups cannot be expected to pay for the fares; and if subsidies are given, then these will be spread very widely, since subway users tend to come from virtually all income groups (Zahavi 1976, p. 69).

31. The elimination of bekjas from central Jakarta is an example of the resulting policy (World Bank 1975b). Another example is the concern in Manila with the impact of jeepneys, low-cost passenger vehicles, and repeated consideration to curb their operations (1975 World Bank data and Roth 1973).

32. The recent switch in urban transport policy in Brazil has been mentioned, as has the example of Singapore. Transport policy in Bogota has also had its progressive aspects (the extensive use of betterment levies, high taxes on automobiles, elimination of a planned limited-access highway, gradual elimination of subsidies on gasoline, employment decentralization, introduction of reserved bus lanes, and so forth). Other examples that could be cited are the cities where the World Bank has financed urban transport projects (Tunis, Kuala Lumpur, Bombay, Abidjan). See also Council for International Urban Liaison (1980a), which contains a review of some recent transport improvement programs in Nairobi, Tunis, San Jose, Bangkok, and cities in Brazil.

33. The cost savings in selected Brazilian cities were cited above; Grimes (1976, p. 17) also cites examples of low-standard streets and paths constructed and maintained without public assistance.

34. For example, for Salvador, Brazil, it has been estimated that "the urban poor constitute 82 percent of bus riders but, because they tend to make longer trips, receive 92 percent of all time savings" (World Bank 1978b, p. 42). For Calcutta or Jakarta—although no hard figures are available—these percentages are likely to be a lot lower.

35. In Manila, between 1960 and 1975 bus fares were changed only in 1960 and 1969; in Kuala Lumpur fares were not changed between 1953 and 1975; in Tunis, no change occurred between 1967 and 1975; in Cairo, no change had been made between 1952 and 1978 (World Bank data).

36. For Karachi an effort was made to estimate the tax component of capital and operating costs for various types of transport modes (USAID 1976, pp. 184–85). The wide range in tax rates does not appear to permit any obvious rational explanation.

37. For a recent evaluation of this tax scheme in Bogota see Doebele, Grimes, and Linn

(1979); similar schemes were in operation in various Latin American countries, albeit with less success (Macon and Manon 1977).

38. Another system of financing urban infrastructure investments, including road construction, is the land readjustment scheme in Korea. For a recent description and evaluation, see Doebele and Hwang (1979); see also chapter 5, below.

39. In some developing country cities (for example, Bombay, Tunis, and Manila), graduated bus fares are actually in use, showing that this practice poses no undue administrative difficulties.

40. Another implication of mass-transit subsidies is that they encourage low-density development and urban sprawl, which in turn tend to increase the cost of providing many urban services, including transport.

41. This is frequently done to protect public mass-transit companies from unwanted competition from private operators, as in Calcutta (Roth 1973) or Recife (World Bank data), or to protect motorized traffic from interference from nonmotorized vehicles, as in Jakarta, where man-powered cycle-taxis (bekjas) were banned from central city streets (World Bank 1975b). Similar restrictive policies were pursued in Malaysia; in Kuala Lumpur, for example, the number of popular trishaws dropped from over 4,000 in 1950 to about 250 in 1974 (Mitsui Consulting Co. 1977, p. 70).

42. A recent decision to permit the operation of minibuses in Kuala Lumpur led to the operation of 400 such vehicles within less than two years (Walters 1979a).

43. The contrast between national government controls on bus fares in Korea and Brazil, to cite two examples, is striking. In Korea, equal fares were until recently imposed throughout all cities irrespective of cost differentials, which have been estimated to be substantial (Beesley and others 1979). In Brazil, regulated bus fares are computed on the basis of formulas (with different coefficients for each metropolitan area and vehicle category) that take into account operating and administrative costs, depreciation, and load factor and allow for a reasonable rate of return (12 percent) on companies' investment. Fares are recomputed twice a year (World Bank data).

44. See also Midgley (1980), who discusses the entire range of traffic management instruments with special reference to the African experience.

45. A successful experiment was conducted in Hyderabad, where commercial banks were encouraged to lend to ricksha operators for the purchase of vehicles (Cousins 1977).

46. For example, the national company providing bus services in Tunis for some time extended substantial subsidies to users without realizing this, because it had failed to allow for depreciation and other nonoperating expenditures in its accounting practice (World Bank 1973b).

5

Urban Housing:
Land, Services, and Shelter

HOUSING is defined here to include not only the shelter structure, but also the lot on which the shelter stands and the services provided to the lot such as water and energy supply, waste disposal, drainage, and fire and police protection. Substantial portions of household budgets are spent on housing and related services, not only among wealthy but also among poor households (tables 5-1 and 5-2). On average, households spend between 15 and 25 percent of their total expenditure on housing (World Bank 1980d), although the share tends to be lower in some countries (especially India) and may vary considerably between and within income groups.[1] The importance of housing in developing countries is further demonstrated by the fact that on average about 4 percent of GDP is devoted to new residential construction in selected developing countries (21 percent of fixed capital formation and 37 percent of total construction; see table 5-3). As with household expenditures, the importance of housing in national income and investment figures varies widely between countries. There also are serious data problems, especially because housing investments in slums and squatter areas are not adequately represented in table 5-3. Moreover, the data do not permit any conclusions regarding differences in housing expenditures and investments across country groupings.[2]

A more clear-cut distinction regarding the importance of housing may be drawn between rural and urban areas. On average, urban dwellers are willing to spend significantly more on housing than are rural dwellers, as is shown in table 5-4 for the case of Peru. In Peru, and very likely elsewhere, this difference applies not only on average, but also for the households among the poorest 40 percent of the population. But there are other reasons why housing is of particular concern in urban areas (World Bank 1980d). In

Table 5-1. *Household Income and Percentage of Household Expenditure on Housing, Utilities, and Transport in Selected Cities, Various Years*

Country, city, and year	Monthly household income (U.S. dollars)	Percentage of expenditure on		
		Housing	Utilities[a]	Transport
Colombia	0.0–23.8	59.3[b]	6.8	4.9[c]
Bogota, 1972	23.9–47.6	24.1	3.3	3.9
	47.7–71.4	23.1	3.5	5.3
	71.5–95.2	21.9	2.7	2.8
	95.3–142.8	22.7	2.8	3.7
	142.9–238.1	26.6	3.0	4.0
	238.2–809.5	24.4	1.9	5.2
	809.6+	22.0	1.5	12.9
Hong Kong, 1973	80.8–303.0	19.8[b]	3.1	4.0
	303.1–606.7	18.4	2.7	4.9
India	0.0–2.70	6.2[d]	n.a.	1.2
Bombay, Calcutta, Delhi,	2.71–3.10	2.5	n.a.	0.6
and Madras, 1964	3.11–3.75	2.8	n.a.	1.3
	3.76–4.38	4.3	n.a.	1.9
	4.39–5.00	3.4	n.a.	2.0
	5.01–5.84	3.7	n.a.	1.4
	5.85–7.09	5.2	n.a.	1.9
	7.10–8.97	5.8	n.a.	3.1
	8.98–11.47	5.3	n.a.	3.1
	11.48–15.64	5.0	n.a.	2.9
	15.65+	7.6	n.a.	5.6
Kenya	0.0–28.0	46.0	n.a.	n.a.
Nairobi, 1968	28.1–42.0	22.0	n.a.	n.a.
	42.1–70.0	15.0	n.a.	n.a.
	70.1–140.0	12.5	n.a.	n.a.
	140.1–280.0	18.5	n.a.	n.a.
	280.1+	15.0	n.a.	n.a.
Korea	0.0–44.4	18.1[b]	10.6	3.6[c]
All cities, 1970	44.5–74.0	16.5	8.6	4.6
	74.1–103.7	16.9	6.8	4.7
	103.8–133.3	17.3	5.7	4.4
	133.4–162.9	18.2	5.4	5.0
	163.0–192.6	18.2	5.0	4.3
	192.7+	19.6	4.7	5.6

n.a. Not available.
Source: Grimes (1976, p. 68).
a. Includes fuel and electricity.
b. Private housing.
c. Purchase and use of transport services and personal equipment.
d. Includes rent and expenditure on repair and maintenance; excludes land purchase.

Table 5-2. *Average Household Expenditures on Housing as a Percentage of Average Income, for the Lowest Third of the Income Distribution, in Selected Countries and Cities*

Country	Average expenditure on housing as a percentage of average household income
Botswana	20.0
El Salvador	12.0
Ethiopia	8.0
India	
Madras	6.5
Baroda	6.8
Indonesia	15.0
Ivory Coast	
Abobo	15.4
Adjame	14.7
Pelieuville	12.8
Jamaica	27.5
Kenya	20.0
Korea	27.0
Morocco	
Douar Doum	13.0
Douar Maadid	22.5
Douar Aajja	23.2
Philippines	10.0
Upper Volta	15.0

Source: Background data for World Bank (1980*a*) compiled by Anthony A. Churchill and Margaret Lycette. See also World Bank (1980*d*).

Table 5-3. *Residential Building Construction as a Percentage of GDP, Fixed Capital Formation, and Total Construction, in Selected Developing Countries*

Region and country	Year	Residential building as a percentage of		
		GDP	Fixed capital formation	Total construction
Sub-Saharan Africa				
Ghana	1972	3.7	43.4	68.4
Kenya	1972	2.4	13.7	29.3
Sierra Leone	1968	3.8	29.6	51.9
Unweighted group average[a]		3.3 (0.8)	28.9 (14.9)	49.9 (19.6)

Table 5-3 (*continued*)

| Region and country | Year | Residential building as a percentage of | | |
		GDP	Fixed capital formation	Total construction
Low-income Asia				
Sri Lanka	1971	8.4[b]	52.4[b]	76.3[b]
Middle-income Asia				
Korea	1972	2.9	13.6	23.1
Philippines	1972	2.2	13.4	34.2
Thailand	1972	3.0	14.0	28.6
Unweighted group average[a]		2.7 (0.4)	13.7 (0.3)	28.6 (5.6)
Latin America				
Chile	1972	2.6	18.8	33.6
Colombia	1972	2.4	13.6	24.9
El Salvador	1971	2.2	17.6	38.0
Guatemala	1968	1.6[c]	12.0[c]	33.9[c]
Honduras	1972	3.4	24.1	44.0
Mexico	1968	10.0[b]	53.4[b]	95.6[b]
Nicaragua	1972	1.3	8.0	18.6
Panama	1972	7.1	23.8	36.9
Uruguay	1971	4.1[b]	28.6[b]	44.4
Venezuela	1972	6.6	24.7	41.1
Unweighted group average[a]		3.7 (2.3)	18.7 (6.2)	33.9 (9.1)
Europe, Middle East, and North Africa				
Greece	1972	7.9	29.7	40.1
Portugal	1972	3.0	13.8	26.6
Spain	1972	3.3	13.7	30.2
Turkey	1971	3.3	20.2	32.6
Iran	1968	2.9[d]	18.8	27.9
Israel	1972	11.4	36.8	59.3
Syria	1972	2.9	19.7	35.0
Cyprus	1972	6.5	34.1	52.0
Unweighted group average[a,e]		5.2 (3.2)	23.4 (9.0)	38.0 (11.9)
Unweighted total average[a,f]		4.0 (2.5)	21.2 (9.1)	37.0 (12.4)

Source: United Nations (1976, table 17).
a. Standard deviation in parentheses.
b. Including nonresidential construction.
c. Private residential construction only.
d. GDP at factor cost.
e. Excluding Guatemala, Mexico, and Uruguay.
f. Excluding Guatemala, Mexico, Uruguay, and Sri Lanka.

Table 5-4. *Average Household Expenditures on Housing as a Percentage of Total Household Expenditure in Peru, 1971*

Item	Percent
All households	
Peru	17.2
Lima	24.9
Large cities	17.9
Medium-size cities	13.4
Rural areas	8.7
Households in the lowest 40 percent of the income distribution:	
Lima	8.2
Urban coast	7.1
Rural Sierra	1.7

Source: Adapted from Thomas (1978, tables 33 and 37–39).

contrast to rural areas, urban areas experience higher population growth rates, worsening health and environmental conditions, and greater need for public involvement in supporting housing development; the greater concentration and visibility in the cities make the problem of inadequate housing politically more urgent than the scattered and less apparent problems of rural housing.

Indeed, the urban housing problem is probably the most visible aspect of the difficulties that developing countries face in their process of transition from rural to urbanized economies and from traditional to modern societies. Sprawling shantytowns, slums, or squatter areas; dilapidated shelter structures patched together from scraps of cardboard, corrugated iron, wood, and some-times bricks; an appalling lack of basic services such as safe water supply, sanitation, and drainage: all these problems are glaringly obvious to anyone living in or visiting the cities of developing countries. Quite clearly a drastic need for improvement exists, but what is an appropriate way to approach the urban housing problem in the developing world? Before this question can be answered, however, the problem itself must be defined.

Accordingly, this chapter first presents an overview of the urban housing sector in developing countries by discussing the major aspects of housing demand and supply and their interaction, which produces the aspects of the urban housing problem typically observed. On the basis of this analysis, the chapter then proposes a definition of the housing problem in developing country cities and suggests a strategy to assist in reducing the problem. To summarize the essence of the argument, it is concluded that the constraint on urban housing lies not in the limits on the demand side, but rather in the inadequate response on the supply side—an inadequacy that has largely been induced by mistaken policies and is therefore subject to remedies through corrective policy action. As a test of the proposed strategy's feasibility, the chapter goes on to present a review of some of the experience gathered in the preparation and implementation of urban development projects financed by the World Bank. The chapter concludes with a summary of major policy implications.

The Urban Housing Sector

Not surprisingly, an analysis of the urban housing sector in developing countries is best carried out first by investigating the nature and determinants of the demand for and supply of housing, and then by considering the interactions of demand and supply and how they create the symptoms of the urban housing problem.

The Demand for Urban Housing

The demand for housing reflects the willingness to pay for a set of attributes or services provided by the physical components of lot and housing structure. The most important of these attributes are access, space, tenure, on-site services, and shelter.

HOUSING ATTRIBUTES AND PREFERENCE PATTERNS. Access defines the accessibility of employment opportunities, of off-site services such as health and education facilities, and of community contacts. Access is important because it permits a household the opportunity of earning an income, of benefiting from social services, and of enjoying community relations with culturally and socially compatible neighbors. These locational advantages, and thus the value of a particular lot, may be affected by changes in the transport system, by the (re-)location of employment opportunities and social service facilities, and by changes in the cultural and social balance of the community.

Space, as reflected by the size of the lot, is important since it represents a constraint on the size of the shelter structure that can be built on it; it limits the extent to which agricultural, commercial, or recreational activities can be carried out on the lot; and it determines the extent of privacy enjoyed.

Tenure has two dimensions. The first is the security of tenure; that is, the protection from being forced to move involuntarily and having to incur costs associated with such a move (moving costs, loss of employment, and so forth). The security of tenure apparently has a considerable influence on the willingness of low-income households to maintain and improve their dwellings. The second aspect of tenure relates to the ownership rights of the asset, which in addition to security convey benefits such as the ability to lease all or part of a lot or house (particularly important for many low-income property owners); the right to carry out commercial activities on the lot (unless prohibited by local ordinances); the ability to reap the capital gains of increases in the property value; the possibility of using the property as collateral when borrowing; and the prestige of being a property owner. Tenure security and ownership rights—and thus the value of property—can be extensively altered by public action such as expropriation or conferral of title, expulsion from squatter land, zoning restrictions on rental or commercial activities, and taxation of rents or capital gains.

The availability of on-site services such as water and energy supply, waste disposal, drainage, and security from crime and fires conveys direct benefits associated with the consumption of these services over and above the costs borne by the user. The benefits derived and costs incurred on account of these services vary with the type of service supplied (for example, in-house water and electricity versus hand-carried water or firewood), with the scale at which the services are provided, and with the pricing policies of the (public or private) supplier. The availability of on-site services, especially piped water and electricity, also makes it possible to carry out productive activities using these services as inputs.

Finally, the shelter structure provides protection from the elements, privacy, convenience, domestic living space, and aesthetic pleasure. It provides an opportunity for earning an income by rental or by commercial and productive activities carried out on the premises.

Beyond the private benefits deriving from these five primary attributes of housing are a number of social benefits. Public health is improved and fire hazards reduced by more spacious, better constructed, and well-serviced housing. Housing provides an incentive for saving and investment, as well as employment opportunities (during construction, and by virtue of the commercial and productive activities carried out in the house and on the lot). Finally, dilapidated housing is an affront to the aesthetic sense of some and to the moral sensitivity of others. Following aesthetic considerations, one would be concerned primarily with the looks of things and be interested mainly with suppressing the symptoms of the housing problem (through slum eradication, "beautification" of cities, and like measures), whereas if following ethical precepts one would be concerned with the consequences of poor housing for the health, productivity, and comfort of the inhabitants and would search out the most effective combination of housing attributes compatible with the preferences of the dwellers and with the availability of public and private resources.

Housing choices vary to a considerable extent with factors such as climate, income, household size and composition, and price. A solid and well-insulated shelter structure is obviously more important where the weather is frequently inclement but is less so in tropical areas; where torrential rains are frequent, drainage is more important than in drier climates. Somewhat less obvious but no less important, preferences tend to differ at different income levels. A common pattern, which was originally postulated by John Turner for selected Latin American cities, is summarized by Mohan (1977, p. 446; see also Dwyer 1975, p. 28):

> The poorest (e.g., fresh migrants) are mainly interested in location. Being near job markets saves on transport costs. In their highly uncertain situation the only security they are interested in is job security. Their meager income only allows for food consumption and other bare essentials in a kind of lexicographic ordering. The only amenity they need is space for sleeping. The next group, with a reasonably stable income but still not well-off, is interested in security of tenure. This group is willing to trade location for security of tenure. A temporary job loss or other economic misfortune does not then mean displacement of residence as well. They are also more interested in space than amenity and are willing to pay for it. Finally the richest income group is more interested in amenity, having a stable income and subsistence essentials. Electricity, plumbing, well-designed houses, and recreation then become important and will be demanded by this group.

Of course, the precise priority ranking of the housing attributes desired may vary, since it also depends on household size and composition and on prices. Thus, the greater is a household's size, the more value will it place on space relative to other attributes. In El Salvador households headed by women have been found to place a greater value on shelter at the time of moving to a new property because they are less able to upgrade their shelter over time (1977 World Bank data). Furthermore, the value of a central location depends on the labor force characteristics and economic activities of the adult household members.[3] Finally, rising land prices are likely to result in a reduced demand for space, in increased investment in structures to accommodate greater density in living, in location of housing at less accessible areas of the city, and in the acceptance of lesser security of tenure.

Two major lessons can be drawn from this discussion of housing preference patterns. First, within the constraints of household budgets, low-income urban dwellers on balance will give high priority to access, space, and some tenure security and service amenities, but they will place relatively less priority on high-quality shelter and services. This latter set of attributes, however, has tended to be emphasized in the traditional public housing policies pursued by governments in developing countries. Second, apart from the broad general preference pattern outlined, the housing preferences of the urban poor will vary across countries, cities, and households.[4] A housing policy that attempts to achieve greatest efficiency in the utilization of economic resources must respect the preferences of the poor, by providing maximum flexibility and beneficiary participation in project and program design so beneficiaries will have as much choice as possible between alternative options for access, lot size, tenure, servicing, and shelter structure.

HOUSING DEMAND AND CITY GROWTH. The demand for housing is intricately related to the growth of cities. Most directly, the growth in population induces an increased demand for all the attributes or services housing can offer (access, space, tenure, services, and shelter). Moreover, the growth in incomes also increases people's willingness to pay for housing, and this in turn further increases the demand for housing services. Assuming unitary population and (per capita) income elasticities of demand for housing at given prices,[5] and taking typical population and per capita income growth rates observed in the cities of developing countries as fluctuating around 5 percent and 3 to 5 percent a year, respectively,[6] one may conclude that, in the absence of price changes or supply constraints, the demand for housing services will increase at a rate of 8 to 10 percent a year.

The pressures on the stock of housing are intensified by competing demands for the major inputs to housing, in particular for urban land. City growth is not only associated with the growth in demand for residential land, services, and structures, but is also accompanied by a rapid expansion of demand for land, services, and structures for commercial and industrial purposes.[7] What is more, land may be demanded not only for services it provides in residential, commercial, and industrial uses, but also as an asset by individuals and corporations (Mohan 1977).[8]

The demand for urban land, services, and structures is thus likely to increase even more rapidly than would be suggested by residential demand alone, and the resultant pressures on the supply of land, services, and construction are considerable in a context of rapid urban growth. The ability of supply to adjust is therefore a crucial question and will be dealt with next.

The Supply of Urban Housing

Increases in the supply of housing services depend largely on increases in the stock of housing available, and thus on the investments taking place in the housing sector. As with all stock adjustments, the adjustments in the housing stock take time, and the more rapid is the increase in the demand for more housing stock, the more likely it is that the supply will not keep up for all of the attributes housing represents. Indeed, the complexities of the demand for housing are matched, if not surpassed, by the intricacy of multiple interactions on the supply side. The following paragraphs first show how numerous agents interact in providing the housing supply; they then review how various constraints impede supply adjustments in response to the rapid increases in housing demand or permit such adjustments only at rising costs.

HOUSING SUPPLY AGENTS. Table 5-5 provides a stylized picture of the urban housing sector in developing countries, showing the common contributors to urban housing supply and distinguishing not only between the major activities required to supply urban housing but also between high-, middle-, and low-income housing. For low-income housing, the subdivision of raw land is typically performed by developers, squatters, or absentee landowners; occasionally it is also done by local governments or public housing agencies. The provision of on-site services to low-income housing is frequently left to owner-occupants, squatters, absentee owners, or renters, especially where

Table 5-5. *Matrix of Housing Supply Agents and Activities*

	Housing supply activities				
Suppliers	*Subdivision*	*Provision of on-site services*[a]	*Provision of off-site services*[b]	*Shelter construction*	*Provision of tenure security*
Private					
Developers	H,M,L	H,M		H,M	H,M,(L)
Owner-occupants	H,(M,L)	L[c]	H[d]	H,M,L	H,M,L
Squatters and occupants of illegal subdivisions	M,L	M,L[c]		M,L	
Absentee owners	(H),M,L	(H),M,L		(H),M,L	(H),M,L
Renters		(M),L[c]		(L)	
Service providers		(M),L[e]	H,M,L[f]		
Public					
Urban government	(M,L)	H,M,L	H,M,L	(M,L)	M,L
Public utilities		H,M,L			
Housing agencies	(H),M,(L)	(H),M,(L)	(H),(M),(L)	(H),M,(L)	(H),M,(L)

H = High-income housing; M = middle-income housing; L = low-income housing. Parentheses indicate that supply activity is of secondary importance.
  a. Water and energy supply, waste disposal, drainage services.
  b. Transport, education, health, security services.
  c. Includes water carrying, private energy supply, waste disposal.
  d. Private automobile transport.
  e. Water and wood carriers; waste collectors.
  f. Transport operators, schools, and health services.

water and firewood have to be hand-carried to the house because of the absence of public services. Off-site services may be provided by private agencies in the case of transport, health, and education, but they are mainly the domain of local authorities, particularly as regards the provision of roads and social services. Low-income shelter construction (and improvement) is generally carried out by absentee landlords for their tenements and by owner-occupants or squatters, who usually improve their housing by staged construction. Renters rarely make significant improvements, and public authorities have in only a few instances (for example, in Singapore and Hong Kong) contributed extensively to the construction of low-income shelter. The responsibility for provision of security of tenure for low-income housing rests generally with the government, which determines the extent to which the insecure tenure of illegal subdivisions, or of squatters on public and private land, is translated into secure freehold tenure. Property owners, of course, determine the extent to which renters can enjoy a relatively undisturbed and secure tenancy.

The picture could be complemented by describing the major suppliers and supply activities for middle- and high-income housing. However, this is not central to the purpose of this study; it suffices to say that high-income housing is usually provided by developers or owner-occupants as subdivision, shelter construction, and provision of tenure; on-site services are provided by the government or the developer; off-site services mainly by the government and by private service agencies (schools, hospitals, and the like). Middle-income housing supply shares aspects of high- and low-income housing, and it is probably the most varied in terms of involvement of different supply agents. The most important aspects are that middle-income households are frequently to be found on illegal subdivisions and among squatters as well as renters (see Vernez 1973 for examples from Bogota) and that public housing programs in the past have tended to benefit mainly middle-income groups.

Overall, there are two conclusions that are important for the remainder of this chapter. First, squatters and occupants of illegal subdivisions make important contributions to the supply of housing, particularly in the provision of on-site services and shelter construction. In fact, shelter construction and improvement generally represent the major form of saving and investment for the groups involved. In contrast, renters rarely contribute to the housing supply and have much less of an option to save or invest in the absence of suitable saving instruments or incentives. Second, urban governments and public utility enterprises are especially heavily involved in the provision of on- and off-site services, and urban governments can play a major role in providing secure tenure of low- and middle-income housing. Public agencies are to a much lesser extent involved in subdivision or shelter construction, and in any case they tend to serve mainly the middle-income groups.[9] Hard figures on the breakdown of construction activities by public and private sector are very scant and quite unreliable; thus these conclusions are mainly based on nonquantitative observation. Table 5-6, for instance, shows that the public sector's share in the construction of *conventional* dwellings is very high in Singapore and quite substantial in Jamaica, Israel, Romania, Yugoslavia, and Tunisia. However, since these figures exclude nonconventional housing, and thus understate the contribution of the private sector that obviously prevails in the construction of nonconventional housing (slums, squatter settlements, and the like), the importance of public housing investments are likely to be severely overstated for some of these countries.

Table 5-6. *Number of Conventional Dwellings Constructed by Public Investors as a Percentage of Total Conventional Dwellings Constructed during 1971–73, in Selected Developing Countries*

Country	Percent
Middle-income Asia	
Singapore	92.3
Latin America	
Colombia[a]	1.2
Honduras[a]	1.2
Jamaica[a]	68.6
Europe, Middle East, and North Africa	
Portugal[b]	10.9
Spain	10.3
Turkey	2.6
Yugoslavia	32.9
Israel	40.5
Morocco	8.1
Syria[b]	6.4
Tunisia	30.0
Romania	38.6

Note: Construction included new construction, partition, conversion, and restoration.
Source: United Nations (1976, table 15).
a. Urban areas only.
b. New construction only.

FACTORS LIMITING INCREASES IN HOUSING SUPPLY. The supply of new housing stock is limited by three types of constraints. For some attributes of housing, the supply is fixed or highly inelastic in the short run but can be expanded at approximately constant costs in the long term; for others, the cost of supply is rising even in the long term; and for yet others, there are transactions costs that may impede the provision of necessary inputs. The first type of constraint operates mainly when cities expand rapidly and when quick adjustments can therefore be made only with rising costs. The second type of constraint is associated mainly with the absolute size of cities rather than their rate of growth. The last type of constraint applies irrespective of city size or speed of growth. These distinctions between constraints are worth bearing in mind in discussions of various specific impediments to adjustments in the supply of raw land, services, and housing structures.

The cost of land may rise because the opportunity cost of rural land may increase as the city expands; some developing country cities, such as Bogota, are located in the midst of fertile agricultural land. In a few cities, such as Hong Kong, land reclamation is the only major way of adding to the urban land area. Subdivision at the urban fringe is frequently impeded by municipal ordinances that do not respond to increases in the demand for urban land, or respond only with substantial lags and in the form of discrete adjustments whose timing cannot be easily predicted by private supply agents. Land conversion, and especially land assembly, may be impeded because of lengthy expropriation proceedings in the case of public demand for land, or because of zoning regulations, land transfer taxes, or land registration requirements (see Dunkerley and others, 1983, for documentation; see also Smith 1977).[10]

More important, however, is that as cities grow the scarcity value of urban land tends to increase. Rising land prices in the urban center as well as at the periphery reflect this phenomenon and serve the essential function of allocating land as a factor of production to its most efficient use. There is frequently a great concern among policymakers in developing countries that urban land prices are rising excessively because of speculation and other market imperfections. However, such concern is generally based on a limited number of observations, particularly of properties at the urban fringe that are converted from rural to urban use and tend to experience the most rapid increases in land values. Careful research of urban land price increases has rarely been carried out, but where reliable data and analysis are available, as in the case of Bogota, Colombia, the evidence clearly shows that *average* land prices in the city have grown roughly in proportion with income over the past twenty years.[11]

Rather than the lack of availability of raw land, it is the lack of land serviced by public utilities and other urban services that creates major bottlenecks. The supply of public services may be constrained by limits on the availability or accessibility of natural resources, particularly in the case of water supply and waste disposal,[12] or because the city is expanding into mountainous or swampy terrain that is more difficult to service.[13] Further constraints on the expansion of public services may result from the lumpiness of the investments required and the lack of capital with which to finance such system expansions. The problem is frequently compounded by high service standards and subsidies, which undermine the financial viability of the public service enterprise and thus limit the expansion of services.

Institutional problems relating to management and planning, imbalanced expansion of production relative to distribution facilities, and political biases in service provision may limit supply response.[14] Some of these adjustment problems in the provision of public services are less serious in the large metropolitan areas because the local governments and public utility enterprises in some instances have better management, planning, and pricing practices and generally easier access to capital.[15]

The construction, improvement, and maintenance of shelter are often constrained in several ways. The supply of material inputs to the construction sector is usually quite inelastic in the short term, although in the longer run supplies tend to adjust to demand at roughly constant real costs (Grimes 1976). The short-term inelasticity of materials supply may mean, however, that during construction booms (such as occurred in Colombia during the early 1970s) prices of materials increase rapidly, limiting especially the expansion of low-income, self-constructed housing (Peattie 1979 and Bender 1975). Labor costs, particularly for skilled labor, may also be inelastic in the short and medium term (Grimes 1976), but more important, especially for low-income housing, tend to be the constraints on the availability of capital to finance the costs of land and shelter structure.

A recent study of housing finance by the United Nations has demonstrated that conventional instruments of housing finance are not accessible to low-income groups because of restrictive eligibility requirements and inappropriate terms (United Nations 1978). This largely explains why poor households generally report very little reliance on debt financing for their housing expenditures (World Bank 1980d, Strassmann 1980). Mortgage markets are generally very thin because artificially low interest rates on formal capital limit the flow of funds to the housing market. Those funds that are made available usually are rationed to higher-income groups (Grimes 1976). Large minimum-size loans and high down payments militate against low-income households. Clouded land titles prevent the use of land as collateral, and lack of steady income and employment makes the poor ineligible. High standards and subsidies limit the expansion of public housing because of budgetary constraints, as has been observed wherever such programs have been pursued.[16] Rent control has been found to impede the supply of housing in Egypt (Wheaton 1978) and India (1978 World Bank data compiled by E. Bevan Waide). Taxes on housing improvements in principle have similar effects, but the low level of property taxation found in most developing countries makes this a relatively minor problem (Bahl and Linn, forthcoming).[17] Finally, one should note that wholesale destruction of slum or squatter areas obviously does not contribute to an increase in the housing stock, but rather destroys considerable investment in housing structures.

Supply and Demand Interactions

For all the reasons cited in the preceding paragraphs, the supply of urban housing in developing countries is severely constrained. Supplies expand over time, but unevenly for the various components or attributes of supply and for different consumer groups, and often only at rising costs. One may further hazard the guess that supply adjustments tend to be more costly the greater the city size and the greater the rate of urban growth. Considering that the aggregate supply of housing, as reflected by the rate of increase in dwelling units from new construction and renovation, has generally not expanded by more than 1 to 3 percent a year (Grimes 1976), but that at unchanged prices demand for housing would be expected to increase by 8 to 10 percent a year (as indicated above), real housing prices will tend to rise in the rapidly growing cities of the developing countries. This leads in turn to overcrowding, lower-quality shelter, poorer services, and worse access than would have been the case had housing supply adjusted more rapidly.[18] For this reason the large and rapidly growing cities tend to experience the greatest slum and squatter problems, the poorest quality of housing, and the worst problems of over-crowding. Of course, to the extent that supply constraints—especially those caused by public action or inaction—are less prevalent in some cities than in others, these problems will differ between cities of similar size and similar growth rates.

To the extent that increased housing costs, overcrowding, and poor housing quality reflect the rising resource costs of providing housing in large and rapidly growing urban areas, as well as the preference patterns of urban dwellers at their prevailing incomes, these symptoms of the urban housing problem reflect an efficient adjustment process. However, it is apparent from the discussion of the supply constraints in the preceding pages that housing supply adjustments are to a large extent influenced by public actions and that there is reason to believe these actions do not necessarily result in efficient resource allocation. Investment, pricing, and regulatory policies in most cities have not been such as to minimize the resource cost of urban development. Rather, they have resulted in higher costs than necessary in infrastructure investments and have rationed high-cost supplies to a few beneficiaries, whereas lower-cost supplies could have been made more widely available, particularly to the urban poor. Inappropriate pricing policies have constrained public service investments and have encouraged overconsumption of services through subsidized prices for those households with access to the services. Finally, regulations and taxes have impeded private supply adjustment. It would therefore be in the interest of a more efficient pattern of urban growth to pursue policies that remove, rather than impose, constraints on the adjustment in urban housing supply.

Distributional considerations support the conclusion of the preceding paragraph. The increases in the costs and prices of housing services associated with a slow supply reaction in the face of rapid demand increases tend to be capitalized into land and structure prices. These capital gains are reaped by property owners. The ownership of urban real estate is likely to be highly concentrated in many developing countries, although there are variations across countries and cities. One important factor relevant to the distribution of urban real estate is the extent to which urban properties are rented or occupied by the owner. When the proportion of rental properties is very high (as in Abidjan, where 80 percent of urban properties are estimated to be rented), the rapid increases in urban property values clearly benefit the upper-income groups.[19] In contrast, where urban landownership is widely distributed, as reflected by a low proportion of rental tenure (for example, in Nepal, Philippines, and Cyprus; see table 5-7), it is likely that the benefits from rising property values are more widely distributed. Table 5-7 shows the distribution of tenure arrangements in urban areas between owner occupancy, rental, and other forms of tenure for forty-six developing countries. The variability between countries, even within country groupings, is considerable. As table 5-8 shows, however, there is a concentration of countries for which owner occupancy accounts for 40 to 50 percent of households, and there are relatively few countries where this percentage falls short of 20 percent or exceeds 70 percent. If nonconventional housing were added, and if one were to count de facto ownership by squatters as owner occupancy, the proportion of owner occupancy might be increased in some countries.

In any case, there can be little doubt that a large proportion of the capital gains in property values that are associated with rapid urban growth in the developing world is garnered by the high-income groups—especially since property taxation and related tax and pricing measures, which would extract some of these capital gains for the general public, are notoriously weak and ineffective with a few exceptions (notably Colombia, Korea, and the island of Taiwan; Bahl and Linn, forthcoming).

Another distributive effect of the slow increase in housing supply in the face of rapidly increasing demand is that low-income groups especially suffer from the effects of crowding, lack of services, and displacement from favored locations close to employment opportunities and social services. Whereas upper- and middle-income groups also have to double up and may have to accept lower-quality services than they might like to, they are generally in a position to preempt the best housing available, even under the worst of

Table 5-7. *Urban Household Tenure in Selected Developing Countries*

Region and country	Year	Distribution of conventional dwellings (percent)		
		Owner-occupied	Rented	Other
Sub-Saharan Africa				
Congo	1958	57.8	42.2	n.a.
Ethiopia	1967	28.1	56.9	15.1
Mauritius	1962	31.3	55.4	13.4
Seychelles	1971	26.9	62.7	10.5
Sudan	1964–66	59.2	28.3	12.6
Zaire	1967	47.4	38.3	14.3
Low-income Asia				
India	1971	47.1	52.9	n.a.
Nepal	1961	75.3	10.7	14.0
Pakistan	1960	48.8	34.2	17.0
Sri Lanka	1971	47.7	47.3	5.0
Vietnam	1962	68.4	28.0	3.6
Middle-income Asia				
Korea	1970	48.4	50.3	1.3
Malaysia				
Sabah	1960	48.8	51.2	n.a.
Sarawak	1960	49.8	50.2	n.a.
Philippines	1967	74.1	19.4	6.5
Thailand	1962–63	38.7	39.6	21.7
Latin America				
Argentina	1960	61.4	31.1	7.5
Bolivia	1963	41.2	47.1	11.6
Brazil	1970	60.0	30.8	9.2
Chile	1970	55.5	31.9	12.7
Colombia	1964	54.1	38.8	7.0
Costa Rica	1963	43.1	48.9	8.1
Dominican Republic	1960	44.9	44.0	11.1
Ecuador	1962	33.9	55.5	10.5
El Salvador	1971	35.3	53.3	11.4
Guatemala	1967	58.6	32.3	9.1
Honduras	1961	38.2	52.6	9.1
Jamaica	1970	29.5	63.2	7.3
Mexico	1970	54.2	} 45.8 {	
Nicaragua	1963	47.5	45.9	6.6
Panama	1970	38.8	52.6	8.7
Paraguay	1962	66.0	19.9	14.1
Peru	1961	39.4	44.7	16.0
Trinidad and Tobago	1957–58	32.4	61.3	6.3
Uruguay	1963	38.9	51.2	9.9
Europe, Middle East, and North Africa				
Cyprus	1973	70.7	29.3	n.a.
Egypt	1960	43.0	57.0	n.a.

Table 5-7 (*continued*)

Region and country	Year	Distribution of conventional dwellings (percent)		
		Owner-occupied	Rented	Other
Greece	1971	56.2	39.5	4.3
Iran	1966	54.9	33.4	11.7
Israel	1971	63.5	33.4	3.1
Jordan	1961	36.6	42.6	20.9
Morocco	1971	28.9	62.8	8.3
Portugal	1960	9.4	86.0	4.7
Tunisia	1966	54.5	32.6	12.8
Turkey	1960	49.3	47.6	3.1
Yugoslavia	1971	46.6	53.4	n.a.

n.a. Not available.
Note: Rows may not add to 100 because of rounding.
Source: United Nations (1976, table 11).

circumstances, by virtue of their superior ability to pay.[20] The poor therefore bear most directly the costs of maladjustments in the housing supply, in the form of loss of access to employment opportunities, poor health and nutrition, and general inconvenience.

Equity and efficiency arguments thus come together in supporting policies designed to increase the supply of urban housing, especially housing for the poor. These policies may involve a removal of constraints on housing supply as well as public incentives for or direct provision of more housing. But two types of questions immediately arise. First, how much housing is required in developing countries, and is it realistic to expect that these housing needs

Table 5-8. *Frequency Distribution of Countries, by Share of Urban Households with Owner Occupancy*

Percentage of urban households with owner occupancy	Number of countries
0–20.0	1
20.0–29.9	4
30.0–39.9	10
40.0–49.9	14
50.0–59.9	9
60.0–69.9	5
70.0+	3
Total	46

Source: Table 5-7.

can be met? And second, which components of housing are appropriately provided by the public sector? What incentives should be introduced? What disincentives or constraints should be removed? The next two sections consider these two sets of questions, respectively.

Estimating Housing Needs

The usual starting point for developing an urban housing policy is to estimate the housing needs for a particular country or city in physical units somehow defined, to estimate the costs of meeting these needs, and then to consider whether and how the required financial resources can be raised, both at the household and at the government level.[21]

The conventional analysis of housing needs starts with a definition of housing attributes that focuses mainly on space, services, and the structural qualities of the housing unit that are regarded as adequate. Usually these attributes involve standards comparable to those commonly found in middle- or even upper-income housing; thus they implicitly reflect not only the income levels of middle-income households but also their preferences in ranking the various attributes of housing. What is more, important attributes such as location, access, and tenure are generally not considered at all in the estimates of housing needs, although these may be among the most important housing attributes for the low-income groups. The conventional procedure for estimating housing needs therefore starts with a set of parameters that reflects neither the ability nor the willingness to pay of significant portions of the urban population.[22]

Given this starting point, it is not surprising to find that conventional housing policies have resulted in houses that are not affordable by the poor. For instance, in Manila in 1975, even with a subsidy ranging from 16 to 44 percent, the cheapest official housing units were not affordable by households in the lower half of the income distribution (1975 World Bank data). In Cairo, official housing is affordable only by the highest 10 percent (1978 World Bank data). Fifty percent of the population and 80 percent of the squatters in Rabat, Morocco, cannot afford conventional public housing (1978 World Bank data). In Indonesia, conventional sites-and-services programs and "low-income" housing are beyond the ability to pay of the poorest 30 to 40 percent of the urban population to be served, *despite* a subsidy estimated to amount to 65 percent of total cost (1978 World Bank data).[23] Since the poor cannot afford publicly constructed housing of this type, the housing units almost invariably have been purchased or leased by high-income groups.

Nor is it surprising to find that public housing programs in the past often have not respected the preferences of poor beneficiaries, especially as regards location and tenure security. The problems encountered in Rio de Janeiro with public housing programs have been well documented by Perlman (1976) and Rush (1974); in particular, the public housing developments were located far from employment opportunities and gave the tenants little security of tenure. Similar difficulties have been encountered in Manila (1975 World Bank data) and elsewhere (Grimes 1976).

Finally, it comes as no surprise that the number of housing units actually built in these kinds of public programs always falls short of the postulated housing needs and that studies of the total budgetary resources required to meet the housing needs must conclude that urban housing in developing countries represents a bottomless pit.

This kind of housing needs analysis is certainly not very useful, and the despair and hopelessness reached at its conclusion can in fact undermine any reasonable effort to deal with the housing problem in developing countries. This does not mean, however, that all housing needs analyses are necessarily useless, as is demonstrated by a recent exercise carried out by Anthony Churchill and Margaret Lycette and summarized in the World Bank's report on shelter (World Bank 1980d). Instead of starting off with some physical standard of adequate housing, they take it as a basic need that all households currently below the poverty line should be brought up at least to the poverty line in total household consumption, including the consumption of housing. Churchill and Lycette then estimate the total public and private investment required to provide housing to all the poor at the standard which those currently at the poverty threshold can afford.[24] Since poverty thresholds are set at different income levels from country to country, the postulated household expenditure on housing varies, as does the physical standard of housing implied by the expenditure figures. These standards are still arbitrary in the sense that they reflect value judgments inherent in the definition of poverty thresholds, which are of course a crucial input to this exercise. The standards, however, are derived so as to ensure that they do not implicitly reflect the income levels of middle- or high-income groups, but so that they define a minimum housing expenditure compatible with incomes at the poverty threshold, up to which all households would be brought over a reasonable time.[25] Furthermore, typical preference patterns at the poverty level are respected in this estimate of housing needs, by using the average propensity to spend on housing by the poor as an estimation criterion. As a result, housing programs that are compatible with these estimates would not require undue distortions in the expenditure baskets of the poor, providing that complementary policies (for example, in the areas of nutrition, health, ed-

Table 5-9. *Financial Implications of a "Basic Needs" Housing Strategy, in Selected Developing Countries, 1980–2000*

Region and country	Required investment		
	Total (millions of 1975 U.S. dollars)	Annual investment as a percentage of government revenue	Annual investment as a percentage of GNP
Sub-Saharan Africa			
Botswana	77	3.3	1.3
Chad	143	7.0	0.9
Ivory Coast	653	3.0	0.7
Kenya	1,482	9.0	1.6
Malawi	110	3.5	0.5
Senegal	210	4.0	0.5
Sierra Leone	76	6.0	1.0
Sudan	738	3.5	0.8
Tanzania	1,700	14.0	3.0
Zambia	37	0.2	0.1
Group total, average[a]	5,226	5.4 (3.9)	1.0 (0.8)
Low-income Asia			
Bangladesh	6,360	70.5	5.6
Burma	910	20.0	3.4
India	32,992	17.0	2.5
Indonesia	9,353	20.0	3.2
Pakistan	2,539	12.0	1.7
Sri Lanka	419	7.0	1.8
Group total, average[a]	52,573	24.4 (23.1)	3.0 (1.4)
Middle-income Asia			
Korea	488	1.0	0.1
Malaysia	717	2.0	0.4
Philippines	2,654	11.0	1.2
Thailand	700	3.0	0.4
Group total, average[a]	4,559	4.3 (4.6)	0.5 (0.5)
Latin America			
Argentina	2,776	9.3	0.7
Brazil	17,794	9.0	1.3
Chile	494	1.1	0.1
Colombia	1,664	10.0	0.8
Costa Rica	122	3.0	0.4
Dominican Republic	485	6.7	1.0
Ecuador	305	4.8	0.6
El Salvador	156	4.8	0.6
Honduras	149	7.8	0.9
Jamaica	202	3.7	0.9
Mexico	20,003	29.0	2.3
Panama	207	4.6	0.7
Group total, average[a]	44,356	7.8 (7.2)	0.9 (0.5)

Table 5-9 (*continued*)

	Required investment		
Region and country	Total (millions of 1975 U.S. dollars)	Annual investment as a percentage of government revenue	Annual investment as a percentage of GNP
Europe, Middle East, and North Africa			
Egypt	1,238	3.5	0.6
Tunisia	894	8.0	1.8
Turkey	4,082	5.0	0.9
Group total, average[a]	6,214	5.5 (2.3)	1.1 (0.6)
Total, average[a]	112,927	9.4 (12.3)	1.3 (1.1)

Source: World Bank data compiled by Anthony Churchill and Margaret Lycette. See also World Bank 1980d.

a. Averages apply to required annual investment as percent of government revenue and to required annual investment as percent of GNP. They are unweighted. Figures in parentheses show standard deviations.

ucation, and so forth) ensure that those below the poverty threshold are brought up to the threshold in their consumption not only of housing, but also of food, clothing, and other essential goods and services.

The budgetary implications of such a basic needs housing strategy can then be estimated, and they are shown in table 5-9.[26] In absolute investment needs, India, Indonesia, Brazil, and Mexico loom very large and jointly account for 71 percent of the investment requirements. The six countries of low-income Asia together account for 47 percent of investment needs. Required annual investment needs expressed as a fraction of government revenue and of GNP are also the highest in this country group. These investments are probably not within the range of fiscal feasibility, and may in part reflect the fact that the propensity to spend on housing is in general substantially below the 20 percent rate assumed by Churchill and Lycette, as shown in tables 5-1 and 5-2, above. It does, however, also reflect the large number of households living in poverty in these countries and the low level of GNP and fiscal resources available to provide even a minimal degree of poverty alleviation. A feasible housing strategy for these countries would therefore have to employ standards even lower than those implied by housing expenditure at the poverty threshold.

With some exceptions (notably, Tanzania and Mexico) the picture looks considerably brighter for most other countries, in that relatively far smaller shares of government revenue and GNP would have to be devoted to a basic needs shelter strategy.[27] Even for the middle-income countries, however, one should not be overly optimistic. In view of the trouble most industrialized countries are having in raising the share of official development assistance from the typical 0.3 percent of GNP to the internationally agreed target level of 0.7 percent, one cannot expect the developing countries to find it easy to shift their budgets so as to devote an additional 0.5 or 1.0 percent of GNP to housing for the poor. The exercise is nevertheless useful in indicating countries that have to be particularly concerned about bringing supply costs down so as to provide housing solutions within reach of everyone, including those below the poverty threshold, and countries for which the fiscal implications of meeting the basic shelter needs of those below the poverty threshold are within the range of feasibility.

In any case, estimates of housing needs not only have to be translated into global, national, or city-specific investment figures but also must be linked with a detailed housing supply strategy that makes allowance for the ability to pay of low-income households and also gives explicit consideration to their preferences for the various attributes of housing (location, space, tenure, services, and structure). The remainder of this section discusses some policy options that can be pursued in an attempt to meet the housing needs of the poor in line with their preferences.

A Housing Strategy for the Urban Poor

Since public resources available for low-income housing are severely limited, the major question for policymakers is how can the public sector best increase supplies or lower costs of housing to the poor through direct intervention. Public sector involvement deserves consideration where there exist substantial economies of scale, externalities, or market imperfections such as monopoly or monopsony power, lack of information, and the like. Without any doubt, the public sector is best equipped to counteract inefficiencies in the housing market that are generated by its own policies. In the absence of significant economies of scale, externalities, or market imperfections, public intervention is not likely to be appropriate, unless it can be shown to have a direct effect in improving the welfare of those below the poverty threshold. Even then, there is good reason to emphasize those areas of public housing intervention where individual households are least able to find solutions for themselves. On the basis of this general principle, three broad kinds of policy instrument will be discussed: first, direct supply of housing services by the government, including public intervention in the urban land market and public provision of services and shelter; second, tax and pricing policies, in particular property taxation and user charges; and, third, regulation and controls.

Public Intervention in the Urban Land Market

In designing urban land policies, the essential point to bear in mind is that land prices serve the important function of allocating land between alternative uses.[28] Unless convincing evidence can be marshalled that the urban land market is not functioning efficiently (for example, because of clear monopoly in landownership or other market futures—often induced by public policy), direct intervention in the land market is not appropriate. There are, however, three conditions under which public intervention regarding urban land may be required. First, monopoly in urban landownership or development may sometimes exist (for example, in El Salvador); second, public sector projects, such as sites-and-services schemes, may require land as an essential input; third, changing land uses, however efficiently, may cause considerable hardship particularly for low-income residents when they are forced to leave rapidly appreciating areas because commercial or industrial development is able to use the land more productively.[29] Monopoly in urban land holdings is quite rare, but where it exists it is difficult to deal with by measures short of major upheaval, since the monopoly landowner usually is also politically powerful. The land needs of public projects have to be directly addressed as discussed in the following paragraphs. In fact, at times these projects are a response to the displacement of poor urban families that are pushed out of their traditional neighborhoods by commercial or other uses, as was the case in Hong Kong. It is important, however, that displaced low-income households are relocated in areas where accessibility to their traditional jobs is not severely disrupted, or that complementary investments in public transport or employment opportunities ensure access to jobs from the new locations.

A major determinant of the public sector's ability to intervene directly in the urban land market is the extent to which land is publicly or privately owned. Where there exist large tracts of public land within the urban area or at its fringe, the government may directly intervene. Where public land is occupied by squatters, the government can combine slum-upgrading programs with efforts to regularize tenure. Vacant public land can be subdivided and made available for housing programs. This approach—in many respects by far the easiest, since it does not involve fiscal resources or complicated acquisition procedures—is not, however, of broad relevance for most cities in developing countries. Although government ownership of urban land is not uncommon, vacant land is generally quite limited and is even more so in locations close to employment opportunities. There exist, of course, special circumstances that permit the use of vacant public land with good accessibility. For example, a conversion of a centrally located military airfield in

Cali, Colombia, to residential use has been discussed as an option to provide improved housing in that city. Although the search for such unused or underutilized public urban land is worthwhile, it is not likely to provide an answer to the long-term housing problem in most cities, including Cali.[30]

The regularization of tenure rights on land owned by the public sector but occupied by squatters is a more common possibility for improving the housing conditions of the squatters—directly by increasing tenure security and providing ownership rights; indirectly by assisting private efforts to upgrade shelter. Tenure security and ownership rights are known to act as incentives for shelter improvement and to permit better access to capital markets, since the new owner-occupants are able to offer their land as collateral. World Bank-funded urban development projects (in Cairo, Manila, Rabat, and Lazaro Cardenas in Mexico, to mention just a few) involve numerous examples of this type of approach. A problem is that this approach may be seen as encouraging more squatting on public land because it would appear to involve ex post sanctioning of land invasions. One way to reduce the political objections to this procedure, and to provide at least some disincentives to squatters, is to require some payment in exchange for the conferral of title. This in turn is likely to be easier to extract if the regularization of land titles is combined with other elements of an upgrading policy—in particular the provision of public services, since the beneficiaries in this case obtain an immediate improvement in their overall living standard, and their willingness to pay is likely to be increased considerably. The case of the World Bank's urban development project in Cairo is particularly interesting in this respect. The payments for regularization of land titles in squatter areas on public land is expected to bring a sizable surplus to the executing agency within a relatively short period, and this surplus in turn may be used to finance upgrading programs for squatter areas elsewhere.

More serious difficulties of public land provision occur where land is privately owned and the government has to acquire land, whether it is vacant, illegally subdivided, or occupied by squatters. In the case of privately owned vacant land, its acquisition and assembly in close proximity to employment opportunities are complicated by the difficulty of finding such land available, in overcoming the private owners' objections to public acquisition or expropriation, and in meeting the financial costs the acquisition of such land frequently involves (unless compensation to landowners is significantly below market prices, which in turn will increase the owners' opposition and tend to delay, if not abort, public action).[31]

Assembly and subdivision of public land tend to be easier at the urban periphery, mainly because larger tracts of vacant land are usually available there, the acquisition of which involves fewer private owners and thus a reduced need for negotiation. Two problems, however, arise. First, peripheral land may not provide accessibility to employment opportunities unless transport improvements are also made or unless concomitant decisions regarding the location of employment and off-site services complement the public land acquisition. Second, there is the question of when to acquire peripheral land. On the one hand, early acquisition results in lower land costs but requires careful planning and the management of public land before it is actually developed. It also ties up public budgetary resources. On the other hand, acquisition at the time of subdivision and development results in higher land costs unless the public sector is willing and able to expropriate the land below market prices. Although there is no simple solution to this dilemma, it is clear that public "land banking," as it has sometimes been called, must be evaluated very carefully and is no easy remedy to the housing problem in developing country cities (Dunkerley and others, 1983).

In the case where private land is occupied by squatters, the problems incurred are akin to those encountered with squatter areas involving public land, except that the regularization of squatter tenure for privately owned land would also have to involve negotiations with and compensation of the private owners (unless the land is expropriated without compensation). The Rabat Urban Development Project financed by the World Bank involves land tenure regularization for squatters on private land. Although public land acquisition in general can take a long time, in Morocco legal instruments permit "provisional public acquisition," a procedure similar to expropriation, which gives the government considerable strength in bargaining over acquisition prices and timing. The existence of a legal framework permitting such public action is obviously important, but it is often absent in developing countries.

Illegal subdivision of privately owned land occurs quite frequently in the cities of developing countries (for example, in Bogota and San Salvador) and consists in the parceling and sale of privately owned land where this is not permitted by municipal zoning ordinances. The implication for the de facto owners is that they do not have the secure tenure of legal landownership and suffer the resultant complications discussed earlier. The problem for local authorities is that frequently they cannot collect property taxes in these areas, since the legal owners have no incentive to pay, and the de facto owners are not even registered in the city's cadastre. Public intervention is in principle relatively easy and involves transferring to the de facto landowners full tenure rights. In practice the matter is, again, not quite so straightforward, since there is the common fear that the ex post sanctioning of an illegal subdivision will encourage more of the same in the future. By extracting a payment for tenure regularization this problem may be circumvented at least in part. Another measure would be to abandon restrictive zoning regulations on the grounds that these are not effective anyway and only hinder the efficient operations of the urban land market. This issue is discussed below.

Three further considerations must be added. First, throughout this study the importance of location and access for the low-income groups has been stressed. Acquisition and subdivision of public land are obviously not the only way in which land tracts with desirable locational characteristics can be made available to poor households. Complementary actions in the areas of transport improvements, decentralization of employment, and off-site service location are policies as important in the long term as direct government intervention in the land market. To provide a maximum of benefits, the use of all these instruments should be planned jointly by the various urban authorities. This, however, is easier said than done, given the common fragmentation of planning and implementation authority in these areas.

Second, considerable cost savings per plot may be realized when the public subdivision is carried out if the average plot size is reduced, particularly in locations where land costs are high. World Bank projects in Mexico, Botswana, and Upper Volta have shown that reducing the lot size below that in conventional public housing programs can substantially reduce project costs and thus permit a program that reaches further down in the income distribution scale while still meeting the preferences of poor beneficiaries. The previously cited examples of Zambia and the Philippines, where beneficiaries were willing to trade smaller lot size for better service levels, and the contrasting experience in El Salvador, where the reverse pattern was observed, indicated also that preferences of project beneficiaries are important in this context and their consideration can contribute significantly to the success (or failure) of a project.

Finally, complementary action to strengthen the cadastral services in urban areas is often a crucial component of public land policy, since the absence of valid land registration, property surveys, and land valuation records impedes the functioning of the land market (that is, interferes with real estate transactions), reduces the usefulness of land as collateral in borrowing, creates uncertainty of tenure rights, and impedes property taxation (Dunkerley and others, 1983). Improvements in the urban real estate registers, however, are often useful only when combined with efforts to regularize tenure rights. Concerted action is therefore critical. Again, fragmentation of responsibility among various public agencies may hamper a coordinated approach in this as in other areas of urban policy action.

This discussion of direct public intervention in the urban land market can be concluded by a brief evaluation of the various possible avenues of action by the criteria set forth earlier. Public, rather than private, initiative is required in the following areas: subdivision of publicly owned land and regularization of land titles for illegal and squatter subdivisions on private and public land; improved cadastral services; and decentralized location of public off-site services and employment opportunities. Public intervention may also be necessary where large-scale displacement of poor households occurs because of redevelopment of their neighborhoods, or where clear monopoly in the urban land market exists. In the former case, provision of alternative sites with appropriate service and access characteristics is desirable; in the latter case, breaking up the monopoly may be the only course of action, even though it may require major political change. These public actions can considerably lower the cost of urban land supply, increase the efficiency of the urban housing market, *and* serve as a vehicle for asset transfers from high- to low-income groups and from the public sector to poor households in a way that will meet with relatively little political opposition.[32] In contrast, the public sector has much less of a clear advantage in the acquisition and subdivision of privately held land or in land banking. As regards land banking, it is not clear that this kind of public intervention in the land market is more efficient than private intervention. In terms of the redistribution of urban landownership and rental incomes, public land acquisition and development may be an effective tool if the political will and the legal machinery exist to impose a far-reaching expropriation of urban real estate at levels of compensation substantially below market prices. This is not likely to be politically feasible in many countries. Instead, various tax and pricing measures must be relied on to achieve a more even distribution of the gains associated with urban land ownership.[33]

Provision of Public Services

Without a doubt, the public sector has a major role in the provision of public services such as water supply, energy, waste disposal, drainage, and road circulation.[34] Economies of scale, externalities, and the possibility of monopoly conditions under private sector provision are well-known arguments for the public provision of urban utility services. Economies of scale and avoidance of monopoly rents are most easily demonstrated for the case of water supply and energy, where comparative information on the cost savings derived from public provision of these services is available.

The concern here is not with the question of economies of scale associated with larger as against smaller size of water supply systems (Saunders and Warford 1976). Rather, the emphasis is on a cost comparison between water available directly from public supplies (either piped in-house or from an easily accessible water tap) and water supplied by carriers or other vendors. Table 5-10 shows that the cost differences are tremendous in most countries or cities for which information is available. Although the base price charged

Table 5-10. *Costs of Public and Private Water Supply in Selected Developing Countries*
(U.S. dollars per cubic meter)

Country or city	In-house connection (public utility)	Water carrier (private vendor)
Nairobi	0.20	1.4–2.1
Senegal	Free	1.6–2.4
Kampala	0.33	1.3–3.0
Upper Volta	0.30	1.0–1.5
Ghana	0.10	1.3–2.5

Note: Ratios of private to public water costs in additional locations are: for Abidjan, 5 to 1; for selected cities in Indonesia, between 2 to 1 and 10 to 1 (World Bank data); for Karachi, 10 to 1 (USAID 1976); and for Lima, between 16 to 1 and 25 to 1 (Thomas 1978).
Source: Vlieger and others (1975, p. 48).

by the utilities in many cases includes considerable subsidies, the difference between the utility's tariff and the vendor's price reflects a combination of increased resource cost and monopoly rent. Monopoly rents can indeed be significant, as has been found recently in Indonesia (1978 World Bank data). The effect on poor households without direct access to public water supply is obvious: they pay a much higher price (for a commodity of lesser quality) than do consumers who are connected to (safe) public supply.[35] The effect on household expenditures can be dramatic. In Lima, households purchasing water from vendors typically spend between 2.6 and 2.7 percent of their incomes on water, whereas those with direct access to piped water spend only between 0.4 and 0.7 percent of their incomes (Thomas 1978). In Indonesia, the poorest households may spend as much as 7 percent of income on water (1978 World Bank data). For energy, the situation is not much different. Thomas (1978) estimates that alternative sources of electric light are over twice as expensive, and Findley (1977, p. 45) reports on a study showing that in Manila "squatters pay more for light using kerosene lamps than those who have electricity." Although quantitative evidence is not readily available, there can be little doubt that economies of scale are also important in the case of other services. They are probably least important in waste disposal, for which it has been shown that small-scale conventional technologies—such as pit latrines or septic tanks for sewage, house-to-house collection for recyclable solid wastes—are frequently cost-effective, private alternatives to publicly provided sewerage systems and garbage collection and disposal (Kalbermatten, Julius, and Gunnerson 1982, 1977 World Bank data compiled by Alfredo Sfeir-Younis).

Externalities can also be an important argument for the public provision of on-site services. Most notable are the health effects of sanitation,[36] and although public supply of water and sewerage services is not necessarily the only way to allow for these externalities (appropriate pricing or regulation might be an alternative), it is one way to bring about a wide acceptance of system connections and service levels that provide the social benefits derived from these services. Services such as road circulation and drainage can be and are frequently installed by developers of higher-income urban housing units even in developing country cities,[37] but their maintenance—and in low-income neighborhoods even their initial provision—generally rests with public agencies because of the public goods nature of these services. To the extent that the externalities derived from on-site and related services are internal to a particular neighborhood—this is certainly the case for road circulation facilities, and to a considerable extent for the external benefits derived from the other services—one can conceive of the public provision of these services again as implying cost reductions to the community. Such reductions increase the efficiency of resource allocation for the community as a whole and yield a fiscal dividend.

Thus, there is little doubt that the public provision of site-related public services can provide important cost reductions as well as increased benefits for the household. But what should the standards be at which the public services are provided? A survey of World Bank sites-and-services projects carried out in 1974 showed that, on average and per plot, reductions in the capital costs of service facilities could be achieved by adopting simpler service standards. For water supply, the average cost of communal standpipes fell in the range of US$30 to US$50 compared with US$80 for individual plot connections.[38] For sewerage, the average cost per plot for a pit latrine was US$20; for a connection to a waterborne sewerage system it was US$180. For neighborhood roads and drainage, three alternative quality standards were compared, yielding average costs of US$150, US$100, and US$25, respectively, for high, medium, and low standards (World Bank 1974b). These estimates give only a general impression of possible cost savings, since subsequent studies of the costs of alternative service standards have shown that a rigorous comparison of costs is not always easily carried out. Furthermore, one must of course be concerned with any differences in benefits in arriving at an overall evaluation of net benefits accruing from alternative standards.

For the case of water supply, Saunders and Warford (1976, p. 125) conclude that "in view of the many possible systems configurations and variations in population density and service costs, it is almost impossible to generalize about the relative cost of household versus standpost supplies." While this is probably true as a general statement, one may nevertheless conclude from the cost data cited above that in cities where average incomes are extremely low, such as in most countries of sub-Saharan Africa and in low-income Asia, community water supplies must almost inevitably be chosen if the costs are to be affordable to the households involved and if public service is to be provided to a substantial portion of low-income households within the government's budgetary constraints (World Bank 1980e). In the middle-income countries, individual house connections are generally affordable by low-income households; to the extent that subsidization is necessary, this poses no undue financial burden on the utility companies because cross-subsidization between users is feasible. This conclusion is confirmed by the selection of water service standards for a large number of urban development projects that have been recently financed by the World Bank.

For the sanitary disposal of wastes, a study of alternative technologies carried out by the World Bank permits the following conclusions:

Fortunately, low-cost alternatives to sewerage exist and work well. When properly constructed and maintained, they provide all the health benefits of sewerage and have fewer adverse environmental effects. They are, in many cases, technologies that had been used for many years in developed countries but were abandoned rather than improved as those countries grew more prosperous. They may not be applicable to parts of the dense, westernized, metropolitan centers of the developing world, where sewerage may remain the most appropriate technology, but they are ideally suited to rural areas, small towns, and metropolitan fringe areas, which closely resemble the environment for which they were originally developed. Their failures are usually attributable to poor design, inadequate education of users, or lack of maintenance—problems that plague sewerage systems as well but can be overcome in developing countries if increased emphasis and attention are given to improving health and sanitation. (Kalbermatten, Julius, and Gunnerson 1982, p. 5.)

Table 5-11 provides a summary of the cost savings feasible by using low-cost technologies. A comparison of those technologies suitable for urban use shows that the ratio of the cost of conventional septic tanks and waterborne sewerage systems to low-cost alternatives, in particular vacuum-truck cartage and low-cost septic tanks, is of the order of 10 to 1. The affordability to low-income households varies accordingly. For the low-cost alternatives, about 5 percent of a typical poor household's income would be required to finance the system at 8 percent interest over five years, while for high-cost systems the proportion is about 50 percent at a rate of interest of 8 percent and financing over twenty years.

In evaluating the desirability of alternative sanitation systems, three further points should be kept in mind. First, at low suburban densities the health benefits of alternative systems suitable for urban use are virtually identical.

Table 5-11. *Total Annual Cost per Household and Affordability*
of Alternative Sanitation Technologies

Technology	Mean cost (1978 U.S. dollars)	Percentage of income of average low-income household[a]
Low cost		
Pour-flush toilet	18.7	2
Pit latrine	28.5	3
Communal toilet	34.0	9
Vacuum-truck cartage[b]	37.5	4
Low-cost septic tank[b]	51.6	6
Composting toilet	55.0	10
Bucket cartage	64.9	6
Medium cost		
Sewered aquaprivy[b]	159.2	11
Aquaprivy	168.0	16
Japanese vacuum-truck cartage	187.7	15
High cost		
Septic tank[b]	369.2	29
Sewerage[b]	400.3	26

Note: Costs include appropriate shadow prices for unskilled labor, foreign exchange, and capital.

Source: Kalbermatten, Julius, and Gunnerson (1982, tables 3-1 and 3-11).

a. Assuming average annual per capita income of $180 and six persons per household.

b. Suitable for urban areas.

At higher densities the sewered aquaprivy allows maintenance of health benefits in almost all locations except high-density, central city areas. Second, all of these alternatives have been used and shown to be functional, although different low-cost systems may have to be used in different countries to allow for differences in climatic and soil conditions or in cultural preferences.[39] Third, water and sanitation services must be considered jointly in designing appropriate investment programs. On the one hand, in-house connections without satisfactory means of disposing of the water after use is likely to negate many of the potential health benefits of improved water supply. On the other hand, high-cost sanitary systems require the use of large amounts of water. Since water production itself is often quite costly, low-cost sanitary systems can also yield savings from lower water use. The best strategy in a joint water and sanitation system involves a phased upgrading of the facilities, starting with communal water taps and improved pit latrines and ending with in-house connections and a pour-flush toilet linked to a small-bore sewer system. By a staged program of this kind, householders can achieve the improvements they desire, at a pace in step with their increasing incomes, over an extended period of time (World Bank 1980e, p. 21; Kalbermatten, Julius, and Gunnerson 1982, ch. 9). The cost savings from such systematic applications of lower-cost water and sanitation technologies are remarkable. It has been estimated that the enormous financial requirements for adequate service coverage of the urban and rural populations in developing countries can be reduced from US$600 billion (in 1978 dollars) to US$300 billion or less (World Bank 1980e, p. 15).

For other services much less information on possible cost savings exists, although again there is evidence that low-cost alternatives are available but frequently unused in developing country cities. For neighborhood roads and drainage, the figures cited above from early World Bank projects are indicative of possible cost savings and have been supported recently in an urban transport project in Brazil (1978 World Bank data). In the case of solid waste collection and disposal, the main technological choices relate to the extent of motor-ization in collection and the technique of disposal. In collection, the use of high-cost options such as compactor trucks should probably be minimized in favor of flat-bed trucks and handcarts; in disposal, sanitary landfills are vir-tually always preferable to expensive and capital-intensive composting facil-ities or incinerators. This is particularly the case where a significant number of low-income people are involved in solid waste collection and disposal activities, as is the case with the *picadores* (pickers) in Medellin, Colombia, and the *zabbaleen* (waste collectors) in Cairo (1977 World Bank data compiled by Alfredo Sfeir-Younis).

In summary, public provision of urban services can provide extensive cost reductions over the private substitutes commonly used by low-income house-holds, and selection of appropriate technologies can further reduce costs to the consumer and the public agency to the point that public services are affordable even by poor households and universal service provision becomes financially feasible in most cities in developing countries. At the same time, no (or only relatively minor) losses in benefits are associated with a switch from high- to low-cost technologies in this area. The case of solid waste collection and disposal is somewhat different from the other services discussed, since public provision of this service may not always be the least-cost solution. Indeed, well-functioning systems of private collection, recycling, and disposal exist in some developing country cities, and their replacement by public systems would very likely result in increased costs. The preferable approach would be to support and strengthen the operations of the private systems.

One common objection raised especially in developing countries to the adoption of basic service standards rather than standards comparable to those in the industrialized countries is that this approach shortchanges the poorer population groups by providing second-rate service. The answer to this objection is simple: experience has shown over and over that where public service standards are set at levels unrealistically high in relation to the poor beneficiaries' ability and willingness to pay, most of the intended recipients of the services have generally not received any service at all. The tradeoff is therefore between higher standards and very limited service access, on the one hand, and lower service standards with often only minor reductions in benefits, but a much wider—if not universal—coverage of poor urban neighborhoods, on the other hand.

Public Provision of Shelter

The public provision of shelter structures does not under most circumstances provide opportunities for cost saving compared with private provision.[40] For low-cost shelter, the experience throughout the cities of developing countries—with the possible exception of Hong Kong and Singapore, which will be discussed separately—has shown that private initiative in shelter construction tends to be preferable. It provides an extremely efficient way of using scarce resources—in the adoption of appropriate standards and technologies, mobilization of low-income savings and investment, and utilization of relatively abundant unskilled labor resources—while conserving scarce management, skilled labor, and capital resources.[41]

With minor exceptions, there exist relatively few externalities or market imperfections in the urban low-cost construction sector, and economies of scale in general do not prevail. In fact, it can be argued that those market imperfections that do exist are imposed mainly by public action, particularly by legal housing standards, zoning requirements, rent control, and the like. Another important constraint on construction of low-income shelter is the lack of access to capital by low-income groups because of lack of collateral, capital rationing as a result of legal constraints on interest rates, lack of mortgage instruments, and so forth. Finally, the lack of accessible serviced land is yet another factor in limiting construction of low-income housing. The appropriate solution to these problems is not, however, to involve the public sector in shelter construction. Rather, the distortions, constraints, and bottlenecks can and should be directly addressed through elimination or adaptation of regulations, through appropriate policies to assist the development of a capital market for housing that is accessible to the poor, and through the provision of land and services in accessible locations.

Appropriate policies in the regulatory field will be discussed below, the issues relating to land and services have already been treated, and only a few words need be said here about capital markets. One way of providing capital for shelter construction is through housing construction loans as part of urban development projects such as slum upgrading and site-and-and-services projects, as is frequently done in projects financed by the World Bank. In the case of the first urban development project in Manila financed by the World Bank, it was found that loans for building materials contributed significantly to the stimulation of private housing investment. In the same project, it was further found that, with regularization of land titles and basic service provision, considerable amounts of informal capital (from relatives, friends, and similar sources) became available to finance acquisition charges for land and costs of shelter construction. This experience exemplifies the importance of land title and service provision in stimulating capital inflows to the low-cost, low-income construction sector. Finally, direct public actions to improve the operations of formal capital markets may also help, including the elimination of the restrictive regulations on commercial banks and savings and loan agencies that prevent them from operating in the mortgage market.[42] These and other actions to promote financial intermediaries for the housing capital market are useful, except the provision of funds at subsidized rates, but the United Nations (1978) survey of housing finance leaves the distinct impression that low-income households in most cases will have to continue to rely on informal capital markets and their own or extended families' savings to finance shelter construction. Improvements in the markets for housing finance are likely to assist more directly middle- and higher-income groups in dealing with their own housing shortages. This may—indirectly, through a trickle-down effect—improve the housing opportunities of lower-income groups by increasing the overall supply of housing.

There are thus no apparent reasons that would strongly suggest that the public sector should be directly involved in the construction of shelter for the urban poor. In fact, there are numerous reasons and a broad range of experience to suggest that public shelter construction does more harm than good. First, given the heterogeneity of people's preferences for the kind of shelter structure and for the speed at which they can or want to improve the quality of shelter, it is not surprising that public housing projects often do not accord with the preferences of the poor (high-rise apartment buildings constructed for the poor in Rio de Janeiro and Caracas are good examples; Perlman 1976, and Dwyer 1975). Public housing projects also tend to distort the household expenditures of beneficiaries in favor of housing to an extent that other necessities of life, especially food, must be seriously neglected [Sudra and Turner (1976) cite case studies for Mexico City]. Second, public investment in shelter substitutes for, and tends to impair, private savings and investment activities because low-, middle-, and high-income groups alike appear to be quite willing and able to finance private housing construction commensurate with their ability to pay, provided that complementary inputs to housing (tenure, space, services, and, to some extent, capital) are readily available. The public resources spent on housing construction would be better used for providing more of these complementary inputs. Third, high-cost public housing units are usually preempted by high- and middle-income households, who then also benefit from the subsidies generally provided with public housing. These subsidies further tie up scarce public funds that could otherwise be used for the provision of serviced land. To the extent that public housing construction programs bid up materials prices, they also tend to harm the self-help, low-cost, low-income construction sector (Wheaton 1978). Finally, public housing projects in the past were often accompanied by the razing or eradication of slums, which actually reduced the housing stock, and demolished the investments of poor households, frequently without substituting feasible housing alternatives.

The major exceptions to this generally negative experience with public shelter construction are the low-income housing programs of Hong Kong and Singapore. A number of factors contributed to their success in significantly improving housing for the poor:[43] (1) standards were chosen at levels that permitted high-rise construction at costs affordable by the poor without substantial subsidies; (2) the public housing units were culturally and socially acceptable to households; (3) the programs were operated at such a large scale that they affected the general level of rents throughout these two cities and thus created a successful trickle-down effect;[44] (4) relatively high per capita incomes in these two cities provided the fiscal basis for such large-scale programs and made standards affordable; (5) the lack of readily urbanized land in these two cities had led to high densities and high land prices and made high-rise construction a necessary element of any large-scale housing program; and (6) both cities possessed the necessary management and technical resources, as well as strong metropolitan governments, to permit the implementation of such housing programs.

A similar combination of circumstances does not generally exist in other cities in the developing world, with the possible exception of cities in Korea and on the island of Taiwan. In fact, incomes are often at such low levels as to exclude the possibility of large high-rise public housing programs, which in any case are not generally well received by the poor. Finally, public management is a very scarce factor in most developing countries, while urbanizable land at the metropolitan fringes tends to be more readily available. Thus, the experience of Hong Kong and Singapore, while reflecting tremendous achievements, does not provide a blueprint for public involvement in shelter construction in other cities of developing countries.[45]

In contrast to direct public provision of housing, taxation and public service pricing are important instruments of urban housing policy. First, they directly affect private decisions regarding the supply of and demand for housing attributes. Second, they provide fiscal resources whose availability at least in part determines the rate of expansion in the stock of housing attributes provided by the public sector. The subsequent paragraphs examine only those tax and pricing instruments that are most directly related to the urban housing market in developing countries; that is, property taxation and public service charges.

Property Taxation

The incidence and revenue potential of property taxation were treated in chapter 3 of this study and need not be considered again. Let it suffice to repeat that urban property taxation can, and in a few developing country cities actually does, play a major role in raising revenues for urban governments without putting a major burden on the poor. Of interest for the present discussion is the effect that property taxation is likely to have on the supply of urban housing by affecting private decisions.[46]

A useful starting point is the taxation of urban land; that is, a site value tax as it is found in Jamaica and Kenya and on the island of Taiwan. The imposition of a general land tax in principle lowers the expected future yield stream on land and would therefore reduce its present value. This lower land price may be important for low-income households that do not have access to a perfect capital market, because it reduces the initial outlay required to purchase land and thus facilitates the acquisition of land for housing. To what extent in practice higher land taxes are capitalized into lower land value, however, has not been empirically verified for cities in the developing world. Evidence from industrialized countries is mixed, but on balance supports the hypothesis that land tax capitalization occurs. Although this may not be the most important of arguments for urban land taxation, at least it provides further support for this tax, since the likely impact of a land tax on land prices would be favorable.

A somewhat different objective is usually pursued in the case of higher taxation of vacant urban land than of built-up land. This type of tax is found in many cities of the developing world, and it is levied to encourage earlier release of vacant land for subdivision and development.[47] Evidence for the island of Taiwan suggests that a tax on vacant land can indeed act as an inducement to land development (Lent 1976). Of course, the use of a vacant land tax presupposes that vacant land is not developed at an optimal rate by the private sector. There is no universal agreement on whether private landowners tend to withhold land from the market beyond the optimal time for its development. In practice, however, one may be able to identify certain zones within the urban periphery where vacant land would, at first glance, appear to involve a loss of economic opportunities. Vacant land taxes could thus be applied selectively to these zones (as has been the practice on the island of Taiwan and in Bogota, Colombia), and could therefore serve as a tool to support land use planning in urban areas. This, however, presupposes that a fairly sophisticated governmental planning apparatus exists, which is obviously not the case everywhere. Therefore, vacant land taxes should probably be used quite sparingly.

Besides taxation of land, property taxation generally also involves the taxation of improvements (that is, buildings).[48] Since the tax on improvements reduces the rate of return that can be earned from the capital invested in the buildings, this tax will provide a disincentive to new construction as well as to maintenance of the structure. It will also tend to reduce the capital value of the improvement at the time of the imposition of the tax. Reducing new construction would diminish the supply of housing in the longer term; reducing capital value of improvements would permit easier access to home-ownership for those who cannot easily raise funds for home purchase in the capital market. As in the case of a land tax, no empirical verifications of these hypotheses are available for developing country cities, although they tend to be supported in general by studies in the industrialized countries. In any case, as long as property taxes are levied at rates as low as commonly found in developing countries, there is little reason to suspect that elimination of the tax on improvements would affect the supply of housing in any significant way (Bahl and Linn, forthcoming). If, however, property taxation were to become a more important revenue instrument for urban governments, as is usually proposed, serious consideration should be given to increasing only the tax on land to avoid any disincentives on housing supply.[49]

Two other forms of property taxation are generally discussed in the literature. Taxes on land transfers are found in many countries (Smith 1977), but only in a few (for example, in Korea), do they contribute significantly to fiscal resources. Nevertheless, these taxes may significantly interfere with the operation of the urban land market by raising the transactions costs, which in turn tends to raise the cost of urban land for housing. These taxes may also encourage evasion of official registration requirements, lead to the underreporting of sales prices, and thus interfere with cadastral and general property tax administration. Property transfer taxes are clear candidates for abolition, especially where the revenue losses are of only minor importance.

The other tax, which is advocated at times on the grounds of efficiency and equity as a major alternative to the conventional property tax, is a tax on the increment in land value. Such a tax is found on the island of Taiwan, in Korea, and in some cities of the industrial world, but its effects on land prices and timing of land development, which are of major concern here, do not appear to be unequivocally in the desired direction, either in theory or practice (Grimes 1974). In any case, the administration of this tax presents considerable practical difficulties that virtually rule it out for most cities of the developing world (Bahl and Linn, forthcoming).

In summary, property taxes in general are not likely to have a significant direct effect on urban housing. Nevertheless, as a rule one should avoid high taxes on improvements, eliminate taxes on property transfers, use special taxes on vacant land with caution, and view proposals for taxation of land value increment with suspicion.

User Charges

For the purpose of this study, user charges are broadly defined to include all charges and levies imposed on the user or beneficiary of a public service, if such charges bear some direct relation to the provision of the service. User charges therefore include public utility tariffs, betterment levies and other plot charges paid because of some public investment that conveys benefits to a property, and land transfers from the private to the public sector in exchange for public service provision.

User charges so defined are important instruments for financing publicly provided components of the urban housing supply. Although all-encompassing figures are not available, it is possible to glean the extent (and variation) of the importance of user charges from different data sources. Table 5-1 (above), for instance, shows that utility charges weigh heavily in the budgets of low-income groups but can account for sizable proportions (approximately 3 percent in Bogota and 5 percent in Korean cities) even for middle-income households.[50] The same pattern of expenditure shares across income groups appears in table 5-12, which shows estimated expenditure shares for water supply in a number of cities.[51] However, for some cities spending on water increases as a proportion of income as one moves up in the income distribution. This is explained in some of these cities, notably Cartagena and Bogota, by the fact that cross-subsidies from high- to low-income consumers are part of the tariff schedules; for other cities, especially Ahmedabad, it is because the figures shown reflect property taxes, rather than user charges.[52] Also notable is the large extent of variation in water charges across cities, with Mexico City showing in general by far the lowest level.

Yet another indication of the potential—and of the varying extent of application—of user charges is shown in table 5-13, which reports the proportion of local government expenditures financed by user charges in selected cities.[53] The importance of user charges varies tremendously among cities: in some cities more than half of all expenditures are financed by user charges; in others user charges make no contribution at all to local budgets. The reasons for this variation are twofold. First, local governments have differing expenditure responsibilities; for example, local authorities in Tunis and Kingston provide virtually no services for which user charges can be levied, whereas

Table 5-12. *Estimated Monthly Water Charges as a Percentage of Estimated Monthly Income, by Income Group, Eleven Selected Cities*

City (year)	Income group (and consumption category by liters)				
	Lowest 20 percent (7,000)	Second 20 percent (15,000)	Third 20 percent (27,000)	Fourth 20 percent (36,000)	Upper 20 percent (40,000)
Addis Ababa (1972)	8.70	7.89	7.70	6.17	2.46
Bogota (1971)	0.67	0.70	1.04	0.83	1.51
Bangkok (1972)	0.49	1.12	2.19	2.02	0.86
Cartagena (1971)	0.97	0.84	1.23	1.25	0.62
Kingston (1971)	1.76	3.04	6.05	3.75	0.81
Lima (1971)	4.96	2.34	1.25	1.41	0.56
Manila (1970)	9.27	1.67	1.65	1.50	0.72
Mexico City (1970)	0.41	0.33	0.38	0.29	0.17
Nairobi (1970)	6.80	5.51	6.00	3.93	1.88
Sao Paulo (1970)	4.71	2.28	3.35	2.85	0.90
Seoul (1972)	0.36	0.32	0.55	0.61	0.49

Note: Water charges are estimated from tariff schedules and estimated water consumption figures for households in the individual cities. Income is the estimated monthly income of households.

Source: Computed by Kenneth Hubbell from survey data; cited in Saunders and Warford (1976, p. 188).

in Colombian cities local authorities are responsible for a wide range of chargeable services. A second reason is the differential application of user charges; for example, Colombian cities levy user charges for water supply, whereas Indian cities finance water supply from property taxation.

The main point to be made on the basis of this rather disparate data base, and on the basis of general impressions and observations, is that the potential of user charges for financing urban services in general, and housing-related public investments in particular, is considerable not only in theory but also in practice. The question then becomes how this potential is best realized in the interest of providing services efficiently to the poor.

Beginning with the efficiency argument for user charges, a strong prima facie case can be made for charging to the user or beneficiary of public services the marginal cost that service provision and use impose on the economy.[54] Subsidization—that is, pricing services below marginal cost—in general will result in consumption up to the point at which the private benefit derived from an additional unit of consumption falls short of the cost that the provision of this additional unit imposes on society. Subsidization encourages location at sites where the benefits derived from such location are below the cost of providing the service there. By making the user aware of the oppor-

Table 5-13. *Percentage Contribution of User Charges to the Financing of Local Government Expenditures in Selected Cities*

City (country)	Year	Percentage of local public expenditure financed by user charges
Francistown (Botswana)	1972	56.1
Kinshasa (Zaire)	1971	—
Bukaru (Zaire)	1971	—
Mbuji-Mayi (Zaire)	1971	—
Lumbumbashi (Zaire)	1972	—
Lusaka (Zambia)	1972	36.9
Kitwe (Zambia)	1975	53.1
Ahmedabad (India)	1970–71	41.8
Bombay (India)	1970–71	38.7
Calcutta (India)	1974–75	—
Madras (India)	1975–76	3.7
Jakarta (Indonesia)	1972–73	15.2
Karachi (Pakistan)	1974–75	2.2
Seoul (Korea)	1971	36.3
Manila (Philippines)	1970	10.0
La Paz (Bolivia)	1975	3.6
Rio de Janeiro (Brazil)	1967	7.2
Bogota (Colombia)	1972	48.5
Cali (Colombia)	1974	57.5
Cartagena (Colombia)	1972	43.3
Kingston (Jamaica)	1971–72	2.7
Mexico City (Mexico)	1968	5.2
Valencia (Venezuela)	1968	13.4
Tehran (Iran)	1974	—
Tunis (Tunisia)	1972	7.1
Average (unweighted)		19.3
Median		7.2

— No user charges levied.
Source: Bahl and Linn (forthcoming).

tunity cost of the service, marginal cost pricing encourages him to avoid excessive use and to consider the economic costs involved in choosing his location of residence (or business). In principle, therefore, where equal costs prevail, individual service recipients should be charged equally, but, by the same token, differential service prices should be charged to consumers and service beneficiaries if service provision to them is associated with differential costs. For example, uniform utility tariffs, which are frequently found in different regions and cities, are not likely to yield efficient provision and use of services, since costs almost certainly vary across regions and cities.[55] Underpricing of public services in the large cities may in fact be one of the reasons for inefficient, rapid urban growth.[56] Similarly, within cities cost differentials can occur both across space and across time. Intracity spatial cost differences are a result of different densities and topological characteristics.[57] Seasonal demand and cost variations occur especially for water and power services, and daily peaks are very common for electricity.

Of course, there are practical limits to an attempt to reflect cost differences in the pricing structure. The determination and application of differential charges themselves involve more resource costs than the application of flat fees, and these costs have to be balanced against the benefits derived from a complex pricing structure. In broad terms, one may conclude from experience in the water and power sectors (Saunders and Warford 1976, Turvey and Anderson 1977) that regionally differentiated prices are virtually always desirable; seasonal pricing for water may sometimes be appropriate; daily peak-load pricing for electricity is generally desirable only for large consumers (that is, for industrial and commercial consumers, but not for the typical residential connection, and especially not for poor households); and intracity spatial differentiation of prices may be desirable in cases where cost differences are substantial and where equity arguments (further discussed below) do not indicate otherwise.[58]

A further and related question is whether service use ought to be metered at all, or whether instead flat charges or taxes should be levied on all service connections. Meters are costly to install, maintain, and read, and their introduction is warranted only where these costs are outweighed by the benefits associated with the reduction in consumption. In Lahore, for instance, a thorough analysis of the decision to meter revealed that, because of the low costs of water supply in that city, installation of water meters was not warranted for residential connections (Warford and Turvey 1974). In other developing country cities where water costs typically are significantly higher, metering has generally been found appropriate, although careful cost-benefit analyses were not frequently carried out. The metering question is particularly complicated in the case of standpipes. Unless the water is sold by attendants (which may well give rise to monopoly rents such as those observed in Indonesia; 1978 World Bank data), individual water charges cannot be used to encourage water conservation. Instead, alternative measures such as flow-limiting devices must be resorted to, although these have not been found universally successful.[59] Although charging for water and the reduction of water waste are important practical problems to be addressed wherever standpipes are used on a significant scale, they generally are not problems that would entirely rule out the introduction of standpipes.

Returning to the mainstream of the argument, the efficiency of user charges has so far been discussed in terms of their effects on service consumption and on location decisions. Marginal cost pricing has, however, the further important benefit of providing a guide for efficient investment decisions by the public authorities. On the one hand, as long as consumers are willing to pay for the incremental cost of adding to service capacity, the benefits from increasing capacity are at least as large as the costs incurred, and investment is therefore warranted (Saunders, Warford, and Mann 1977). On the other hand, if no such measuring rod is available because services are subsidized, authorities will have a hard time in determining whether benefits outweigh costs, since benefits are often difficult if not impossible to estimate. Moreover, because at subsidized prices excess demand is likely to be generated for the service, the users whose demands are unsatisfied at the prevailing low prices will strenuously argue for increased supplies, although this may not be warranted on efficiency grounds. The same point can be made with respect to the effect of user charges on service standards. If users have to pay for the cost of the service according to quality, they will chose that level of quality commensurate with their ability and willingness to pay; what is more, public agencies will have an incentive to provide services at standards reflecting people's willingness to pay. Where subsidies are widely applied, this incentive will generally be absent at the level of the household and of the public agency. This, indeed, is one of the major reasons the World Bank has stressed the elimination of *general* subsidies as a guiding principle in the design and implementation of its urban development projects.

Another reason for eliminating subsidies relates to the fiscal implications of user charges. Subsidies directly reduce the financial resources available for service extension. They raise the cost of service provision per household indirectly by encouraging service standards in excess of the willingness and ability to pay of the beneficiaries, and thus again reduce the possible service coverage, given the public budget constraint. World Bank experience—in the field of public utility pricing especially, but also elsewhere in the housing field—strongly suggests that *general* subsidization of major housing attributes leads not only to inefficiency in resource allocation but also to serious fiscal constraints on the public agencies. General subsidies thus limit the extent to which public services can contribute to increases in housing supply, especially for the poor (Grimes 1976, Ray 1975, Shipman 1967, Turvey and Anderson 1977, World Bank 1973).

The case of water supply in Jakarta in the recent past has provided a particularly drastic example (Linn, Smith, and Wignjowijoto 1976). The failure to levy and enforce cost-covering charges created a dire financial situation for the municipal water company, which therefore could not provide adequate service to its customers and expand service to new customers. Since customers' willingness to pay was further eroded by poor service, a vicious circle was set up, similar to the one discussed in chapter 4 in the case of bus fares.

A contrasting example of effective user charges is the experience with valorization charges in Bogota, Medellin, and Cali, Colombia, and with the land readjustment schemes in Korean cities. Valorization charges are betterment levies designed to recoup the cost of municipal infrastructure investments from the owners of properties whose values are increased by the investment programs. In Bogota, for instance, valorization programs have financed the construction of major arterial highways, neighborhood road improvements, and major sewerage programs. The revenues raised have been substantial and in some recent years have rivaled the local property tax in importance (Doebele, Grimes, and Linn 1979). Particularly interesting is the component of the valorization program that is designed specifically for the upgrading of streets in low-income neighborhoods. This program relies on extensive community inputs of initiation, planning, implementation, and financing. It has made major contributions to improving the accessibility of low-income neighborhoods in Bogota and has been the most consistent component of the valorization program in providing steady, self-financing growth.

Land readjustment schemes in Korea involve the public assembly of numerous small parcels of raw land without monetary compensation to the owners. This land is serviced and subdivided for urban use and then returned to the original owners in proportion to the value of their land contribution. Some of the land is retained by the public authority and sold at market prices to permit the recovery of the development cost.[60] The scale at which these schemes are carried out is impressive. As of 1976, some 45 percent of all urban land in Korea classified for residential purposes was covered by completed or ongoing land readjustment schemes. Although the system has evidently been successful in opening up new land for urban uses, and thus has assisted significantly in increasing the supply of housing and in raising public funds, it appears to have conveyed its direct benefits mainly to middle- and high-income landowners. Some trickle-down effect may have occurred, given the large scale of the exercise, to the extent that the scheme reduced general urban land prices and rents below the levels that would have prevailed in its absence.

Discussion of the advantages of charging for services to cover their incremental costs has not considered the issues of externalities or equity (except that it was argued that *general* subsidies in service pricing will tend to reduce the poor's access to services). A case can be made, however, for *selective* subsidization either on grounds of externalities or on grounds of poverty alleviation. Since the arguments for subsidies on either grounds overlap considerably, it is best to treat them jointly. The focus will be on water supply pricing, but similar arguments could be made for other services.

The main externality derived from improved housing supply is the improvement in health associated with better services and more space per household. Since one person's bad health may affect others' and may require public sector intervention in providing curative health services, the social value of investments in and consumption of housing services is not adequately reflected at low income levels by the household's willingness to pay. For water supply, it is fairly well established that a daily consumption of 20 to 40 liters per capita provides virtually all possible health benefits that can be derived from safe water (Kalbermatten, Julius, and Gunnerson 1982). An incentive should therefore be given to consumers to encourage them to consume at least this amount of safe water, in case they will not or cannot do so at their prevailing incomes. This has been one of the major reasons for the introduction of the so-called life-line tariffs in many developing countries.[61] A life-line tariff on water would consist of a very low tariff for an initial consumption block equivalent to, say, 20 to 40 liters per capita daily, with consumption beyond this amount charged at full marginal cost. Since water consumers with house connections typically consume more than 40 liters per capita daily even at low incomes (table 5-14), the subsidy provided by the life-line tariff in practice is inframarginal to consumption but acts as an incentive for connection to the system. This is indeed desirable, since consumption from standpipes often is at the lower limit of the amount required for health purposes (table 5-14).[62]

In fact, it may be argued that considerably more attention should be given to connection fees than has customarily been the case. For some countries, for example, Colombia (Linn 1976a) and in Cameroon, Indonesia, and

Table 5-14. *Daily Urban Water Consumption*
from Community Water Supplies
(liters per capita daily)

World Health Organization region	House connections		Public standpipes	
	Minimum	Maximum	Minimum	Maximum
Africa	65	290	20	45
Central and South America	160	380	25	50
Eastern Mediterranean	95	245	30	60
Algeria, Morocco, Turkey	65	210	25	40
Southeast Asia	75	165	25	50
Western Pacific	85	365	30	95
Average	90	280	25	55

Note: Average daily consumption rounded to nearest 5 liters.
Source: Saunders and Warford (1976, table 5.4, p. 124).

Liberia (World Bank data), it has been shown that connection fees are very high and in some cases substantially exceed direct connection costs, and that as a result legal connections especially by low-income groups are discouraged and clandestine connections are made more attractive. In Surabaya, Indonesia, the minimum connection fee is twice the average connection cost (1978 World Bank data). In some Colombian cities it was found that new consumers effectively subsidize existing consumers because of the high connection fees charged (Linn 1976a). This taxation of connection fees counteracts any subsidies provided through life-line tariffs and is particularly pernicious when these charges are lump-sum charges that require payment in full immediately upon connection. Given the lack of accumulated savings and the extremely limited access to capital markets typical of poor households, those not serviced by in-house connections are effectively excluded from connecting to the system, even where the layout of the system permits them to do so. It is thus not surprising that Selowsky (1979b) and Meerman (1979) found for Colombia and Malaysia, respectively, that a significant number of households without water connections lacked access because of insufficient demand rather than because of insufficient supply.

The case of public service pricing in four Colombian cities illustrates the implications of utility tariffs that involve extensive subsidies between consumers but that tend to exclude new, usually low-income consumers by high connection fees. Table 5-15 demonstrates that cross-subsidization between users permits redistribution of income from the highest- to middle-income groups, but the lowest two population deciles benefit very little from this subsidy scheme because they are mostly not connected to the utilities, including water supply and sewerage, electricity, telephones, and solid waste collection. Cali represents an exception, since there the local utility enterprise has long engaged in an aggressive program of system expansion, with subsidized connections in low-income neighborhoods ensuring a nearly universal effective demand for connections. As a result, utility service coverage is high in Cali, and the cross-subsidies on service use reach down quite low in the income distribution scale.

The upshot of the preceding arguments is that care needs to be taken not to counteract the effects of life-line rates (which tend to encourage connection) by imposing high connection fees (which tend to discourage connection). There is, however, the different question of whether subsidization of in-house connections will, for given fiscal resources, always yield the greatest possible benefits in improved public health or ameliorated poverty. In cities of low-income countries where large proportions of the population are often not even served by standpipes within reasonable proximity to their houses, and where only middle- and upper-income groups can afford to pay even for subsidized house connections, subsidized connections benefit relatively high-

Table 5-15. *Public Service Subsidies (Taxes) as a Percentage of Income,*
by Population Group, and Change in Gini Coefficients,
in Four Colombian Cities, 1974

Item	Bogota	Barranquilla	Cali	Medellin
Population decile				
0–10	0.18	—	0.20	1.3
10–20	0.40	0.12	1.90	1.6
20–30	0.34	0.92	1.50	3.1
30–40	1.95	0.61	1.40	3.7
40–50	1.47	0.26	1.10	2.4
50–60	1.18	0.22	0.80	1.9
60–70	0.70	(0.02)	(0.03)	1.5
70–80	0.24	(0.44)	(0.07)	1.2
80–90	(0.42)	(0.56)	(0.30)	(0.5)
90–100	(1.24)	(0.66)	(1.50)	(0.7)
Gini coefficient of income distribution				
Without charges	0.5103	0.4145	0.4308	0.4593
With charges	0.5070	0.4129	0.4261	0.4533

Note: Figures without parentheses are subsidies; those with parentheses are taxes (negative subsidies).

Source: Gutierrez (1975, annex tables 4–7, 11).

income groups and reduce the resources available to provide standpipes. In this setting, in-house connections should not be subsidized (or at least not heavily); instead, standpipe provision could be subsidized in the interest of improved health and poverty alleviation.[63]

In addition to the case of water supply, there are other examples where selective subsidies can be effectively used in the interest of efficiency and poverty alleviation. World Bank projects have shown, for instance, that in sites-and-services and slum-upgrading projects it is possible to levy differentially higher plot charges above cost on particularly desirable lots (for example, those on corners, easily accessible, or designed for commercial and industrial use). The resultant surplus can then be applied to lower charges on other plots, thus permitting poorer households to bid for them than would otherwise have been possible. For example, in Morocco in a recent World Bank project that used this type of cross-subsidization, 90 percent of all households in the project area could afford to participate in upgrading; without the cross-subsidization, only 70 percent could have afforded participation (1978 World Bank data).[64]

Selective subsidization can thus improve projects to provide better housing for the poor, but such subsidies must be carefully designed and monitored to ensure that they do not accrue to households to which externality arguments do not apply or which fall outside the poverty group, and to prevent such subsidies from undermining the financial viability of the public agency supplying the subsidized service. It is furthermore important to bear in mind that major departures from conventional practices in public service pricing generally have to be introduced gradually. The arguments raised in chapter 4 in the discussion of the institutional and political constraints on bus-fare reform apply here with equal force. Efficient, equitable, and fiscally sound user charges are a goal that should be worked toward, but there are practical limits to the speed with which this goal can be reached.[65]

Regulations and Controls

Governments can and often do attempt to guide urban development in general, and the development of housing in particular, through the use of various regulation and control instruments.[66] The experience in developing countries in this area, however, has not in general been very encouraging because of a lack of clear definition of goals for these instruments, a lack of realism in their design and application, a lack of information that would guide their use, a lack of manpower and skills for design and implementation, and a lack of political will or of control over corruption sufficient to ensure implementation. This harsh indictment does not in most cases reflect a lack of effort among developing country governments. Rather, it reflects the inherent weaknesses of these tools in an environment where they are either inappropriate (for example, rent control), or where the resources for their design and implementation are extremely limited (for example, zoning, subdivision control, and building codes). There is some evidence, however, that regulation, control, and planning are beginning to be viewed in a more effective manner that considers clearer articulation of goals, more realistic targets, and a greater readiness to limit private property rights in the public interest (Dunkerley and others, 1983). The following paragraphs will review only briefly how some of the instruments of regulation, control, and planning have contributed in the past to aggravate the urban housing problems in developing countries by placing limits on the speed with which housing supply could expand.

Given the high density of urban development, private decisions regarding land use and building activity have important ramifications not only for the decisionmaker himself but also for households, firms, and local governments alike. In principle, the main goal of regulation and control measures is to ensure that private decisionmakers act in a way that maximizes the social or external benefits and minimizes the social or external costs associated with their actions.

Land use zoning, for example, traditionally has tried to separate industrial from residential land use to protect residential areas from noise, pollution, heavy traffic, and the like. But zoning regulations, particularly in developing country cities, should be designed to encourage an adequate mix of residential, commercial, and industrial uses in order to increase access to employment opportunities for the poor and to reduce the need for public and private outlays for transport. The uncritical application of zoning ordinances bor-rowed from industrial countries is likely to lead to an overly segregated land use, especially for low-income areas in the developing countries, because at lower incomes lesser emphasis tends to be placed on environmental and aesthetic qualities and greater emphasis on ease of access to employment.[67]

Regulations and controls on subdivisions have the purpose of ensuring that the layout of a neighborhood conforms with commonly postulated standards for road space and design, lot size, and public areas (parks, schools, play-grounds, and the like). These measures also have the objective of guiding the timing and location of urban development in ways that are compatible with timely public provision of infrastructure at minimal cost. In principle these regulations and controls are desirable, since neighborhood layouts are difficult and costly to change after initial subdivision and since the cost of public provision of infrastructure can be greatly increased by inappropriate timing and location or urban subdivisions. In practice, however, subdivision regulations have generally been applied too inflexibly, so that they have required high standards for space and services. Thus, the poor could not possibly comply with them: low-income groups had the option either to engage in illegal subdivision and land invasion, or, where subdivision laws and ownership rights were relatively strictly enforced (for example, in Nai-robi), to crowd into the limited urban space, thus further raising high rents and worsening already serious overcrowding. In the end, none of the purposes of subdivision control and regulation is served by this approach. Instead, a much more flexible solution is required in which the government guides the location and timing of subdivisions only to the extent that private households have the resources to comply with the rules and public agencies have the resources to enforce them. Public regulatory action in this area is closely linked with policies for public land use development and service provision and should therefore be explicitly coordinated with them.

Building codes are yet another prevalent form of regulation and control of housing development. They are typically designed to reduce fire and health hazards and to provide for privacy and open space. It is obvious from housing conditions observable in slum areas of developing country cities that the high standards frequently required in housing design cannot and are not re-spected;[68] where they are, overcrowding of the existing housing stock negates the benefits that might have been reaped from the codes in the absence of overcrowding.

Because building codes, like most of the regulations regarding land use and subdivision, are honored mainly in the breach, one may feel inclined to regard them as largely innocuous and irrelevant. They can, however, have extremely undesirable effects on the housing conditions for the poor. Apart from creating overcrowding and elevated rents that benefit a few property owners where the rules are enforced, these regulations tend to lead to clouded land titles and lack of secure tenure; they are used as legal instruments permitting the bulldozing of low-income neighborhoods;[69] and they play a role in determining the standards employed in public housing programs. A revision of zoning and subdivision regulations and of building codes can therefore be of primary importance in many cities of developing countries.

Another form of regulation frequently found is rent controls, used, for instance, in India (Bahl 1975, Mohan 1974), Egypt (Wheaton 1978), and El Salvador (1978 World Bank data compiled by Marisa Fernandez-Palacios). These controls are imposed ostensibly to restrain rents where they have risen rapidly as a result of urban growth and the failure of housing supply to keep up with demand. This is one particularly unfortunate attempt to solve an urban problem by treating its symptoms, ignoring its causes, and thereby making matters worse. Despite the fact that rent controls are frequently circumvented by illegal payments by renter to owner (Mohan 1974, Wheaton 1978), the return to housing investment and maintenance becomes more uncertain, and where owners do adhere to the law the return is lowered in absolute terms. Therefore, the willingness of owners to invest in new buildings or maintain old structures tends to dwindle.[70] Furthermore, since illegal rent payments frequently take the form of lump-sum payments at the beginning of the tenancy, low-income households that do not have access to capital are disadvantaged and become less mobile. Another problem has arisen in El Salvador, where low-income households are frequently evicted because prevailing laws permit higher rentals only at a time when tenants change (1978 World Bank data compiled by Marisa Fernandez-Palacios). Finally, in countries where property taxes are levied on rental values, the controlled rents generally must be used as a basis of tax assessment. This significantly reduces the level and buoyancy of property tax revenues (Bahl 1975) and thus limits the ability of local authorities to expand public services. The housing shortage, which initially was the reason for the introduction of rent control, is therefore only made worse.

Urban Development Projects: Recent World Bank Experience

At the time of preparation of the World Bank's (1975c) *Housing* Sector Policy Paper, only ten projects in urban housing and development had been appraised and approved for financing by the Bank. As of June 1980, forty-three urbanization projects had been processed, among them seven that constituted follow-ups to earlier projects and thus built directly on the experience gathered during the implementation of them. Moreover, a major in-depth monitoring and evaluation program of selected urban projects has been underway for five years, and routine monitoring and evaluation components have been included for virtually all urban projects. As a result, a considerable body of evidence has been compiled regarding the feasibility of the basic elements of the strategy originally outlined in the World Bank's (1972) *Urbanization* Sector Working Paper. Much of this evidence still needs to be sifted through carefully, and a full-fledged evaluation is beyond the scope of this paper, but a few tentative points can be presented here from the Bank's experience in designing low-income housing programs.

Between mid-1972 and mid-1980 the World Bank helped twenty-nine developing countries to provide approximately 310,000 sites-and-services lots and to improve some 780,000 lots through urban upgrading efforts. Assuming ten persons per lot, which is likely a conservative figure, over 10 million people were expected to benefit from these projects at a total project cost of about US$2.5 billion.[71] During the same period, shelter components (sites and services, upgrading, and off-site infrastructure for shelter sites) accounted for 56 percent of total costs; special transport and other infrastructure investments for 16 percent; community facilities (including schools, health facilities, and related programs) for 6 percent; and employment support programs for 12 percent. Technical assistance outlays added another 10 percent to make up total cost (table 5-16). These projects will be briefly reviewed for their ability to reach the poor, their affordability, and their replicability.

The World Bank projects' ability to reach the poor is defined quite narrowly for the purposes of this preliminary evaluation, which is concerned merely with how far down in the income distribution the projects were expected to reach to make improved housing affordable to the urban poor. The first three columns of table 5-17 show this information and provide a comparison with conventional public housing programs in the countries where the projects were carried out for the years 1972 to 1978.[72] The data indicate that in all the countries the Bank-financed projects were designed to reach income groups considerably lower in the distribution than were the conventional housing programs.[73] The data also show that upgrading programs tend to have a better record than sites-and-services projects in their intended effect on poor households, although the difference is not always significant.

Evidence on the actual location of project beneficiaries in the income distribution has recently become available through the World Bank's effort to monitor and evaluate the effects of selected urban housing projects. Table 5-18 summarizes the available information for a total of six project sites in El Salvador, Zambia, and the Philippines.[74] The first observation is that there

Table 5-16. *Total Cost Breakdown of World Bank Urbanization Projects, at Appraisal, Fiscal Years 1972–80*
(percent)

Component	1972–80	1972–75	1976–78	1979–80
Shelter[a]	56.2	52.0	51.6	60.4
Sites and services	30.0	32.5	20.1	37.8
Upgrading	21.9	14.2	26.3	19.6
Special transport components	8.2	9.0	12.9	3.9
Other physical components[b]	7.7	15.2	8.8	4.7
Community facilities and programs[c]	6.1	8.1	8.4	4.1
Employment support programs[d]	11.8	5.3	8.1	17.0
Technical assistance[e]	10.0	10.4	10.2	9.8
Total	100.0	100.0	100.0	100.0
Total project cost (millions of U.S. dollars)[f]	2,469.1	341.8	956.2	1,171.1

Note: Columns may not add to 100.0 percent because of rounding.

Source: Computed from World Bank data compiled by C. Clifford and L. Cooper on the basis of appraisal reports.

a. Sites and services, upgrading, and off-site infrastructure for shelter sites.

b. Infrastructure not servicing shelter sites.

c. Includes schools, health facilities, nutrition and family planning programs, and other community facilities and programs.

d. Includes aid to small-scale enterprises, markets, and industrial and commercial development components.

e. Includes project-related management assistance, design/engineering/supervision, monitoring and evaluation, and studies and forward planning.

f. Estimated as at appraisal, including allowance for physical and price contingencies.

is considerable variation in effects across project sites even within countries and cities, an indication that project design and local conditions can have a major influence on the extent to which the poor benefit from urban housing projects. (See also Sanyal, Valverde, and Bamberger 1980; and Bamberger, Sae-Hau, and Gonzalez-Polio 1980). Second, although the sites-and-services projects shown in table 5-18 reached households in the lowest income quintile, at one site in Zambia the households in that quintile were not reached in proportion with their share in the overall income distribution. The upgrading projects did somewhat better in that over 20 percent of their beneficiaries fell into the lowest income quintile. Nevertheless, the major difference in the effects upgrading and sites-and-services projects are likely to have on the very poor is that upgrading projects generally reach a larger total number of beneficiaries. Third, many of the projects have experienced considerable leakage of their benefits to households in the top half of the income distribution. To the extent that the programs were designed to improve the

Table 5-17. *Poverty Impact, Cost Recovery, and Affordability: Comparison of World Bank Projects with Conventional Public Housing Programs*

Region, project, and date of approval by World Bank's Board of Executive Directors	Poverty impact: lowest percentile of population reached		
	Sites and services (1)	Upgrading (2)	Conventional public housing[c] (3)
Sub-Saharan Africa			
Botswana I (4/74)	27	21	n.a.
Botswana II (5/78)	26	5	60
Ivory Coast (11/76)	14	5	n.a.
Kenya I (5/75)	22	—	n.a.
Kenya II (4/78)	24	1	n.a.
Senegal (9/72)	47	—	n.a.
Tanzania I (7/74)	31	14	n.a.
Tanzania II (7/77)	20	5	n.a.
Upper Volta (1/78)	n.a.	n.a.	n.a.
Zambia (1/74)	17	15	n.a.
Low-income Asia			
India			
Calcutta I (8/73)	—	n.a.	n.a.
Calcutta II (12/77)	20	—	n.a.
Madras (3/77)	9	8	—
Indonesia I (9/74)	12	1	n.a.
Indonesia II (10/76)	—	1	30–40 (50)[d]
Middle-income Asia			
Korea (1/75)	19	—	n.a.
Philippines (4/76)	33	22	>50
Thailand (6/78)	25	11	n.a.
Latin America and Caribbean			
Bolivia (10/77)	10	2	n.a.
Colombia (5/78)	16	8	n.a.
El Salvador I (10/74)	17	—	n.a.
El Salvador II (4/77)	18	9	n.a.
Guatemala (6/76)	10	—	n.a.
Jamaica (5/74)	30	11	n.a.
Mexico (4/78)	17	7	75
Nicaragua (5/73)	15	—	n.a.
Peru (4/76)	14	7	n.a.
Europe, Middle East, and North Africa			
Egypt (6/78)	23	22	90
Morocco (2/78)	20	5	n.a.

n.a. Not available.   — Not applicable.   ⋯ Zero or negligible.

Source: World Bank appraisal reports and information compiled by C. Clifford.

a. Excluding all nonshelter costs (see note *a* in table 5-19).

b. Nominal interest rate, not allowing for inflation or different payment periods.

Percentage of shelter costs recovered[a]			Interest rate (percent)[b]		World Bank project	
Sites and services (4)	Upgrading (5)	Conventional public housing (6)	World Bank project (7)	Conventional public housing (8)	Charges as percentage of household income (9)	Cross-subsidization (10)
n.a.	n.a.	n.a.	7.0–8.0	n.a.	14–23	Yes
81	100	n.a.	8.25–9.0	8.0	15–20	Yes
70	50	n.a.	9.0–13.0	13.0	25–32	No
100	—	n.a.	8.5	6.5	25	Yes
100	90	n.a.	8.5	6.5	30	Yes
100	—	n.a.	7.0	11.0–13.0	8	—
100	—	n.a.	6.0–9.0	6.0	15	Yes
75	75	n.a.	6.0	8.0	15	Yes
100	100	n.a.	8.5	8.5	22	No
80	80	n.a.	7.5	6.25	25	Yes
—	100	n.a.	5.0	5.0	n.a.	No
100′	—	n.a.	8.5	8.5	20	Yes
100	100	n.a.	12.0	10.0–11.0	13	No
n.a.	—	50	12.0	8.0–9.0	20	—
—	0–30	35	—	n.a.	—	—
100	—	n.a.	12.0	8.0	25	No
100	100[e]	56–84	12.0	6.0–8.0	26	Yes[f]
100	80	n.a.	12.0	15.0	13–30	Yes
78	100	50	10.0	3.0–6.0	32–50	No
63	63	n.a.	13.8	14.0–18.0	24	Yes
100	—	n.a.	6.0–8.0	5.0–10.5	25	Yes
83	100	n.a.	6.4	2.0–3.0	10–20	No
100	—	n.a.	4.0	8.0–11.0	20	No
n.a.	n.a.	n.a.	8.0–12.0	11.0	33	Yes
98	81	n.a.	15.0	6.0–8.0	20	No
100	—	n.a.	5.0	6.0–14.0	20	Yes
100	100	65	12.0	10.0–12.0	20	No
100	100	25	7.0	3.0	7–20	No
67	79	n.a.	7.0	9.0	25	Yes

c. Including subsidies.

d. Without subsidies on structures, but not including land costs.

e. Not including land costs.

f. Higher charges for lots on corners and major roads; approximately one-third of total project cost borne by commercial and industrial properties.

Table 5-18. *Urban Housing Projects in El Salvador, Zambia, and the Philippines: Location of Participants in the Income Distribution*
(percent)

| | Sites and services | | | | Upgrading | |
| | El Salvador | | Zambia | | | |
National urban income percentile	Somsonate (1977)	Santa Ana (1976)	Lilanda (1980)	Matero (1978)	Philippines (1979)	Zambia (1976)
0–20	6	11	28	18	27	38
21–40	38	32	26	38	24	22
Upper 60	56	57	46	44	49	40
41–60	37	38	16	14	23	17
60+	19	19	30	30	26	23
Total	100	100	100	100	100	100

Source: Keare and Parris (1981).

overall conditions in the urban housing markets, such leakage is not a serious concern. To the extent that housing programs are designed mainly to alleviate poverty in the lower half of the income distribution, however, improvements in project design should be sought to limit the extent to which higher-income groups preempt a significant share of the project benefits. Lower standards, improved selection procedures, amended cost recovery schemes, and similar measures may help in reducing the leakage. Realistically, however, one must expect some leakage to continue even with the most careful control measures; this is particularly the case in upgrading projects, where the preexisting distribution of residents in a project site, not project design and allocation criteria, largely determines the composition of beneficiaries. The success or failure of low-cost housing programs as a means to help the poor must be measured relative to other programs designed to alleviate poverty (for example, programs in the areas of health, education, and nutrition). Measured in these relative terms, low-cost urban housing programs would appear to represent quite an effective instrument for poverty alleviation.

The interesting questions are, of course, how the World Bank's urban projects achieved their relatively good distributive effect when compared with conventional housing programs, and to what extent the Bank projects are replicable. Low-income groups were not, in general, reached by extensive subsidization of beneficiaries. In fact, as columns (4) and (5) of table 5-17 indicate, with the exception of the Indonesian case (which will be discussed separately), all the projects listed have sought substantial, if not full, recovery of shelter costs from plot holders.[75] In contrast, conventional public housing programs have been supported by significant subsidies, as shown in column (6) of table 5-17. This conclusion is confirmed by columns (7) and (8) of the table, which indicate that nominal interest rates charged in World Bank projects were frequently above those charged in conventional housing programs. About half the projects shown in table 5-17 relied on subsidies internal to the project (column 10). With only few exceptions, plot charges were not expected to exceed 25 percent of household income among the intended beneficiary groups, and this indicates the affordability of the projects for the intended groups.

The key to this achievement lay in the drastic reduction of costs per plot compared with those of conventional public housing programs, as can be seen from the last four columns of table 5-19. This cost reduction in turn was feasible because of reduced standards. World Bank projects generally do not involve the construction of complete houses, although some of the sites-and-services projects provide so-called core structures, such as minimal structures for sanitary facilities on the lot (wet cores) or, for higher-cost lots, minimal one-room structures (core units). Components of upgrading projects have not in general provided any structures (the first Calcutta project in

Table 5-19. *Standards and Shelter Costs of World Bank Urbanization Projects*

Region, project, and date of approval by World Bank's Board of Executive Directors	Total number of plots (1)	Percentage of plots		Percentage of plots with	
		Sites and services (2)	Upgrading (3)	Communal water and non-waterborne sewerage (4)	Individual water and waterborne sewerage (5)
Sub-Saharan Africa					
Botswana I (4/74)	2,800	64	36	100	—
Botswana II (5/78)	6,734	41	59	96	4
Ivory Coast (11/76)	8,835	43	57	—	100
Kenya I (5/75)	6,000	100	—	—	100
Kenya II (4/78)	23,147	76	24	11	89
Senegal (9/72)	15,600	100	—	87	13
Tanzania I (7/74)	19,400	92	8	92	8
Tanzania II (7/77)	34,788	59	41	100	—
Upper Volta (1/78)	11,306	11	89	100	—
Zambia (7/74)	28,851	41	59	89	11
Low-income Asia					
India					
Calcutta I (8/73)	n.a.	n.a.	n.a.	—	100
Calcutta II (12/77)	8,187	100	—	—	100
Madras (3/77)	57,434	60	40	77	23
Indonesia I (9/74)	96,930	8	92	92	8
Indonesia II (10/76)	107,700	—	100	100	—
Middle-income Asia					
Korea (1/75)	1,893	100	—	—	100[d]
Philippines (4/76)	18,119	17	83	—	100
Thailand (6/78)	4,471	67	33	—	100
Latin America and Caribbean					
Bolivia (10/77)	9,775	57	43	—	100
Colombia (5/78)	62,640	23	77	12	88
El Salvador I (10/74)	7,000	100	—	—	100
El Salvador II (4/77)	8,800	91	9	9	91
Guatemala (6/76)	18,000	56	44	—	100
Jamaica (5/74)	8,750	69	31	—	100
Mexico (4/78)	5,768	31	69	100	—
Nicaragua (5/73)	6,400	100	—	—	100
Peru (4/76)	15,463	6	94	—	100
Europe, Middle East, and North Africa					
Egypt (6/78)	9,823	47	53	49	51
Morocco (2/78)	9,330	10	90	34	66

n.a. Not available.   — Not applicable.

Source: Appraisal reports and data compiled by C. Clifford, except for column on cost of conventional public housing, which is derived directly from appraisal reports.

a. Derived by dividing shelter cost by number of plots; costs are as of date of appraisal and do not include special components, community facilities, employment-generation component,

Plot size (square meters)		Shelter costs per plot (U.S. dollars)[a]			Unit cost of cheapest conventional public housing (U.S. dollars)
Sites and services (6)	Upgrading (7)	Sites and services[b] (8)	Upgrading[b] (9)	Total[c] (10)	(11)
375	Variable	502	297	571	n.a.
330	—	1,449	201	905	n.a.
100–200	150–500	5,238	3,971	4,856	n.a.
100–140	—	1,800	—	2,817	2,310
100–250	100–350	1,592	2,034	1,853	n.a.
150	—	397	—	455	1,600
288–370	300	4,762	1,482	5,619	n.a.
—	200–300	585	568	578	n.a.
240–360	240–360	241	239	363	n.a.
324	Variable	1,074	1,692	1,279	1,320
n.a.	n.a.	n.a.	1,778	n.a.	n.a.
32–243	—	1,478	—	1,478	n.a.
40–223	20	192	118	192	n.a.
80–200	87	954	323	381	n.a.
—	170	—	59	59	n.a.
116–231	—	1,479	—	2,218	1,500
35–240	Variable	1,688	831	1,038	4,217
70–100	80	2,636	746	2,035	n.a.
90–135	60	1,220	380	931	4,750
54–64	n.a.	361	296	337	n.a.
60–128	—	1,157	—	1,229	3,000
160–260	60–120	1,399	50	1,455	2,800
76–130	n.a.	1,835	631	1,389	n.a.
100–140	n.a.	3,064	221	2,182	n.a.
113–137	200	1,342	1,357	1,543	3,300
110	—	1,531	—	1,531	1,845
120–200	110–140	259	709	1,442	7,400
45–72	n.a.	953	384	814	3,570
60–80	62–95	3,644	1,012	1,490	5,000

technical assistance, or contingencies.

b. Does not include off-site infrastructure.

c. Includes off-site infrastructure.

d. Individual water and nonwaterborne sewerage services were provided in this project.

1973 is the only exception), although materials loans were made available in approximately half of them. This difference between sites-and-services components and upgrading components explains to a large extent the fact that the former are usually more expensive than the latter, and that without subsidies the former therefore are not affordable by households at incomes as low as is the case with upgrading projects. Between 1976 and 1978 particularly, the World Bank financed urbanization projects that placed higher emphasis on upgrading than on sites-and-services components, as indicated by the changing cost shares for these two approaches (table 5-16). This reflects the growing awareness that, in the poor countries especially, upgrading projects provide a feasible way of assisting a substantially greater number of households than do sites-and-services projects (World Bank 1980d).

Other sources of cost savings in urbanization projects financed by the World Bank have been the frequent adoption of communal water supply facilities (for example, standpipes and nonwaterborne sewer systems); smaller lot size than that of conventional public housing programs; and low-cost standards for road circulation (for example, heavier reliance on footpaths than on streets). Standards and costs generally were lower in projects carried out in the low-income countries (that is, in most of sub-Saharan Africa and low-income Asia). This difference is dictated by the extremely low levels of per capita income among the urban poor in these country groups and reflects the sensitivity of project design to the different levels of ability and willingness to pay.

The replicability of urbanization projects, and thus their ability to reach all or most of the world's urban poor over time, depends to a large extent on how low standards (and therefore costs) are set and on the extent to which costs are recovered from project beneficiaries. But these are not the only constraints on replicability, as some of the World Bank projects have shown. One problem relates to the availability of raw land for sites-and-services projects in reasonable proximity to employment opportunities. Project replication may involve higher land costs, which in turn adversely affect the affordability of the project by the poor groups, or it may require a more distant location from employment opportunities. In this latter case the attractiveness of the project to low-income groups is reduced unless transport improvements accompany the project or new employment opportunities are generated close to the project site. A somewhat different problem that also involves the issue of land affects the replicability of upgrading projects. As discussed earlier, tenure regularization tends to be easiest where slums are located on public land. Usually these areas are tackled first in upgrading programs. When follow-up projects then turn to squatters on private land, the whole question of tenure regularization becomes more difficult to resolve and will generally involve greater political obstacles, danger of delays, and budgetary costs than was the case initially.

Another limitation on the replicability of low-cost housing programs, even where costs are fully recovered in the long term, is the problem of limited availability of capital for such programs in the short term. The government's overall housing strategy is important in this context. As long as scarce capital is devoted to major high-cost housing programs, the availability of funds for low-cost housing projects is obviously limited, and the pace and scale of replication of such programs are considerably impaired.

Finally, the ability of housing agencies and of other related governmental units to raise revenues from other sources is a crucial determinant of the replicability of low-cost housing programs. This is the case not only because the ability to raise revenues governs the availability of funds for the provision of shelter and related services but also because it determines the extent to which complementary components can be implemented (components such as community facilities, employment supports, and technical assistance, the costs of which are not usually recouped directly from the beneficiaries). A strengthening of the fiscal base of local governments is of central importance and has been of concern in various World Bank projects (for example, in Kenya, India, the Philippines, and Indonesia).

The Indonesian experience with low-income housing programs is a particularly interesting example for several reasons. The so-called Kampong Improvement Program began in 1969 in Jakarta as an attempt by Indonesian authorities to deal with the overwhelming slum problems of that city on a large scale. The scale of the program was indeed impressive. During its first phase (1969–74), approximately 20 percent of the slum areas (kampongs), accounting for some 60 percent of the urban area of Jakarta, were upgraded, 16.5 percent during the second phase (1974–76), and a further 25 percent were expected to be upgraded during the third phase (1976–79). Improved infrastructure and communication for some 61.5 percent of all slum areas in Jakarta would be provided over a ten-year period (1978 World Bank data). The number of plots and households involved in this program is very large (see table 5-19), and there apparently has been a notable improvement in the overall housing conditions in Jakarta, not only improved service availability but also reduced overcrowding. The standards and costs of services provided were very low (as indicated in table 5-17) but nevertheless included paved footpaths, roads, drainage, water supply, sanitation, primary schools, and health clinics. In a departure from usual Bank practice, project costs were not directly recovered from project beneficiaries but were borne by the local government in Jakarta, which initiated a major effort to increase its fiscal resources, especially through significant improvements in property tax-

Table 5-20. *Estimated Economic Rates of Return
on World Bank Urbanization Projects*
(percent)

Region, project, and date of approval by World Bank's Board of Executive Directors	Rate of return		
	Sites and services	Upgrading	Industrial/ commercial
Sub-Saharan Africa			
Botswana I (4/74)	—	—	—
Botswana II (5/78)	15.0–22.0	16.0	15.0
Ivory Coast (11/76)	30.0	30.0	—
Kenya I (5/75)	19.0	—	—
Kenya II (4/78)	17.0	—	13.0
Senegal (9/72)	18.0	—	—
Tanzania I (7/74)	10.0–14.5	10.0–14.5	—
Tanzania II (7/77)	35.0	20.0	—
Upper Volta (1/78)	37.0	24.0–31.0	—
Zambia (7/74)	16.0	12.0	—
Low-income Asia			
India			
Calcutta I (8/73)	—	10.0	—
Calcutta II (12/77)	17.0	16.0	26.0
Madras (3/77)	15.0	18.0	—
Indonesia I (9/74)	17.0	—	—
Indonesia II (10/76)	—	67.0,>100[a]	—
Middle-income Asia			
Korea (1/75)	17.0–22.0	—	17.0
Philippines (4/76)	25.0	25.0	42.0
Thailand (6/78)	17.0	24.0	—
Latin America and Caribbean			
Bolivia (10/77)	16.0	27.0	—
Colombia (5/78)	10.0	10.0	—
El Salvador I (10/74)	20.0	20.0	20.0
El Salvador II (4/77)	18.0	—	—
Guatemala (6/76)	16.0	—	—
Jamaica (5/74)	13.0–15.8	—	—
Mexico (4/78)	28.0	22.0	—
Nicaragua (5/73)	12.0–14.0	—	—
Peru (4/76)	32.2	—	34.4
Europe, Middle East, and North Africa			
Egypt (6/78)	16.0	23.0	—
Morocco (2/78)	19.0	21.0	—

Source: World Bank appraisal reports.
a. 67 percent for Jakarta, >100 for Surabaya.

ation.[76] As a result, property tax resources increased more than fourteenfold between 1971 and 1975 (admittedly from a very low base), and all locally raised revenues (that is, revenues excluding transfers from the national government) increased more than fourfold during the same period (1976 World Bank data). In summary, the Kampong Improvement Program in Indonesia provides a unique example of the potential for improvement in low-income housing conditions even where average incomes are quite low.

World Bank experience can also throw light on the extent to which the objectives of efficiency and equity (poverty alleviation) can jointly be met through low-cost urbanization projects. Table 5-20 records the estimated rates of return on the sites-and-services, upgrading, and industrial/commercial development components of the urbanization projects financed by the World Bank between 1972 and 1978. In most cases, the projects' rates of return are above reasonable estimates of the opportunity cost of capital in these countries, which is likely to fall somewhere in the range of 10–15 percent. The estimation procedures for these rates of return are necessarily rough, relying, as they do, on estimated increases in rental or capital values of the improved lots. If anything they tend to underestimate the benefits derived from these projects, since they cannot measure the external benefits generated, particularly improvements in public health. One may therefore conclude that programs to improve the housing conditions of the urban poor through the provision of low-cost services in general do not appear to involve a tradeoff between efficiency and equity, since both objectives are served by these projects.[77]

The experience with urbanization projects financed by the World Bank also extends to other areas. It is important to address the urban poverty problem not only by focusing on improvements in the physical infrastructure; complementary components—in particular transport improvements, better public utility system, and provision of basic social services such as education, health, nutrition, and family planning—must be part of an overall strategy of improving the welfare of the urban poor. Integrated urban development projects, which encompass many of these components, are therefore now the rule rather than the exception, and what preliminary experience is available— particularly from follow-up projects such as in Indonesia and the Philippines and from preliminary results of the World Bank's monitoring and evaluation exercise for selected urban projects (World Bank 1979b)—indicates the general validity of this approach. Other lessons from experience have included the realization that community participation in project design and implementation is important and that women play an essential role in any attempt to improve the lot of the urban poor in developing countries. It is too early, however, to attempt a comprehensive evaluation of World Bank experience in these areas.[78]

Summary of Policy Implications

Throughout much of this chapter the focus has been on the policy dimension of urban housing in developing countries. These policy results are summarized below.

Diagnosis of the Urban Housing Problem

Design of urban housing policy must begin with the recognition that housing is a multidimensional commodity that includes the shelter structure, the lot on which the shelter stands, the infrastructure services provided to the lot, and access to off-site services, amenities, and employment opportunities. Housing policy must respect private preferences for desired combinations of housing attributes if it is to meet consumer demand. The urban housing problem is caused by the inability of housing supply to match rapid increases in housing demand, and this in turn creates rising costs, lack of services, overcrowding, and poor access to employment opportunities. Public intervention should be designed to minimize the barriers to expansion in housing supply by removing biases against increases in the private housing stock and by providing those dimensions of housing which the public sector is best equipped to supply—in particular public services at standards that are affordable by the poor. The major areas for public intervention are direct investment, pricing, and regulation.

Public Supply of Housing Services

Public supply of housing services may involve intervention in the urban land market, provision of public services, public construction of shelter, and improvements in the system of housing finance.

INTERVENTION IN THE URBAN LAND MARKET. The urban land market, and in particular urban land prices, serve to allocate scarce urban land to the most productive uses. Artificially depressing urban land prices or other means of interfering with the functioning of the land market are likely to lead to misallocation of urban land resources. The main role of public intervention therefore is (1) to regularize land tenure where clouded titles are a major impediment to private housing investment; (2) to assist selectively in subdivision of new land, particularly for the benefit of poor urban households displaced from central city locations by expansions in commercial uses of land; (3) to limit private monopolies in urban land markets; and (4) to develop effective land registry and cadastral records. Large-scale land banking is not likely to be an effective tool of urban management, given the limits of public managerial capacity and the scope for corruption and abuse.

PROVISION OF PUBLIC SERVICES. Public service provision is the major area for public intervention in the urban housing market. Extension of public services throughout a city is the most effective policy instrument for expanding the supply of urban housing, dampening land price increases, and stimulating private investment in shelter. In serving the urban poor, low-cost technologies need to be sought to ensure that public investments are affordable to the beneficiaries, that investment and operating costs are recoverable through user charges, and that service expansion is thus replicable. Particularly for water supply and sanitation, careful phasing of gradual improvements in service levels commensurate with the economic development of a neighborhood can cut public investment costs by more than half, without serious losses of the major benefits derived from service provision.

PUBLIC CONSTRUCTION OF SHELTER. Shelter construction is best left to the private sector, except where high-rise residential construction is required by extreme scarcity of urban land, where it is socially acceptable to the prospective users, and where it is within the capacity of urban public management. The conditions that have prevailed in Hong Kong and Singapore are not likely to be found in many other cities. In fact, most public housing construction programs have failed to provide significant increases in the housing stock and housing improvements specifically for the poor. Destruction of shelter structures in eradicating slums, squatter areas, and the like is to be avoided wherever possible.

IMPROVEMENTS IN HOUSING FINANCE. The poor tend to borrow little for investment in housing. To a certain extent they can be helped directly by selective improvements in housing finance instruments, in particular the provision of small home-improvement loans. A general improvement of the conventional housing capital market, which is likely to benefit the middle-income consumers most directly, may increase the housing opportunities for the urban poor by increasing the overall housing stock.

Taxation and Service Pricing

Property taxes are not likely to have a significant direct effect on urban housing supply, but high taxes on buildings should be avoided because of their disincentives for new contruction and maintenance. Taxes on property transfers should be eliminated, special taxes on vacant land should be used only with caution, and proposals for the taxation of land value increments should be viewed with some suspicion because of their poor track record in practical feasibility.

In contrast, user charges have a major role to play in encouraging an efficient allocation of demand, efficient private location decisions, and efficient public investment patterns for urban public services. In general, estimates of the marginal cost of service provision can offer a rough guide to efficient service pricing, but the cost of administration limits the fine tuning in the pricing structure, particularly in the case of small consumers. General subsidies for urban services should be avoided because of their detrimental effects on efficiency, revenues, and equity. Selective subsidies, in particular life-line tariffs, can be defended on grounds of externalities or poverty alleviation. For water supply, careful consideration must be given to the appropriate vehicle of reaching the most deserving households. Subsidization of house connections is likely to be feasible and desirable in middle-income developing countries, but subsidization of standpipes will be preferable in the low-income countries.

Regulation and Control of Urban Housing

Regulations regarding urban land use, subdivision, and building standards in developing countries are honored mainly in the breach, but nevertheless they can cause clouded land titles and are cited to justify the bulldozing of slums and to maintain elevated standards for public housing and service provision. Rent controls are counterproductive, since they generally fail to achieve their goal of lowering rents and tend to restrict the housing supply, to impede mobility, to reduce access to housing by the poor, and to limit property tax revenues. Overall, regulatory intervention in the urban housing market in developing countries should be kept to a minimum.

Comprehensive Approaches for Urban Housing

Comprehensive public programs to come to grips with the lack of housing in the cities of developing countries are no longer in the experimental stage; they have successfully been developed by a number of urban governments whose efforts have often been supported by international institutions such as the World Bank. These programs usually involve a judicious mixture of slum upgrading—consisting mainly of improving basic infrastructure services in existing low-income areas—and new land development for low-income residential use by new urban residents as well as those displaced by changes in urban land use. If service standards are kept low and costs are recovered through beneficiary charges, such programs can benefit large numbers of the urban poor while effectively contributing to the efficient allocation of a country's and city's resources. Such programs also can and should be designed to intervene in related policy areas, particularly in improving employment opportunities and access to transport in poor neighborhoods, and in extending basic health care and other social services.

Notes to Chapter 5

1. Estimating household expenditures on housing is inherently difficult for a number of reasons, including the difficulty of separating investment from recurrent expenditures and of estimating imputed rents for owner-occupants and squatters. Therefore, the figures shown in tables 5-1 and 5-2 should be taken as merely indicative of general orders of magnitude.

2. The higher average proportion of residential construction in GDP found for Europe, the Middle East, and North Africa is explained by the fact that three countries (Greece, Israel, and Cyprus) have shares much higher than the remaining countries in the group.

3. Sudra and Turner (1976) report on a number of household case studies in Mexico City that reflect the impact of the importance of household characteristics other than income level in determining housing preferences.

4. For example, in the Philippines and in Zambia low-income households that have had an option to trade off lot size against level of servicing have opted for smaller lots with higher service levels, whereas the reverse was the case in El Salvador (1978 World Bank data).

5. The former assumption presupposes that there are no economies of scale in the consumption of housing, which is reasonable; the latter probably represents an upper limit but is not likely to be much mistaken (Grimes 1976).

6. City population growth rates are well known (see Renaud 1981, Hauser and Gardner 1980). Much less is known about the growth of incomes generated in cities, but it is probably safe to say that they grow at least as rapidly as national per capita incomes in most countries.

7. In twenty-one selected developing countries for which data are available (see table 5-3), residential construction on average (unweighted) accounts for 37 percent of total construction, indicating the importance of competing demands for construction inputs from nonresidential sources.

8. The large land holdings in Bogota of the *beneficiencias*, a group of semiofficial entities providing health services, are a good example of a case where portfolio preferences have dominated land demand decisions in an urban area, with large vacant land tracts in central locations as a result.

9. For example, in Manila (World Bank 1975c) and in Cairo, Abidjan, and cities of Indonesia (World Bank data).

10. In the case of San Salvador, for example, it was found to be extremely difficult to assemble tracts of land within the urban area large enough for an urban development project (1977 World Bank data).

11. For the case of Bogota, see McCallum (1974) and Mohan and Villamizar (1980); for a more general discussion of urban land prices and their role in urban development, see Ingram (1980).

12. Linn and Valverde (1981) find that water and sewerage service costs increase with city size across middle- and large-size cities in Colombia. World Bank data compiled by Alfredo Sfeir-Younis have shown that most Colombian cities find it increasingly difficult to find sites for solid waste disposal within the urban area or in close proximity.

13. In Cali, for instance, it was found that the average incremental cost (AIC) of supplying water to high-lying areas is approximately 30 percent above that for the rest of the city (Linn 1976b). For Nairobi, the AIC for water and sewerage services in high-lying areas was approximately 20 percent above those in low-lying areas (McLure 1977).

14. A recent study on the urban sector in Indonesia found that underdeveloped water distribution systems led to losses of water in some cities, whereas in others water production shortages impeded the quantity and quality of water distributed (1978 World Bank data). In San Salvador, the implementation of the first sites-and-services project financed by the World Bank was hampered by the delayed expansion in water production for the city and by the resulting difficulties in connecting the project site to the city's water system (1977 World Bank data).

15. This accounts to some extent for the fact that large cities are usually better served by public utilities than are smaller cities and towns. Demand factors have also been found to contribute, however, in the case of Colombia (Selowsky 1979b) and Malaysia (Meerman 1979).

16. For example, in Zambia and Colombia (World Bank data), Mexico (Sudra and Turner 1976), and Egypt (Wheaton 1978), to name just a few countries.

17. It could, however, become a problem with heavily increased reliance on urban property taxes, which is frequently suggested for developing country cities. A site value tax, such as that recently introduced in Jamaica, would avoid this problem. These questions are further discussed in the next section.

18. Follain, Lim, and Renaud (1979) found that for Korea overcrowding is particularly heavy among low-income groups, but that it affects middle- and higher-income groups as well.

19. Unfortunately, there appears to exist no quantitative evidence on the income levels of absentee landlords in developing country cities. Nevertheless, it is reasonable to assume that urban absentee landlords are found mainly among the highest-income groups, except where public agencies own the land.

20. This has important implications for the trickle-down hypothesis in urban housing. Increasing the housing supply for middle- and upper-income groups may not lead to increases in housing supply at the lower end of the income scale, since the higher-income groups may merely reduce their crowding, without releasing shelter units for the poorer income groups (Follain, Lim, and Renaud 1979). Indeed, to the extent that higher- and middle-income groups compete for the same inputs into their housing, increased emphasis on higher-income housing may drive costs and prices up for low-income houses.

21. A recent example for Jamaica is in Jamaica Ministry of Finance and Planning (1977); for Indonesia, in 1978 World Bank project data. See also Dwyer (1975) for a summary of conventional estimates of housing needs in developing countries.

22. The following statement reflects well the common practice: "In Jamaica it is felt that 30 square meters (323 sq. ft.) is inadequate for a household and that 420 sq. ft. should be the minimum floor area, bearing in mind the average family size. The standard of 420 sq. ft. is that used by the Ministry of Housing" (Jamaica Ministry of Finance and Planning 1977, p. 3.23). The report goes on to show that at this standard 61 percent of households cannot afford public housing in Jamaica (p. 3.27).

23. World Bank project data contain similar examples for Mexico, El Salvador, and Ivory Coast. Other examples are the cities surveyed by Grimes (1976), especially Nairobi, Bogota, Ahmedabad, and Madras. See also table 5-17 below.

24. An affordable housing expenditure was defined to represent 20 percent of household income, on the basis of empirical observations indicating that this was the typical propensity to spend on housing by the poor in developing countries.

25. Churchill and Lycette take the year 2000 as their target date.

26. In their data for World Bank (1980d), Churchill and Lycette emphasized that their

estimates, based on a number of broad assumptions, are merely indicative of the general order of magnitude of required investments.

27. This is confirmed by Selowsky's estimate of subsidy needs for a basic housing policy in the middle-income countries (Selowsky 1979*a*).

28. Many of the issues raised here are treated at much greater length in Dunkerley and others, 1983.

29. This has occurred, for example, in San Salvador, where centrally located tenement housing (*mesones*) has been displaced by commercial development (1978 World Bank data compiled by Marisa Fernandez-Palacios). In Hong Kong, squatters were moved on a grand scale into public housing to make room for commercial development (Drakakis-Smith and Yeung 1977).

30. Even where public land in good locations appears in principle to be available for conversion, problems are usually encountered in practice because of the need to negotiate land transfers between different public agencies, which may have different perceptions of the relative priorities of urban land use. This is a case where serious delays may be caused by fragmented public authority.

31. The difficulties encountered in San Salvador in attempting to assemble sufficient land for the sites-and-services projects financed by the World Bank are an example of the problems incurred in land assembly in large urban areas.

32. These actions involve not only benefits but also costs. A cost-benefit evaluation, even if only quite rough, should therefore precede the implementation of these actions. In any case, only public action is feasible in these areas, since private substitutes are not available.

33. Urban land was nationalized a few years ago in Tanzania and Zambia, but "the means of distributing this land to low-income groups are yet to be devised" (World Bank 1980*d*, p. 6).

34. Other services such as telephone service, police and fire protection, and recreation also warrant public intervention. These will not be discussed in detail because telephone service, for instance, is not of primary importance in providing housing for the poor and because little is known of the supply conditions for the other services.

35. The World Bank's data on Indonesia also indicate that consumers are often sold well water (of presumably lower quality than piped water) when they believe they are receiving water from the municipal pipes. More frequently, water has to be carried by household members over considerable distances from the source to the house (World Bank 1980*e*), or waiting lines are long at the public taps, with consequent loss of valuable time (1980 World Bank data compiled by Emmanuel Mbi and Tim Campbell).

36. See Saunders and Warford (1976) for a survey of the evidence of the health effects of water supply and sewerage disposal facilities. Available studies indicate that substantial health benefits can indeed be reaped from water and sewerage services, but that the relation is complicated by other factors affecting public health in developing countries, in particular the prevailing hygienic practices, and by the difficulty of economically quantifying such benefits. For a thorough treatment of the subject, see Kalbermatten, Julius, and Gunnerson (1980 and 1982); Feachem and others (1983); World Bank (1980*e*); and the series of World Bank reports entitled *Appropriate Technology for Water Supply and Sanitation* (1980–81).

37. In Colombian cities, all urban developers are required by law to install water supply and sewerage reticulation systems as well as drainage and circulation facilities. In practice, these regulations can be enforced only in high-income developments, however.

38. Warford and Julius (1977, p. 338) also report on a recent World Bank study for a densely populated city in the Yemen Arab Republic, where it was found that "moving from a 100-meter to a 50-meter standpipe spacing more than doubled per capita distribution costs, while moving from 50-meter radii standpipes to patio-connections more than quadrupled per capita costs."

39. In Botswana, for example, the World Bank found aquaprivies not to be socially acceptable, pit latrines could not be used because of poor soakage, and waterborne sewerage systems were too expensive. An alternative low-cost, dry sanitation system therefore had to be installed. For other sociocultural factors affecting choice of sanitation technologies, see Kalbermatten, Julius, and Guinnerson (1982, ch. 5) and Elmendorf and Buckles (1980).

40. This section draws especially on Grimes (1976), Payne (1977), and Vernez (1973).

41. For example, in the case of the first urban development project financed by the World Bank in Manila, it was found (according to preliminary estimates) that private investment in substantial house construction was done by hired artisans and family labor at a cost per unit 20 to 50 percent below that of similar work done using normal contracting methods by the government.

42. Grimes (1976) cites Turkish regulations preventing commercial banks from making mortgage loans and other examples of the more typical practice of pegging interest rates artificially low.

43. See Dwyer (1975), Grimes (1976), and Drakakis-Smith and Yeung (1977) for further discussions of the experience in Hong Kong and Singapore. Actually, the programs of Hong Kong and Singapore differed from each other in some important respects, despite many similarities; for an excellent comparison, see Drakakis-Smith and Yeung (1977).

44. Between 1960 and 1975 some 230,000 public housing units were built in Singapore, and by 1980 approximately 70 percent of the population is expected to live in publicly constructed housing (Laquian 1980).

45. Laquian (1980), however, predicts that eventually the high population growth rates of the large cities in developing countries will make high-density living, and thus high-rise construction, a likely outcome as in Hong Kong and Singapore.

46. For a more extensive treatment of the issues, see Bahl and Linn (forthcoming) and Donald C. Shoup's chapter in Dunkerley and others (1983).

47. For example, the island of Taiwan, Colombia, Brazil, Argentina, Venezuela, Bolivia, Botswana, Ivory Coast, Tunisia, Peru, Ecuador, Chile, Syria, Turkey, and Senegal (Bahl and Linn, forthcoming).

48. Indeed, in some countries or cities heavier taxes are levied on improvements than on land (for example, in Rio de Janeiro, Seoul, and a number of Zambian cities; Bahl and Linn, forthcoming).

49. Short of a total revision of property taxation, this cannot be easily implemented in countries where the property tax is levied on rental value rather than on capital value.

50. An extreme case was recently observed in Monrovia, Liberia, where utilities accounted for 17 percent of higher-income and 23 percent of lower-income household budgets (1980 World Bank data compiled by Emmanuel Mbi and Tim Campbell).

51. The data in table 5-12 are generated on the basis of rather sweeping assumptions regarding household consumption patterns and income distribution; they are therefore merely indicative of the general range of budget shares.

52. In India and Pakistan, but also in a number of other Asian countries, water supply is predominantly financed from property taxes.

53. In contrast to the previous two tables, user charges here reflect the broad definition used in general in this study. However, since only local agency budgets are reflected in table 5-13, the full extent of the contribution of user charges to public revenue cannot be deduced even from this table.

54. See Ray (1975) for a general discussion of the issues arising in the pricing of public services in developing countries; Saunders, Warford, and Mann (1977) for the case of water and sewerage pricing; Turvey and Anderson (1977) for electricity pricing; and Walters (1968) for road user charges. Alfredo Sfeir-Younis of the World Bank's Agriculture and Rural Devel-

opment Department has compiled data on solid waste collection and disposal pricing. These sources deal extensively with the practical question of marginal cost definition and measurement, which must vary from service to service because of different extents of lumpiness of investment and related problems. This question is not addressed in this paper.

55. For example, for water supply and sewerage services in nine cities in Colombia a cost differential of 200 percent was observed between the lowest-cost and the highest-cost city (Linn 1967a); see also Saunders and Warford (1976).

56. The extent of the response of migrants and investors to public service subsidies is not empirically verified for developing countries (see Renaud 1981). However, there can be little doubt that in a case like Mexico City, where water in particular is heavily subsidized (one indication for this is given in table 5-12, above, for water supply), the elimination of these subsidies would encourage a more efficient growth pattern for the city and support official efforts to obtain regional decentralization.

57. Examples for water supply in Nairobi and Cali were cited above; there the cost differentials are a result of the need for supplementary pumping to higher-lying areas.

58. In Nairobi, where high-income households tend to live in high-cost areas, it may be desirable to charge them a higher price than in the rest of the city (McLure 1977); in Cali, where low-income households are concentrated in the high-cost areas, this may not be desirable (Linn 1976b).

59. Saunders and Warford (1976) discuss the spotty experience with alternative devices. The following example presents a colorful demonstration of some of the practical difficulties encountered in preventing misuse and waste in the case of standpipes: "Another wastage-limiting device for public standposts that makes use of a reservoir and float mechanism operates essentially as a siphoning tank for water (used in Gabon and Cameroon). In this case, on the outside of a tank there is a nipple connected to a fixed tube extending inside the tank down into the water. Each water consumer brings his own plastic tube which is inserted over the outside nipple. The consumer then sucks on the tube until water begins to flow. The disadvantage with this means of dispensing water is that little children, who enjoy making gurgling noises, have a considerable propensity to blow into the nipples, thus contaminating the water. Also, the tubes used by individual consumers tend to become contaminated rapidly" (Saunders and Warford 1976, p. 183).

60. See Doebele and Hwang (1979) for a recent overview and evaluation of the land readjustment system in Korea. The information presented here draws on this source.

61. According to Warford and Julius (1977), this type of tariff has been adopted in twenty-one of the thirty-six developing countries that have borrowed from the World Bank in the water supply sector and have metered connections.

62. See also Warford and Julius (1977), who report that in one East African city average consumption at standpipes is only 14 liters per capita daily, while even for the lowest-income groups consumers use an average 100 liters per capita daily when they have a house connection.

63. Although no hard evidence is available, it is reasonable to suspect that the health improvement from the provision of one standpipe to, say, 100 households exceeds the health improvement that can be obtained by upgrading service for *one* household from easy access to a standpipe to an in-house connection.

64. Other examples include projects in the Ivory Coast and the Philippines. A similar principle is also adopted in the Colombian valorization scheme discussed earlier. Cross-subsidization has made it possible to carry out major valorization projects also involving, among other areas, low-income neighborhoods (Doebele, Grimes, and Linn 1979).

65. The comparison of World Bank experience in two Indonesian cities is instructive. In Jakarta, plot charges in slum upgrading did not exist at the time the first two projects were financed by the World Bank. It was therefore decided to finance the projects by improving the

city's property tax system, which indeed happened. In Surabaya, in contrast, where beneficiary contributions to defray the cost of similar upgrading had an established history and acceptance, such charges could in part be relied upon to finance the Bank's urban development project in that city (1976 World bank data).

66. The following discussion of controls and regulations draws on Dunkerley and others (1983), where a more extensive treatment of the issues may be found.

67. Dunkerley and others (1983) cite the case of Bangkok, where the recently adopted new land control law emphasizes conventional zoning based on studies by local city planners of the practices in Washington, D.C., and Paris.

68. In Turkey, for instance, German building codes were originally adopted (Dunkerley and others, 1983).

69. A somewhat different phenomenon has occurred in San Salvador. Low-income rental units called *mesones* cannot legally be reconstructed or repaired, with consequent decline of their quality (1978 World Bank data compiled by Marisa Fernandez-Palacios).

70. For Egypt, for example, qualitative evidence indicates that the housing stock has suffered from the existence of rent controls (Wheaton 1978, 1978 World Bank data).

71. These figures reflect estimates at the time of appraisal. They are drawn from an unpublished survey of World Bank appraisal reports carried out by C. Clifford and L. Cooper.

72. The percentile figures are approximate and show only minimum values. They do not imply that all benefits of the projects and programs were actually concentrated at these percentiles in the income distribution.

73. For the case of Indonesia, one needs to add that the projects financed by the World Bank were a continuation of the Kampong Improvement Program in Jakarta, which had been initiated by Indonesian authorities in 1969 and served as a model for the efforts supported by the World Bank starting in 1974.

74. The estimates shown in table 5-18 are subject to considerable uncertainty and should be taken merely as reflecting the broad picture.

75. Community facilities, special project components not related to shelter provision, and technical assistance overheads were generally not recovered by plot charges, although in some projects some of these cost items were charged to plot holders.

76. This can be justified by the low unit costs of the project compared with the costs of collection of charges; the improved property tax system actually led to an indirect cost recovery from beneficiaries, since the property value base was promptly reassessed, especially in the upgraded areas (Linn, Smith, and Wignjowijoto 1976).

77. A recent ex post analysis of the economic rates of return in a sites-and-services project financed by the World Bank in El Salvador confirmed the results of the ex ante estimates shown in table 5-19, above. The ex post rates of return fell between 28 and 33 percent (1978 World Bank data compiled by Marisa Fernandez-Palacios).

78. See World Bank (1975d and 1979c) for further elaborations on community participation and the role of women in urbanization projects.

6

Urban Social Services:
Education, Health, Nutrition,
and Family Planning

PUBLIC INVOLVEMENT in the provision of social services, especially those relating to education, health, nutrition, and family planning, is a well-established practice in all developing countries. Serious policy issues arise in the delivery of urban social services because of their important effects on labor productivity and on the human welfare of the urban poor, because of the difference between urban and rural needs for social services, and because of the traditionally heavy emphasis on social service provision in urban areas. What is more, urban local government customarily plays a much greater role in the provision of social services than is the case in rural areas, where national or provincial authorities generally carry primary, if not in fact exclusive, responsibility for these services. The scope for local initiative in improving urban social services is therefore often considerable, and local efforts in this area need to be actively supported.

The World Bank has recently provided extensive overviews of the general issues and policies in the area of human development—education, health, nutrition, and fertility—in its *World Development Report, 1980* (World Bank 1980*a*) and in Sector Policy Papers on education (World Bank 1980*b*) and health (World Bank 1980*c*). This chapter draws extensively on these documents and on earlier work (World Bank 1974*a* and 1975*a*) in its general position on human development, but in line with the general tenor of this volume the emphasis here is on the urban dimensions of the issues.

The Social Service System

The starting point of this discussion of urban social services must be the close interrelations among all the services considered here, as well as their links with other aspects of the urban economy, especially with other urban services. Figure 2 shows a schematic representation of this linkage, which will briefly be discussed as a basis for subsequent analysis of policy issues relating to each of the major social services.

Figure 2. *System Linkage of Urban Human Resource Development*

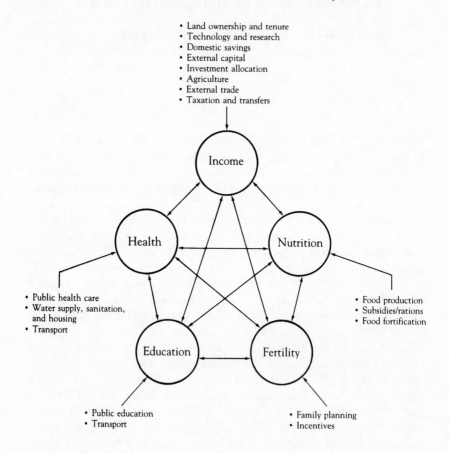

Source: World Bank (1980*a*), figure 5.6, p. 69.

Beginning with education and its relation to other social services, it is well established that higher levels of education tend to be associated with lower fertility levels (Boulier 1977, Anker 1978) and that family planning programs, to be fully effective, must be complemented by specific educational and training efforts for the family planning clients and for the staff in charge of the services. At the same time, reduced fertility lowers the demands on the educational system of a country or city because of the consequent decline in the school-age population. At the household level, it has been found that there is a negative correlation between family size and the intelligence quotient (IQ) of each additional child (Boulier 1977). Education and training programs are essential in improving nutritional practices, especially in instructing low-income women on the value of breastfeeding and on the preparation of balanced and uncontaminated food for infants and children.[1] Schools have also customarily been used as a conduit to improve the nutrition of children; for example, through school feeding programs and milk distribution. At the same time, it is well known that poor nutrition affects the ability of children to benefit from educational programs; furthermore, school feeding programs can be used as an incentive for poor families to enroll their children. Similarly, an important dimension of any health program must be educational efforts to improve personal hygiene and health-related family practices, since transmission of many diseases, particularly gastrointestinal illnesses, is often related to poor hygiene (Feachem and others, 1983). In turn, improved health will increase school attendance and the ability and motivation of children to learn (World Bank 1975a, 1980c).

The links between health, nutrition, and family planning are particularly close, making it a cluster of urban services best treated as a single sector. On the one hand, improved health, as measured by reduction in morbidity or increase in life expectancy, is known to lead to a reduction in fertility, albeit with a variable time lag (World Bank 1975a, 1980c). On the other hand, a reduction in household size tends to increase overall family health (Boulier 1977); more specifically, the reduction in the number of births and an increased spacing of children contribute to improved maternal and infant health and nutrition (Boulier 1977, World Bank 1975a). Poor nutrition is a major cause in increasing susceptibility to illnesses, and malnutrition is itself a major cause of morbidity and death (Austin 1980). At the same time, certain illnesses, especially those affecting the gastrointestinal tract, reduce the ability of the human body to absorb a given nutritional intake; others (especially fevers) are associated with excessive calorie loss.

The role of women, infants, and children is central in this education-health-nutrition-family planning complex. Maternal pre- and postnatal health and nutrition, as well as maternal health and nutrition practices in general, directly affect the health and nutritional well-being of the infant and thus its chance for survival during the critical first year. Indirectly, maternal health determines the infant's future health and intellectual capacity (Selowsky 1976). Social service programs should therefore be specifically designed to reach this crucial target group (Reutlinger and Selowsky 1976, Selowsky 1978).

Besides the internal links within the system of education, health, nutrition, and family planning, there is important linkage between individual social services and other factors. For instance, improved sanitation (water supply, sewerage, and solid waste disposal) has important effects on the health of the urban population, but these health benefits can be reaped in full only if improved sanitation is combined with educational measures aimed at improving the personal hygiene of urban dwellers (World Bank 1975a, 1980c). The quality of housing, in particular the extent of crowding, is closely related to health, since with high density the likelihood of contamination and disease transmission is considerably increased (World Bank 1980c). The physical accessibility of education, health, and family planning facilities is especially important for the urban poor (Basta 1977), and this calls for either community-level provision of these services or improvements in the urban transport system.

Finally, probably the most important external linkage of the education-health-nutrition-family planning complex is its relation to the level of income. Higher incomes—at the household, city, and national levels—are associated with significantly improved levels of education, health, nutrition, and family planning in a pattern of two-way causation. Better education, health, nutrition, and family planning increase productivity and reduce the drain on household resources associated with poor health and large household size; in contrast, higher incomes permit greater household, municipal, and national expenditures to achieve and maintain good educational, health, and nutritional levels and may directly affect the parental decisions regarding reproduction. Indeed, what for a poor family is a vicious cycle—where low income induces poor education, health, nutrition, and family planning and leads again to low income—is for a high-income family a self-reinforcing cycle where high income yields good education, health, nutrition, and family planning and perpetuates high income.

The main policy question is therefore how to help the poor to break the vicious cycle in which they are entrapped. The rationale behind such a policy is not only an ethical one—that is, the alleviation of poverty—but also one of efficiency. The synergistic interactions of education, health, nutrition, and family planning imply that private and public resources—food, educational, health, and sanitation services, as well as family planning efforts— are largely wasted unless a comprehensive effort is made to assist the poor to break out of the vicious circle in which they find themselves (see Austin

1980, pp. 78–84). In fact, public intervention in the field of social services is most appropriate in the case of the urban poor, but much less necessary among the better-off. The poor are particularly affected by lack of information on health, nutrition, and family planning and are especially unable to utilize cost reductions associated with economies of scale. Furthermore, public intervention is crucial, given the importance of negative externalities in the vicious cycle of low income, high fertility, and poor education, health, and nutrition identified above. Related to this point is another. Subsidies in the provision of social services for the poor can be justified on the basis of economic externalities of the social service system as well as on the basis of the normative concept of basic needs. Efficiency and equity concerns therefore overlap very closely in this field.

Before considering a detailed evaluation of social service policies, three further general comments must be made. First, as with all urban public services, particular attention must focus on ways and means to reduce the cost of social service provision by looking for efficient, low-cost standards and by an improvement in organization and management. Second, many of the policy recommendations for social services cut across the urban-rural classification, and in this respect are not special to the urban environment. Nevertheless, there are a number of differences between the rural and urban social service system that warrant a separate examination of the urban context. Finally, many of the policy decisions affecting social service provision are taken at the level of the national, or at least provincial, government rather than at the city level. As will be argued below, however, local authorities and communities should be encouraged to participate in the planning and delivery of these services for poor communities, and in many countries and cities they already do so, thus creating room for city-level initiative and action.

Education

After World War II a rapid expansion of education services occurred throughout the world, including the developing countries, where education has long been thought of as providing a way out of collective, as well as individual, poverty (World Bank 1974a, 1980b). Public expenditures on education have become important in many countries when measured in relation to GNP (among developing countries, Algeria reached the highest proportion of 7 percent of GNP; World Bank 1974a, table 3). For a number of developing countries, education absorbed more than a quarter of all public expenditures (World Bank 1974a), and in various cities of developing countries urban governments spent over a quarter of their budgets on education-

related services (Bahl and Linn, forthcoming). As a result, student enrollments rose rapidly in most developing countries, and considerable advances
were made in improving student enrollment ratios at all levels of education,
in reducing illiteracy, and in creating, in some countries at least, significant
domestic scientific elites which compete vigorously with the scientific estab-
lishments of the industrial countries. India's achievements in nuclear physics
and in medicine are a notable example.

However, it appears that the enthusiasm with which the heavy emphasis
on education was embraced in the developing countries during the 1950s
and 1960s waned during the 1970s as it became apparent that education is,
after all, not a panacea for the problems of development, at least not as it
was designed during the first twenty-five years after World War II. One of
the problems incurred in some developing countries was the rising unemployment rate among the better-educated (Phillips 1978) coupled with the
brain drain of highly trained specialists to the industrialized nations.

Another problem that became apparent during the early 1970s was that,
despite the great advances made in most developing countries, many of them,
and especially the low-income countries, were "approaching the limits of
their financial capability without having achieved even a minimum education
for the majority of their populations" (World Bank 1974a, p. 28).[2]

Finally, it also became clear that, although some sections of the population
in developing countries made considerable progress in educational achievements, large segments were little affected by the educational efforts. Not
surprisingly, these were mainly the rural poor, but also to a considerable
extent the urban poor. All forms of higher education were found to benefit
mainly the higher-income groups, not only the benefit of access—which was
extended mainly to the children of high-income groups, who thus derived
the fiscal dividend of increased future earnings above cost incurred—but also
the benefit from the substantial subsidies generally accorded to higher education [see Selowsky (1979b) on Colombia and Jallade (1977) on Brazil].
Expenditure on primary education was found to be generally distributed in
favor of lower-income groups (at least relative to the existing income distribution), and in fact sufficiently so to make the overall incidence of education
spending and financing progressive in the sense of providing low-income
households with net subsidies relative to their incomes greater than those
accorded to the rich [see Meerman (1979) on Malaysia and Selowsky (1979b)
on Colombia]. In absolute terms, however, the high-income groups received
an equal or even larger net subsidy than the poor. If returns to education
are a function of absolute spending per child, then there can be little doubt
that conventional education in the developing countries has helped strengthen
the position of those groups that are already well educated.[3] Since early
dropouts are particularly prevalent among low-income groups, and since a

certain number of years appears to be required to convey a minimal amount of conventional education, the benefits derived by the poor dropout are even lower than the already low expenditures made on his behalf.

In sum, a number of observers recently have begun to question the efficacy of conventional education in reaching broad development goals, a view reflected in the following statement by Harbison (1977, p. 149):

> Clearly, the overall design of the strategy for development will be the major force determining labor force mobility, alleviation of low-end poverty and narrowing of income variances. Education and learning programs have only minor impacts. A country's learning system is logically derived from an overall development strategy based upon explicit or implied goals; it is seldom the initiating force in the building of such a strategy.

Along with the suggestion that education be placed in the overall context of development objectives and strategies as one of many policy instruments is the increasing realization that the education system itself needs to be restructured to attain the goals of improved efficiency and equity in development (World Bank 1974a, 1980b).

Increasing the Efficiency of the Education System

Research on the social rates of return from different levels of education in developing countries has demonstrated that primary education has a social rate of return usually substantially in excess of any reasonable rate of return to capital and that the social rate of return from primary education exceeds generally the social rate of return from higher levels of education (Selowsky 1979a, Psacharopoulos 1980, World Bank 1980a). This permits two conclusions. First, efficiency would be increased by spending more resources on primary education; second, higher education is overextended relative to primary education.

A related issue is the question of education finance, in particular the financing of higher education. Apart from equity considerations, it is believed that the subsidization of higher education exceeds those levels justified by marginal externalities of higher education, especially for the wealthy, and thus leads to inefficient allocation of resources because private education costs are set below social costs (Harbison 1977). Demand for higher education therefore exceeds the optimal level, and—given the common phenomenon of excess demand leading to excessive (that is, inefficient) investment patterns—supply also tends to be overextended. The proposed remedy is to price higher education at social cost (Harbison 1977). Indeed, public secondary education is not always free in developing countries. For instance, in Colombia, Indonesia, and Korea, parents of secondary school students pay school fees; in the first two countries these are graduated with income.[4] But there is some fear that charging for higher education will increase the extent of reliance on private schools, especially among the wealthy, lower the quality of public relative to private education, and thus lead to increased inequality.[5] This issue is quite complex and is far from resolved, but if it is possible to maintain public higher education at a quality close to that of its private competitors, *and* if means can be found to help low-income individuals attend high schools, private or public (for instance, through student loans, scholarships, and the like), the dangers of a regressive long-term incidence of fees for higher education are likely to be considerably reduced.

Besides attempts at restructuring the overall balance between primary and higher education, the 1970s saw calls for improvements within each level of education (Harbison 1977, World Bank 1974a, 1980b). Of particular concern has been the fact that existing curricula and teaching practices predominantly focus on giving the student the wherewithall to progress from one level to the next higher level, rather than on tailoring the education programs to the needs of the majority of the students who will leave the school system upon graduation from a particular level. As a result, it has been suggested that skill training, as well as functional literacy and numeracy training, be emphasized at all levels of education rather than continue emphasis on general education, and that less reliance be placed on external curricula and examination standards imported from industrialized countries such as Britain, France, and the United States (Harbison 1977, Jamacia Ministry of Finance and Planning 1978, Phillips 1978, World Bank 1974a). The upshot has been the development of the concept of "basic education," the essence of which is summarized in the World Bank's *Education* Sector Working Paper (World Bank 1974a, pp. 29–30):

> Basic education is an attempt, despite severe resource constraints, to meet the needs of substantial portions of the population who do not have access to even minimal educational opportunities. It is a supplement, not a rival, to the formal education system, and is intended to provide a functional, flexible, and low-cost education for those whom the formal system cannot yet reach or has already passed by. Although the primary cycle may be its principal vehicle in many countries, it differs from the conventional concept of universal primary education in three major respects:
>
> (i) The objectives and content of basic education are functionally defined in terms of "minimum learning needs" of especially identified groups, and not as steps in the educational hierarchy (i.e., primary level).
>
> (ii) The "target groups" of basic education are not necessarily school-

age children. They may vary according to age (children, youths, adults) and socioeconomic characteristics (rural-urban groups, women, participants in particular development programs).

(iii) The "delivery systems" of basic education will take different forms in different countries (restructured primary schools, nonformal programs, or various combinations of the two) adapted to the needs of different clienteles and to constraints upon resources. The costs will play a predominant role in the choice of educational technologies of basic education programs.

One of the difficulties with the concept of basic education is that in urban areas the spectrum of basic skills required by the population is much greater than in rural areas, where functional education and training can largely be tailored to help the farmer improve his planting or livestock-raising techniques, including the use of fertilizers, tools, machinery, and irrigation water. The scope for translating a relatively clearly defined set of skills immediately into productivity improvements is therefore greater in rural than in urban areas, where complementary factors of production are not as readily available or are linked with a much wider range of activities (Phillips 1978). Given the more varied skill needs in urban areas, a greater variety is required in education, and an even greater concern with analyzing the labor demand conditions appears to be warranted in urban areas than in rural areas if the urban education system is to produce the right type of skills.[6] At the same time, however, the economic returns from educating urban dwellers appear to lie significantly above those associated with rural education (Berry 1980). The rewards for a carefully designed and implemented urban education system are therefore considerable.

One way of achieving more effective urban education is to link basic education programs as far as possible with other urban development programs—such as projects providing shelter and urban infrastructure, small-scale enterprise and handicraft development programs, and nutrition and health programs—that meet important training and education needs and that provide a ready context for functionally oriented education and training efforts (World Bank 1980b). This also applies to more advanced training programs (such as those to train medical auxiliaries for community health posts, basic education teachers, local government administrators, accountants, real estate appraisers, and the like), which are geared to provide particular skills required for the implementation of various urban programs. Obviously, such an education system is considerably more difficult to design and to implement than a system of conventional education that has been borrowed, textbooks and teachers included, from the developed countries. And one does well to remember the caveat expressed by Morawetz (1977,

p. 53): "Yet although governments have been proposing for up to 100 years that education ought to be tailored to local needs, it seems to be difficult in practice to implement these suggestions satisfactorily."[7]

There are further steps that can and should be taken to increase the efficiency of the education system, including higher student-teacher ratios where these are low and a scaling down of training requirements for school teachers (it has been found that, within fairly wide boundaries, student achievement does not appear to vary significantly with class size and teacher training; World Bank 1974a). Another very important area for improvement of efficiency is reduction of the dropout rate, since, as mentioned above, dropouts (especially at the primary school level) do not reach the minimum threshold of learning required to absorb and retain the basics of literacy, numeracy, and other fundamental skills. Measures to reduce the dropout rate are best analyzed in the context of a discussion of how the education system can be directed to meet the needs of the urban poor, since the propensity for dropping out of school is much higher in children from low-income groups than in those from middle- or high-income families (World Bank 1974a).

Education for the Urban Poor

The improvements in urban education systems in developing countries that were suggested above in the name of economic efficiency also can increase educational opportunities for the urban poor.[8] Changing the balance between primary and higher education, reforming school financing practices, adapting education design to emphasize functionally oriented basic education, and attempting to reduce the dropout rate and increase access to education would all directly or indirectly produce benefits for the poor, as long as care is taken in educational program and project design to ensure that the poor are actually reached. Indeed, it is probably correct to claim that the more effectively the public education system caters to the needs of the poor, the more efficient is the use of public resources devoted to education. The following paragraphs therefore discuss the steps that may be taken to improve the access of the urban poor to educational facilities and the return which they can obtain from education.

The question of access to education and the net benefits that are expected from education are very closely related. Unless there are physical constraints on mobility or discriminatory constraints on school entrance (based, for instance, on location, race, nationality, or social status), the decision to seek or not to seek education involves comparing the costs incurred with the benefits derived, subject to the family's budget constraint. The budget constraint is particularly binding for the lowest-income groups, and thus an important question is how to lower the costs of education to them.[9] One important way to do this is to locate schools in poor urban neighborhoods and thus to reduce transport costs from prohibitively high levels. In many cities of developing countries schools are very scarce in the squatter or slum areas. In Greater Cairo, for instance, primary school spaces are available to only 20 percent of the school-age population in the low-income fringe areas, whereas the city-wide average is 75 percent (1978 World Bank data). In seventeen low-income neighborhoods in Cartagena, Colombia, the number of schools per thousand inhabitants in 1972 was 0.33, whereas it was 0.44 for the city as a whole (Linn 1975).

Lack of physical accessibility is not, however, the only source of potentially prohibitive costs for poor students and their families. Out-of-pocket expenditures for required school uniforms, school lunches, textbooks, and materials may be considerable, not to mention the opportunity cost of lost time that children (or adult students) could use for domestic chores (such as infant supervision, water carrying, and so forth) or jobs. Meerman (1979) has estimated that in Malaysia for one student the out-of-pocket expenditures alone (not counting the opportunity cost of time) amount to 13 percent of household income in the lowest population quintile of the income distribution and 11 percent in the next higher quintile. Thus, even where education is free, as in Malaysia, the privately incurred costs may well prevent low-income parents from sending their children to school or may induce them to take their children out of school before graduation. School enrollment could therefore be increased, and the dropout rate in many cases lowered, by reducing out-of-pocket expenses (for instance, by providing free school lunches, books, and materials). It is important, however, to weigh the gains in increased enrollment of low-income students derived from these policies against the gains that could have been achieved by investing an equivalent amount of resources in building and staffing schools in low-income areas. In countries and cities where physical access to schools and the number of available school places are already quite high in low-income areas, incentives such as those mentioned above to induce greater enrollment and lower dropout rates are likely to be the preferable approach. In contrast, in countries and cities where schools are largely absent in low-income neighborhoods, these incentives would not significantly help the poor but would subsidize predominantly the better-off students and would also inhibit the construction and staffing of schools in low-income areas because of the overall budget constraint.

In addition to lowering private education costs to low-income groups, the benefits that the poor derive from education can be increased in various ways. Improvements in school facilities, especially the reduction of crowding and the scheduling of fewer shifts, increase the quality of education.[10] Improving curriculum design to provide relevant skills combined with appropriate teacher training and a sufficient supply of textbooks will also raise the returns from all types of education available to the urban poor. But complementary policy actions outside the education field also have important implications for the returns from education. Improvements in the health and nutrition status of children have been shown to reduce absenteeism and dropout rates and to increase the learning capacity of students while they are in school (World Bank 1974a). At an even more general level, the returns from schooling for the low-income student (and for society) depend significantly on the overall demand for unskilled and semiskilled labor. Unless this demand expands, increased schooling may do no more than drive down the private and social returns of education (as discussed above in chapter 2).

Finally, the institutional framework within which educational services are provided for the urban poor deserves consideration. First, community participation in some form—for example, in course selection and curriculum design, choice of language, recruitment of teachers—is likely to be an important ingredient in ensuring that the education provided meets the needs of the community and is regarded as a community asset rather than as an intrusion. Second, local governments in developing country cities frequently have extensive involvement in the provision, operation, and financing of school facilities and complementary services (for example, transport; Bahl and Linn, forthcoming). Their role needs to be carefully studied and their capacity to provide the kinds of education and complementary services outlined above needs to be strengthened. The major responsibility for the education sector in most developing countries, however, rests with national or provincial authorities. It is at this level that issues of basic policy—such as the balance between primary and higher education curriculum design, education finance, or teacher training—must be dealt with for urban and rural education alike. Although community participation, local government involvement, and integrated urban development projects are virtually always essential instruments in the implementation of education policies, particularly if they are to reach the urban poor, the national (provincial) government needs to set the overall priorities and provide the appropriate sectoral planning and resource support to permit local urban action to work effectively.

Health, Nutrition, and Family Planning

Health, nutrition, and fertility are particularly closely interrelated, in terms of their mutual interactions and the opportunities for joint action in these areas within an integrated human development program. Each of these three areas has been the subject of extensive research, much of which has been surveyed in World Development Report, 1980 (World Bank 1980a) and in other World Bank studies.[11] The present section will focus mainly on the area of health; nutritional and family planning issues and policies are treated only in passing.

Policy Issues and Approaches

Health problems in developing countries vary considerably between continents, countries, regions within countries, and even within cities. However, certain fundamental similarities in health conditions exist among all developing countries. These were succinctly recapitulated in the World Bank's *Health* Sector Policy Paper (World Bank 1975a, p. 22):

> The core health problems throughout the developing world, except among middle- and upper-income urban groups, are fecally transmitted diseases, airborne diseases, and malnutrition. These three elements interact cumulatively and synergistically. This is particularly true for those below the age of five but also applies to the older age groups. Improved water supply and sanitation check the fecally related disease cycles. More spacious, well-ventilated living conditions cut down the transmission of airborne and fecally transmitted diseases. Better nutrition reduces susceptibility to infection and greatly diminishes the severity as well as the duration of illness; it is of special importance for infants and young children.

One may compare this diagnosis of the major health problems in the typical developing country with that of the typical developed country. As shown in table 6-1, the predominant causes of death in the latter are degenerative diseases (cancer, circulatory system diseases, and the like) and traumatic injuries; in the former the infectious, parasitic, and respiratory diseases are the most important causes of death.

Because infectious diseases are far more effectively controlled by preventing

Table 6-1. *Percentage Distribution of Deaths, by Cause, in Selected Model Populations*

Cause	Model developing country	Model developed country
Infectious, parasitic, and respiratory disease	43.7	10.8
Cancer	3.7	15.2
Circulatory disease	14.8	32.2
Traumatic injury	3.5	6.8
Other causes	34.3	35.0
All causes	100.0	100.0

Source: World Bank (1975a), table 3.

their incidence than by treating their symptoms (World Bank, 1975a), one would expect that developing countries are emphasizing preventive, rather than curative, measures in health care. In fact, however, public health expenditure in developing countries are heavily biased in favor of curative care (table 6-2), and within this category the emphasis is on in-hospital rather than out-patient treatment (Rao 1974, World Bank 1975a).[12]

Table 6-2. *Composition of Public Health Expenditures in Selected Developing Countries*
(percentage)

Country	Year	Preventive care	Curative care	Training and research
India	1965/66	37.0	55.5	7.5
Sri Lanka	1957/58	23.3	74.4	2.3
Colombia	1970	18.7	79.3	2.0
Chile	1959	18.3	77.7	4.0
Venezuela	1962	18.0	76.5	5.5
Israel	1959/60	14.3	81.1	4.7
Kenya	1971	5.2	83.8	11.0
Tanzania	1970/71	4.9	80.3	4.4

Source: Rao (1974, table VII.2).

Besides this bias toward curative care, analyses of developing country health conditions and policies usually also detect a bias in favor of urban areas, in the sense that health services (as measured by the availability of hospital beds or doctors per population) are relatively more abundant in urban than in rural areas (World Bank 1975a, Oftedal and Levinson 1977), whereas common indicators of morbidity, life expectancy, and nutrition show that urban dwellers, on the average, are better-off than the rural population (World Bank 1975a, Basta 1977). Yet, before jumping to any conclusions, one must bear in mind two important factors that complicate the picture.

First, Basta (1977) and Lee and Furst (1980) have persuasively demonstrated that average indexes of health and nutritional conditions in urban areas can be misleading. Indeed, the available evidence indicates that the inhabitants of slum and squatter areas fare significantly worse in health and nutrition than is shown by city averages (see table 1-12 above), with the result that there is good reason to suspect that the urban poor are as badly off in health as are the rural poor.[13] As regards nutrition, there is convincing evidence that the urban poor are frequently worse off than the rural population (table 1-11, above).[14] As long as the urban poor live in overcrowded housing with no access to safe water and disposal of human and solid waste and with only limited availability of preventive health care, they are likely to be seriously affected by ill health. This problem is compounded by the fact that the nutritional intake of the urban poor in general tends to be lower and less well balanced than that of the rural poor because of greater availability of food items with poor nutritional value (Basta 1977). The fact that relatively few mothers breastfeed their infants during the crucial first year of life and frequently dilute commercial baby formulas with unsafe water creates particularly serious health and nutritional problems among the urban poor (Reutlinger and Selowsky 1976). Urban dwellers, especially those among the lower-income groups, are also particularly susceptible to traffic accidents and occupational injuries because of poor urban traffic management and low standards of job safety (Golladay and Liese 1980).

The second factor to consider is that, although curative health services (as reflected by the distribution of conventionally trained doctors and nurses and the availability of hospital beds) are indeed highly concentrated in urban areas, the access to these facilities is frequently quite limited for the urban poor because of the high costs of medical attention and medication, lack of information, and the physical as well as cultural inaccessibility of modern curative medical care. Moreover, the distribution of preventive and basic curative care of the kind provided by community public health clinics and similar neighborhood institutions is, at least in some developing countries, biased in favor of rural areas. In Jamaica, for example, the ratio of basic health staff per population served is lower in the Kingston metropolitan region than in the country as a whole (Jamaica Ministry of Finance and Planning 1978). For Malaysia, Meerman (1979) concludes that public expenditures for health favor rural areas and small towns over the large cities. Although rural and small-town bias is not likely to be the rule in all developing countries—Selowsky (1979b) demonstrates, for example, that the reverse is true in Colombia—one nevertheless needs to be cautious in presuming that the health and nutritional needs of the urban poor are necessarily better (let alone adequately) served by prevailing policies than are the needs of the rural poor.

Whatever the precise balance between urban and rural poor in the relative benefits they receive from public health policies in developing countries, there can be little doubt that neither of these two groups has been served well by the prevailing emphasis on urban-based modern curative medicine. Matters are made worse by the costs of modern medical technology, which are high, both in outlays for medical facilities and for medical training (World Bank 1975a).[15] Also, the cost effectiveness of conventional curative medical care has been shown to be inferior to that of preventive methods for the health problems prevalent in developing countries. For example, Rao (1974, p. 150) cites a study for Morocco that demonstrates "that the costs of saving a life average US$2,500 in general hospitals but only US$40 with mass vaccination programs." One may therefore conclude that public provision of health care in developing countries has generally been inequitable and inefficient, and that significant changes are required to make public health services more efficient and equitable in both rural and urban areas.

A Basic Urban Health Strategy for Developing Countries

A comprehensive strategy for basic health in the cities of developing countries should involve the following five components.

First, the conventional focus on high-technology curative medical care, with the associated emphasis on degenerative diseases, should be replaced by preventive efforts to reduce the incidence of the diseases most prevalent in developing countries (for example, infectious, parasitic, and respiratory diseases). This would not mean abandoning modern curative services, but it would mean providing them without subsidy and without heavy commitment of public capital. Health insurance systems, private medical education, and the like could provide a framework for continued provision of curative health services.

Second, the switch from curative to preventive health care should be associated with a switch from in-patient treatment in large hospitals to out-patient treatment in community-based, smaller health centers, which also would be charged with the preventive and promotional functions of a basic health care system, including maternal and child health care, immunization, family planning, nutrition programs, and health education. Indeed, the comprehensive approach of integrated health-nutrition-family planning services is essential to a basic health system. The need for a "pyramidal structure" of health care has been emphasized in World Bank studies (1980c); it consists essentially of three levels: the community health worker, the neighborhood clinic, and the referral hospital. Extensive contacts between these three levels are essential, with the lower levels providing medical care wherever possible but referring cases beyond their ability to the next higher level.

Third, the development of such a basic health care system would require changes in medical training. The conventional emphasis on highly trained, specialized, and costly medical staff should give way to the development of a staff of community health workers, who receive a broadly based, but quite rudimentary, training in the area of health, nutrition, and family planning.[16]

Fourth, a basic health care system should pay particular attention to those population groups most directly affected by the prevalent diseases and malnutrition; for example, the poor in general, and among them especially infants and pregnant and lactating women. The basic health needs of these groups are the most severe, their ability to seek prevention and treatment from private sources is the most limited, and the external benefits from public intervention are the most significant.

Fifth, a basic health program should also give explicit consideration to the sanitary needs of the urban population. It is well established that improved water supply and waste disposal systems are essential ingredients to a program of improving public health, particularly in urban areas. At the same time, general public health programs are required to provide the maximum benefits from investments in sanitary infrastructure (World Bank 1975a).

There is evidence that various developing countries have begun to shift from the traditional focus on conventional curative health care toward the kind of basic health system outlined in the preceding paragraphs. For example, in 1972 Jamaica initiated a system of "primary health care" that included all the components of basic health care suggested here (Jamaica Ministry of Finance and Planning 1978). In the wake of the observation that the health conditions in its major cities are worsening, Brazil has begun a reevaluation of its health strategy and has increased efforts to provide some elements of basic health care to the lower-income groups (Webb and Pfeffermann 1978). Also, a number of recent urban development projects financed by the World Bank (for example, in Indonesia, the Philippines, Botswana, and Colombia) have given a prominent role to basic health care components.

The example of the Jamaican primary health care system is particularly interesting because of its comprehensive design and because it has been in operation for a number of years.[17] The structure of this system is summarized in figure 3. The system operates out of community-based health centers in locations easily accessible to the poor and relies heavily on the services of community health aides and nurse practitioners. The former, of whom 1,169 had been trained between 1972 and 1978, "are members of the community who are trained for 6–8 weeks to do field work [home visiting] at primary care level, providing maternal and child care, family planning and nutritional services" (Jamaica Ministry of Finance and Planning 1978, p. 5.8). Nurse practitioners were recently introduced to take over some paramedical functions traditionally executed by physicians. The focus of the preventive and promotional programs are sharply slanted toward the needs of the most vulnerable groups (pregnant and lactating mothers, infants, and children). The results of the program were judged to be encouraging, but they still fall short of fully meeting the basic health needs of Jamaica, mainly because of insufficient resources, especially in the Kingston metropolitan area. Also, some difficulties were encountered in the selection of health aides from the communities; as a result, assignments were uneven across the city and the training program suffered a slowdown. The work of these aides also appears to be complicated by a continuing uncertainty regarding their role and their relation

Figure 3. *Primary Health Care System in Jamaica*

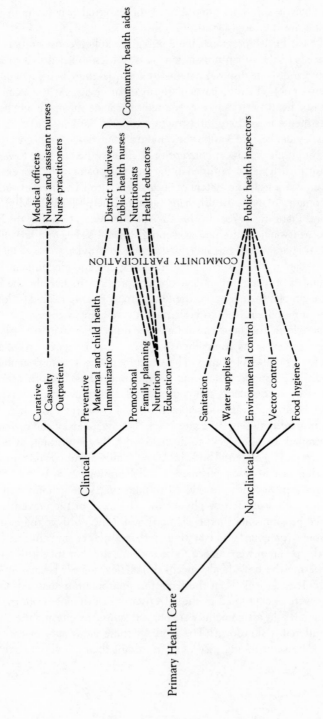

Primary Health Care

Clinical

Curative
— Casualty
— Outpatient

{ Medical officers
Nurses and assistant nurses
Nurse practitioners

Preventive
— Maternal and child health
— Immunization

District midwives
Public health nurses
Nutritionists
Health educators

} Community health aides

Promotional
— Family planning
— Nutrition
— Education

COMMUNITY PARTICIPATION

Nonclinical

— Sanitation
— Water supplies
— Environmental control
— Vector control
— Food hygiene

Public health inspectors

Source: Jamaica Ministry of Finance and Planning (1978).

to the conventional health staff. Jamaica, like most of the developing countries, still has a long way to go in implementing an effective basic health care system, but at least the direction of change appears correct.

Although problems of implementation will always need to be overcome in practice, World Bank "experiences in lending for health components confirm that basic health care can be provided at affordable cost. Health care properly conceived and operated, and low in cost, can be of as high a quality as physician-dominated care" (World Bank 1980c, p. 58).

Summary of Policy Implications

One of the most important areas of policy intervention shaping the course of economic development in the developing countries is the area of human resource development. A recent survey of research on the relation between economic growth and human resources came to the following conclusion: "The correct program of human resource investments will depend on individual country situation and will have to consider the opportunity cost of capital and the current state of human resources. Nevertheless, it does seem clear that investing in people can be an efficient way of both eliminating poverty and increasing the growth rate of output for many developing countries" (Hicks 1980, p. iv).

Six major conclusions for policy design emerge from the preceding sections of this chapter; they apply to all four areas of human resource development: education, health, nutrition, and fertility. Of course, among these areas details will differ, and in different countries and even in different cities within the same country appropriate balances may have to be struck in applying the general lessons. Nevertheless, the general lessons are useful in focusing on the major areas of concern, which are briefly summarized below.

• First, education and health programs need to shift emphasis away from higher-level services to basic services in the interest of greater efficiency and equity of delivery.

• Second, human resource policies must recognize that certain groups in the population (especially infants and young children) are subject to particularly high risks; and that women are especially important as target groups for social service provision because of the crucial role they play within families in determining the effectiveness of education, health, nutrition, and family planning programs.

• Third, constraints on the demand for social services must be recognized and, where possible, minimized. Physical accessibility of social service facilities is a particular problem in rural areas, but poor accessibility also limits the use of social services by the urban poor. The location of social service facilities close to, or preferably within, poor neighborhoods is essential. Private out-of-pocket expenses frequently associated with use of social services is another constraint on the demand for these services by the poor. Well-targeted attempts to reduce these costs for poor users should be encouraged. Similarly, the loss of forgone earnings from the use of social services, particularly education, can be reduced by such measures as job-related training, dispensaries near the work place, and the like. Cultural barriers to the use of social services must also be recognized and measures taken to overcome them (for example, the use of indigenous languages and the incorporation of traditional health care practices in basic health care programs).

• Fourth, complementarities within and among social services need to be exploited in program design and implementation. The complementarity between teachers, textbooks, and physical plant is essential in education, as is the complementarity of community health workers, neighborhood clinics, and referral hospitals in a basic health care system. School lunch programs can serve the goals of improved child nutrition and better school attendance among the poor. A basic health care system can serve as a vehicle for nutrition education and instruction in family planning.

• Fifth, social service delivery must attempt to work toward institutional integration at the local level so that benefits from the complementarities among the services may be realized. Local authorities and communities themselves have to get directly involved, not only to help articulate an effective demand for these services but also to provide the institutional framework within which the activities of specialized national or provincial government agencies can be integrated. In urban areas in developing countries the local authorities frequently are already quite heavily involved in the delivery of social services. Their function must be understood, and ways must be found to improve their effectiveness.

• Finally, attention needs to be paid to the question of cost recovery from service beneficiaries. Cost-covering user charges for high-level services (modern hospital care and higher education) should be developed wherever possible for the wealthier beneficiaries, and some (albeit minimal) fees even for use of basic health services may be appropriate to limit inessential use.

Notes to Chapter 6

1. Cochrane, O'Hara, and Leslie (1980) have reviewed recent research in this area and found that higher literacy rates are associated with lower mortality rates, even after allowing for other factors such as income, and that maternal education level is a particularly strong determinant of child mortality and nutrition levels.

2. The importance of the overall resource constraint in limiting the potential of reaching conventional education goals in a representative developing country was also demonstrated by Hultin and Jallade (1975).

3. See Jallade (1977) for an analysis of the long-term incidence of education in Brazil.

4. The author has compiled data for Colombia; see Linn, Smith, and Wignjowijoto (1976) for Indonesia and Bahl and Wasylenko (1976) for Korea. In Indonesia, primary school fees are also levied. Since 1972 these fees are no longer paid directly by parents to the schools attended by their children, but are paid to the local government, which distributes the funds between the schools more in accordance with school needs than with the neighborhoods' ability to pay.

5. "A policy of direct, progressive pricing according to which the level of subsidization decreases as income rises may be more equitable in the *short term* but is likely to foster life-long income inequalities in the future" (Hultin and Jallade 1975, p. 26).

6. A recent World Bank project for urban development in Egypt, for instance, set up training centers to offer courses in furniture making and woodworking, leatherworking, welding and metalworking, and production of handicrafts.

7. By way of example, Morawetz notes that "in Ghana . . . this subject was stressed in every major education report from 1842 until independence in 1957" (Morawetz 1977, p. 53).

8. For a recent review of issues and data on the relations between education, urban labor markets, and urban poverty, see Berry (1980).

9. The emphasis on costs and benefits in this discussion is not to be interpreted as limiting it to financial costs and benefits. For instance, one important cost may be the loss of cultural identity where education is carried out in a language other than the native language of the student. Similarly, the possible psychic benefits and prestige of possessing an education may be just as important as the increased earnings.

10. In Jakarta, schools in low-income areas operated on the basis of four two-hour shifts daily in 1976, and this was seen as a major reason for declining enrollment rates (1976 World Bank data). However, other cases have also been reported where existing facilities have been underutilized and where the use of daily double shifts could have significantly increased the capacity of the educational system (World Bank, 1980a, 1980b).

11. See Golladay and Liese (1980), Birdsall (1980), Cochrane (1979), Cuca (1979), Selowsky (1979a), Austin (1980), World Bank (1975a, 1980c).

12. These figures do not, apparently, include outlays for sanitation (water supply, sewerage, and solid waste disposal), which could be counted among preventive health measures. See Feachem and others (1983).

13. The urban health program in some developing country cities appears in fact to be growing. In Kingston, for instance, increases in the incidence of tuberculosis have been registered in recent years (Jamaica Ministry of Finance and Planning 1978); in Sao Paulo, infant morbidity is rising, there is a resurgence of malaria and the bubonic plague, and meningitis in 1974 took on epidemic proportions (Webb and Pfeffermann 1979); in Manila, the incidence of cholera and tuberculosis appears to be on the rise (1976 World Bank data).

14. The nutritional deprivation of the urban relative to the rural poor has been confirmed in recent studies for India (Katona-Apte 1977), Peru (Thomas 1978), and Jamaica (Jamaica Ministry of Finance and Planning 1978). See also Lee and Furst (1980).

15. The cost of educating a physician in developing countries frequently ranges between $25,000 and $80,000, and a sizable portion of the locally trained doctors tend to emigrate to the industrialized countries. It is not untypical to find that medical doctors emigrating per year account for more than 20 percent of the total annual medical graduates (World Bank 1975a).

16. Oftedal and Levinson (1977) report that "in Malaysia auxiliaries cost 75 percent to 85 percent less than a doctor per working day."

17. This review is based on Jamaica Ministry of Finance and Planning (1978).

References

The word "processed" describes works that are reproduced from typescript by mimeograph, xerography, or similar means; such works may not be cataloged or commonly available through libraries, or may be subject to restricted circulation.

Ahluwalia, Montek S. 1974. "Income Inequality: Some Dimensions of the Problem." In *Redistribution with Growth*. Edited by Hollis Chenery and others. London: Oxford University Press.

Andors, Stephen. 1978. "Urbanization and Urban Government in China's Development: Toward a Political Economy of Urban Community." *Economic Development and Cultural Change*, vol. 26(3), pp. 525–45.

Anker, Richard. 1978. "An Analysis of Fertility Differentials in Developing Countries." *Review of Economics and Statistics*, vol. 60(1), pp. 58–69.

Austin, James. 1980. *Confronting Urban Malnutrition*. Baltimore, Md.: Johns Hopkins University Press.

Bahl, Roy W. 1975. "Urban Public Finances in Developing Countries: A Case Study of Metropolitan Ahmedabad." Urban and Regional Report no. 77–4. World Bank, Washington, D.C. Processed.

————. 1977. *Urban Property Taxation in Developing Countries*. Occasional Paper no. 32. Maxwell School, Syracuse University.

Bahl, Roy W., and Johannes F. Linn. Forthcoming. "Urban Public Finance and Administration in Developing Countries." Washington, D.C.: World Bank. Processed.

Bahl, Roy W., and Michael J. Wasylenko. 1976. "Urban Public Finances in Developing Countries: A Case Study of Seoul, Korea." Urban and Regional Report no. 77–3. World Bank, Washington D.C. Processed.

Bamberger, Michael, Umnuay Sae-Hau, and Edgardo Gonzalez-Polio. 1980. "Evaluation of the First El Salvador Sites and Service Project." Urban and Regional Report no. 80–12. World Bank, Washington, D.C. Processed.

Basta, Samir S. 1977. "Nutrition and Health in Low Income Urban Areas of the Third World." *Ecology of Food and Nutrition*, vol. 6, pp. 113–24.

213

Beardsley, John R. 1980. "Assisting the Smallest Economic Activities of the Urban Poor: Final Workshop Report." Program for Investment in the Small Capital Enterprise Sector (PICES), Phase I. ACCION International/AITEC, Washington, D.C. Processed.

Beesley, M., C. Turner, P. Gist, and K. B. Whang. 1979. "Korean Urban Sector Study: Options for Secondary City Urban Transport." Urban and Regional Report no. 79–2. World Bank, Washington, D.C. Processed.

Beier, George, Anthony Churchill, Michael Cohen, and Bertrand Renaud. 1975. *The Task Ahead for the Cities of the Developing Countries.* World Bank Staff Working Paper no. 209. Washington, D.C.

Bender, Stephen O. 1975. "Low Income Housing Development in Bogota." *Rice University Studies,* vol. 61(4), pp. 97–111.

Berry, Albert R. 1975. "Open Unemployment as a Social Problem in Urban Colombia: Myth and Reality." *Economic Development and Cultural Change,* vol. 23(2), pp. 276–91.

————. 1980. "Education, Income, Productivity, and Urban Poverty." In *Education and Income.* World Bank Staff Working Paper no. 402. Washington, D.C.

Bird, Richard M. 1976. *Charging for Public Services: A New Look at an Old Idea.* Toronto: Canadian Tax Foundation.

————. 1978. *Intergovernmental Fiscal Relations in Developing Countries.* World Bank Staff Working Paper no. 304. Washington, D.C.

Bird, Richard M., and Luc H. De Wulf. 1973. "Taxation and Income Distribution in Latin America: A Critical Review of Empirical Studies." International Monetary Fund *Staff Papers,* vol. 20(3), pp. 639–82.

Birdsall, Nancy. 1980. *Population and Poverty in the Developing World.* World Bank Staff Working Paper no. 404. Washington, D.C.

Bougeon-Maassen, Francine, and Johannes F. Linn. 1975. "Urban Public Finances in Developing Countries: A Case Study of Metropolitan Kingston, Jamaica." Urban and Regional Report no. 77–7. World Bank, Washington, D.C. Processed.

Boulier, Bryan L. 1977. "Population Policy and Income Distribution." In *Income Distribution and Growth in the Less-Developed Countries.* Edited by Charles R. Frank, Jr., and Richard C. Webb. Washington, D.C.: Brookings Institution.

Bromley, R. J. 1977. "Organization, Regulation and Exploitation in the So-called 'Urban Informal Sector': The Street Traders of Cali, Colombia." Paper presented at the Institute of British Geographers, Developing Areas Study Group, Conference on "The Urban Informal Sector in the Third World." London. Processed.

Burki, S. J., D. G. Davies, R. H. Hook, and J. W. Thomas. 1976. *Public Works Programs in Developing Countries: A Comparative Analysis.* World Bank Staff Working Paper no. 224. Washington, D.C.

Chelliah, Raja J., Hessel J. Baas, and Margaret R. Kelly. 1975. "Tax Ratios and Tax Effort in Developing Countries, 1969–71." International Monetary Fund *Staff Papers,* vol. 22(1), pp. 187–205.

Churchill, Anthony A. 1972. *Road User Charges in Central America*. Baltimore, Md.: Johns Hopkins University Press.

Cochrane, Susan H. 1979. *Fertility and Education: What Do We Really Know?* Baltimore, Md.: Johns Hopkins University Press.

Cochrane, Susan H., Donald J. O'Hara, and Joanne Leslie. 1980. *The Effects of Education on Health*. World Bank Staff Working Paper no. 405. Washington, D.C.

Cohen, Michael. 1978. *Urban Growth and Economic Development in the Sahel: Prospects and Priorities*. World Bank Staff Working Paper no. 315. Washington, D.C.

Council for International Urban Liaison. 1980. *The Urban Edge*, vol. 4, no. 2 and 5.

Cousins, W. J. 1977. "Urban Community Development in Hyderabad." *Social Action* (India), vol. 27(3), pp. 324–334.

Cuca, Roberto. 1979. *Family Planning Programs: An Evaluation of Experience*. World Bank Staff Working Paper no. 345, Washington, D.C.

De Wulf, Luc H. 1975. "Fiscal Incidence Studies in Developing Countries: Survey and Critique." International Monetary Fund *Staff Papers*, vol. 22(1), pp. 61–131.

Doebele, William A., and Myong Chang Hwang. 1979. "Land Policies in the Republic of Korea with Special Reference to Decentralized Development." Urban and Regional Report no. 79–4. World Bank, Washington, D.C. Processed.

Doebele, William A., Orville F. Grimes, Jr., and Johannes Linn. 1979. "Participation of Beneficiaries in Financing Urban Services: Valorization Charges in Bogota, Colombia." *Land Economics*, vol. 55(1), pp. 73–92.

Drakakis-Smith, D. W., and Yen-man Yeung. 1977. "Public Housing in the City-States of Hong Kong and Singapore." Occasional Paper no. 8. Development Studies Centre, Australian National University, Canberra.

Dunkerley, Harold B., and others. 1983. *Urban Land Policy: Issues and Opportunities*. New York: Oxford University Press.

Dwyer, D. J. 1975. *People and Housing in Third World Cities*. London: Longman.

Elmendorf, Mary, and Patricia Buckles. 1980. *Appropriate Technology for Water Supply and Sanitation*. Vol. 5, *Sociocultural Aspects of Water Supply and Excreta Disposal*. Washington, D.C.: World Bank

Fapohunda, O. J., J. Reijmerink, and M. P. van Dijk. 1975. "Urban Development, Income Distribution and Employment in Lagos." World Employment Programme Research Working Paper. International Labour Office. Geneva. Processed.

Feachem, Richard G., David T. Bradley, Hemda Garelick, and D. Duncan Mara. 1983. *Sanitation and Disease: Health Aspects of Excreta and Wastewater Management*. World Bank Studies in Water Supply and Sanitation, no. 3. Chichester: John Wiley and Sons.

Findley, Sally. 1977. *Planning for Internal Migration*. U. S. Department of Commerce, Bureau of the Census. Washington, D.C.

Follain, James R., Jr., Gill-Chin Lim, and Bertrand Renaud. 1979. "The Economics of Housing Crowding in Developing Countries." Draft. Department of Economics. University of Syracuse, Syracuse, N.Y.

Friedmann, John, and Flora Sullivan. 1974. "The Absorption of Labor in the Urban Economy: The Case of Developing Countries." *Economic Development and Cultural Change*, vol. 22(3), pp. 385–413.

Garza, Gustavo, and Martha Schteingart. 1978. "Mexico City: The Emerging Megalopolis." In *Metropolitan Latin America: The Challenge and the Response*. Edited by Wayne A. Cornelius and Robert V. Kemper. Beverly Hills, Calif.: Sage.

Golladay, Frederick, and Bernhard Liese. 1980. *Health Problems and Policies in the Developing Countries*. World Bank Staff Working paper no. 412. Washington, D.C.

Gomez-Ibanez, Jose Antonio. 1975. "Federal Assistance for Urban Mass Transportation." Ph.D. dissertation. Harvard University, Cambridge, Mass.

Grimes, Orville F., Jr. 1974. *Urban Land and Public Policy: Social Appropriation of Betterment*. World Bank Staff Working Paper no. 179. Washington, D.C.

———. 1976. *Housing for Low-Income Urban Families*. Baltimore, Md.: Johns Hopkins University Press.

Gutierrez de Gomez, Marta Izabel. 1975. "Politica Tarifaria y Distribucion de Ingresos." Colombian National Planning Department. Bogota. Processed.

Harberger, Arnold C. 1977. "Fiscal Policy and Income Redistribution." In *Income Distribution and Growth in the Less-Developed Countries*. Edited by Charles R. Frank, Jr., and Richard C. Webb. Washington, D.C.: Brookings Institution.

———. 1978. "Basic Needs versus Distributional Weights in Social Cost-Benefit Analysis." Background notes for a seminar presented at the World Bank. University of Chicago. Processed.

Harbison, Fredrick H. 1977. "The Education-Income Connection." In *Income Distribution and Growth in Less-Developed Countries*. Edited by Charles R. Frank, Jr., and Richard C. Webb. Washington, D.C.: Brookings Institution.

Hauck Walsh, Annemarie. 1969. *The Urban Challenge to Government*. New York: Praeger.

Hauser, Philip M., and Robert W. Gardner. 1980. "Urban Future: Trends and Prospects." In *Population and the Urban Future*. Report on an international conference, Rome, Italy, September 1–4, 1980. United Nations Fund for Population Activities.

Hicks, Norman. 1980. *Economic Growth and Human Resources*. World Bank Staff Working Paper no. 408. Washington, D.C.

Hultin, Mats, and Jean-Pierre Jallade. 1975. *Costing and Financing Education in LDCs: Current Issues*. World Bank Staff Working Paper no. 216. Washington, D.C.

Ingram, Gregory K. 1980. "Land in Perspective: Its Role in Structure of Cities." Urban and Regional Report no. 80–9. World Bank, Washington, D.C. Processed.

Ingram, G. K., and A. Carroll. 1979. "The Spatial Structure of Latin American Cities." Urban and Regional Report no. 79–9. World Bank, Washington, D. C. Processed.

International Labour Office. 1976. *Growth, Employment and Equity: A Comprehensive Strategy for the Sudan*. Geneva. Processed.

Jallade, Jean-Pierre. 1977. *Basic Education and Income Inequality in Brazil: The Long-Term View*. World Bank Staff Working Paper no. 268. Washington, D.C.

Jamaica Ministry of Finance and Planning. 1977. "Urban Growth and Management Study: Interim Report." National Planning Agency, Kingston. Processed.

———. 1978. "Urban Growth and Management Study: Interim Report no. 3." National Planning Agency, Kingston. Processed.

Joshi, Heather, Harold Lubell, and Jean Mouly. 1976. *Abidjan Urban Development and Employment in the Ivory Coast.* Geneva: International Labour Office.

Kalbermatten, John M., DeAnne S. Julius, and Charles G. Gunnerson. 1982. *Appropriate Sanitation Alternatives: A Technical and Economic Appraisal.* Baltimore, Md.: Johns Hopkins University Press.

———. 1980. *Appropriate Technology for Water Supply and Sanitation.* Vol. 1. *Technical and Economic Options.* Washington, D.C.: World Bank.

Kalbermatten, John M., DeAnne S. Julius, Charles G. Gunnerson, and D. Duncan Mara. 1982. *Appropriate Sanitation Alternatives: A Planning and Design Manual.* Baltimore, Md.: Johns Hopkins University Press.

Katona-Apte, Judit. 1977. "Urbanization, Income and Socio-Cultural Factors Relevant to Nutrition in Tamil Nadu." *Social Action* (India), vol. 2(3).

Keare, Douglas H., and Scott Parris. 1981. "Evaluation of Shelter Programs for the Urban Poor: Principal Findings." Urban and Regional Report no. 81–25. World Bank, Washington D.C. Processed.

Keesing, Donald B. 1979. *Trade Policy for Developing Countries.* World Bank Staff Working Paper no. 353. Washington, D.C.

Laquian, Aprodicio A. 1980. "Issues and Instruments in Metropolitan Planning." In *Population and the Urban Future.* Report on an international conference, Rome, Italy, September 1–4, 1980. United Nations Fund for Population Activities.

Lee, Che-fu, and Barbara G. Furst. 1980. "Differential Indicators of Living Conditions in Urban and Rural Places of Selected Countries." Applied Systems Institute, Washington, D.C.

Lee, Kyu Sik. 1979. "Intra-Urban Location of Manufacturing Employment in Bogota." Urban and Regional Report no. 79–10. World Bank, Washington, D.C. Processed.

Lent, George E. 1976. "Taiwan's Land Tax Policy." International Monetary Fund, Fiscal Affairs Department Working Paper no. FAD/76/2. Washington, D.C. Processed.

Linn, Johannes F. 1975. "Urban Public Finances in Developing Countries. A Case Study of Cartagena, Colombia." Urban and Regional Report no. 77-1. World Bank, Washington, D.C. Processed.

——— 1976a. *The Distributive Effects of Local Government Finances in Colombia: A Review of the Evidence.* World Bank Staff Working Paper no. 235. Washington, D.C.

———. 1976b. "Estimation of Water Supply Costs in Chile, Colombia." Urban and Regional Report no. 76–14. World Bank, Washington, D.C. Processed.

———. 1976c. "Education and Health Services in Metropolitan Bogota, Colombia. Organization, Service Levels, and Finance." Draft. World Bank, Washington, D.C. Processed.

————. 1976d. "Public Transportation and Housing in Bogota: Organization, Service Levels and Financing." Draft. World Bank, Washington, D.C. Processed.

————. 1977. *The Incidence of Urban Property Taxation in Developing Countries: A Theoretical and Empirical Analysis Applied to Colombia.* World Bank Staff Working Paper no. 264. Washington, D.C.

————. 1979. "Urbanization Trends, Polarization Reversal, and Spatial Policy in Colombia." Urban and Regional Report no. 79–01. World Bank, Washington, D.C. Processed.

————. 1979b. "Automotive Taxation in the Cities of Developing Countries." *Nagarlok Urban Affairs Quarterly* (India), vol. 11(1), pp. 1–23.

————. 1980. "Urban Finances in Developing Countries." In *Urban Government Finance: Emerging Trends.* Edited by Roy Bahl. Urban Affairs Annual Reviews, vol. 20. Beverly Hills, Calif.: Sage.

Linn, Johannes F., Roger S. Smith, and Hartojo Wignjowijoto. 1976. "Urban Public Finances in Developing Countries: A Case Study of Jakarta, Indonesia." Urban and Regional Report no. 80–7. World Bank, Washington, D.C. Processed.

Linn, Johannes F., and Nelson A. Valverde. 1981. "Public Service Costs and City Size: The Case of Urban Water Supply and Sewerage Cost Functions in Colombia." Paper presented at the Eastern Economic Association Meetings, Philadelphia, Penn., April, 1981. Processed.

Lipton, Michael. 1977. *Why Poor People Stay Poor: Urban Bias and World Development.* Cambridge, Mass.: Harvard University Press.

Lubell, Harold. 1974. *Calcutta: Its Urban Development and Employment Prospects.* Geneva: International Labour Office.

Macon, Jorge, and Jose Merino Manon. 1977. *Financing Urban and Rural Development Through Betterment Levies.* New York: Praeger.

Mazumdar, Dipak. 1976. "The Urban Informal Sector." *World Development,* 4(9), pp. 655–79.

————. 1979. *Paradigms in the Study of Urban Labor Markets in LDCs: A Reassessment in the Light of an Empirical Survey in Bombay City.* World Bank Staff Working Paper no. 366. Washington, D.C.

Mazumdar, Dipak, and Masood Ahmed. 1978. *Labor Market Segmentation and the Determination of Earnings: A Case Study.* World Bank Staff Working Paper no. 278. Washington, D.C.

McCallum, J. Douglas. 1974. "Land Values in Bogota, Colombia." *Land Economics,* vol. 50(3), August, pp. 312–17.

McGee, T. C., and Y. M. Yeung. 1977. *Hawkers in Southeast Asian Cities: Planning for the Bazaar Economy.* Ottawa: International Development Research Centre.

McGreevey, William Paul. 1980. *Third World Poverty.* Lexington, Mass.: Lexington Books.

McLure, Charles E., Jr. 1975. *Taxation and the Urban Poor in Developing Countries.* World Bank Staff Working Paper no. 222. Washington, D.C.

————. 1977. "Average Incremental Costs of Water Supply and Sewerage Services: Nairobi, Kenya." Urban and Regional Report no. 77–13. World Bank, Washington, D.C. Processed.

McLure, Charles E., Jr., and Wayne R. Thirsk. 1980. "The Inequity of Taxing Iniquity: A Plea for Reduced Sumptuary Taxes in Developing Countries." *Economic Development and Cultural Change*, vol. 26(3), April, pp. 487–503.

Meerman, Jacob. 1977. *Meeting Basic Needs in Malaysia: A Summary of Findings.* World Bank Staff Working Paper no. 260. Washington, D.C.

————. 1979. *Public Expenditure in Malaysia: Who Benefits and Why.* New York: Oxford University Press.

Midgley, Peter. 1980. "Urban Transport and Traffic Management: How to Utilize Benefits and Avoid Unnecessary Investments." Paper presented for the IRF Fourth African Highway Conference, Nairobi, Kenya, January 20–25, 1980. Processed.

Mitsui Consultants Company. 1977. *Public Transport Requirements in Intermediate Size Cities.* Tokyo. Processed.

Mohan, Rakesh. 1974. "Indian Thinking and Practice Concerning Urban Property Taxation and Land Policies." Research Program in Economic Development Discussion Paper no. 47. Princeton University, Princeton, N.J. Processed.

————. 1977. "Urban Land Policy, Income Distribution and the Urban Poor." In *Income Distribution and Growth in the Less-Developed Countries.* Edited by Charles R. Frank, Jr., and Richard C. Webb. Washington, D.C.: Brookings Institution.

————. 1980. *Workers of Bogota: Who They Are, What They Do, and Where They Live.* World Bank Staff Working Paper no. 390. Washington, D.C.

Mohan, Rakesh, and Rodrigo Villamizar. 1980. "The Evolution of Land Values in the Context of Rapid Urban Growth: A Case Study of Bogota and Cali, Colombia." Urban and Regional Report no. 80–10. World Bank, Washington, D.C. Processed.

Morawetz, David. 1977. *Twenty-five Years of Economic Development: 1950 to 1975.* Baltimore, Md.: Johns Hopkins University Press.

Oftedal, Olan T., and F. James Levinson. 1977. "Equity and Income Effects of Nutrition and Health Care." In *Income Distribution and Growth in the Less-Developed Countries.* Edited by Charles R. Frank, Jr. and Richard C. Webb. Washington, D.C.: Brookings Institution.

Payne, Geoffrey K. 1977. *Urban Housing in the Third World.* Boston: Routledge and Kegan Paul.

Peattie, Lisa. 1979. "The Organization of the 'Marginals'." *Comparative Urban Research*, vol. 7(2), pp. 5–21.

Perlman, Janice E. 1976. *The Myth of Marginality: Urban Poverty and Politics in Rio de Janeiro.* Berkeley: University of California Press.

Pfeffermann, Guy Pierre, and Richard C. Webb. 1979. *The Distribution of Income in Brazil.* World Bank Staff Working Paper no. 356. Washington, D.C.

Phillips, H. M. 1978. "Education and Training Programs and Projects for the Urban Poor." World Bank, Education Department. Washington, D.C. Processed.

Preston, Samuel H. 1979. "Urban Growth in Developing Countries: A Demographic Reappraisal." *Population and Development Review*, vol. 5(2), June, pp. 195–216.

Psacharopoulos, George. 1980. "Returns to Education: An Updated International Comparison." In *Education and Income*. World Bank Staff Working Paper no. 402, Washington, D.C.

Rao, D. C. 1974. "Urban Target Groups." In *Redistribution with Growth*. Edited by Hollis Chenery and others. London: Oxford University Press.

Ray, Anandarup. 1975. *Cost Recovery Policies for Public Sector Projects*. World Bank Staff Working Paper no. 206. Washington, D.C.

Renaud, Bertrand. 1981. *National Urbanization Policy in Developing Countries*. New York: Oxford University Press.

Republic of Colombia–IBRD–UNDP. 1973. Bogota Urban Development Study. Phase II. Departamento Administrativo de Planeacion Distrital, Bogota. Processed.

Reutlinger, Shlomo, and Marcelo Selowski. 1976. *Malnutrition and Poverty: Magnitude and Policy Options*. Baltimore, Md.: Johns Hopkins University Press.

Risden, O. St. Clare. 1979. "Property Tax Reform: A History of Jamaica's Experience with Land Taxation Based on the Site Value System." In *The Taxation of Urban Property in Less Developed Countries*. Edited by Roy W. Bahl. Madison: University of Wisconsin Press.

Robson, William A., and D. E. Regan. 1972. *Great Cities of the World. Their Government, Politics and Planning*. London: Allen and Unwin.

Roth, Gabriel J. 1973. "Regulation of Buses in Cities." *Highway Research Record 476*, pp. 21–29.

Rush, Barney S. 1974. "From Favela to Conjunto: The Experience of Squatters Removed to Low-cost Housing in Rio de Janeiro, Brazil." Honors thesis. Harvard College, Cambridge, Mass.

Sant'Anna, Anna, Thomas W. Merrick, and Dipak Mazumdar. 1976. *Income Distribution and the Economy of the Urban Household: The Case of Belo Horizonte*. World Bank Staff Working Paper no. 237. Washington, D.C.

Sanyal, Bish, Nelson Valverde, and Michael Bamberger. 1980. "Evaluation of the First Lusaka Upgrading and Sites and Services Project." Urban and Regional Report no. 80–13. World Bank, Washington, D.C. Processed.

Saunders, Robert J., and Jeremy J. Warford. 1976. *Village Water Supply*. Baltimore, Md.: Johns Hopkins University Press.

Saunders, Robert J., Jeremy J. Warford, and Patrick C. Mann. 1977. *Alternative Concepts of Marginal Cost for Public Utility Pricing: Problems of Application in the Water Supply Sector*. World Bank Staff Working Paper no. 259. Washington, D.C.

Schaefer, Kalman, and Cheywa Spindel. 1976. *Sao Paulo: Urban Development and Employment*. Geneva: International Labour Office.

Selowsky, Marcelo. 1976. "A Note on Preschool-Age Investment in Human Capital in Developing Countries." *Economic Development and Cultural Change*, vol. 24, pp. 707–20.

————. 1978. *The Economic Dimensions of Malnutrition in Young Children.* World Bank Staff Working Paper no. 294. Washington, D.C.

————. 1979a. *Balancing Trickle Down and Basic Needs Strategies.* World Bank Staff Working Paper no. 335. Washington, D.C.

————. 1979b. *Who Benefits from Government Expenditure: A Case Study of Colombia.* New York: Oxford University Press.

Shipman, Harold R. 1967. "Water Rate Structure in Latin America." *Journal American Water Works Association,* vol. 59(1), pp. 3–12.

Shoup, Donald C. 1983. "Land Taxation and Government Participation in Urban Land Markets: Policy Alternatives in Developing Countries." In *Urban Land Policy: Issues and Opportunities.* Edited by Harold B. Dunkerley. New York: Oxford University Press.

Smith, Roger S. 1974. "Financing Cities in Developing Countries." International Monetary Fund *Staff Papers,* vol. 21(2), pp. 329–88.

————. 1975. "Highway Pricing and Motor Vehicle Taxation in Developing Countries: Theory and Practice." *Finanzarchiv* N. F., vol. 33, pp. 451–74.

————. 1977. "Land Prices and Tax Policy." *American Journal of Economics and Sociology,* vol. 36(4), pp. 337–50.

Squire, Lyn. 1981. *Employment Policy in Developing Countries: A Survey of Issues and Evidence.* New York: Oxford University Press.

Squire, Lyn, and Herman G. van der Tak. 1975. *Economic Analysis of Projects.* Baltimore, Md.: Johns Hopkins University Press.

Strassmann, W. Paul. 1980. "Housing Improvement in an Opportune Setting: Cartagena, Colombia." *Land Economics,* vol. 56(2), May, pp. 155–68.

Streeten, Paul, and Shahid Javed Burki. 1978. "Basic Needs: Some Issues." *World Development,* vol. 6(3), pp. 411–21.

Sudra, Tomasz, and John F. C. Turner. 1976. "Housing Priorities and Demand of Lower Income Households in Mexico City." Urban and Regionl Report no. 76–5. World Bank, Washington, D.C. Processed.

Thomas, Vinod. 1978. *The Measurement of Spatial Differences in Poverty: The Case of Peru.* World Bank Staff Working Paper no. 273. Washington, D.C.

Thoss, Rainer, and Johannes F. Linn. 1978. "The Spatial Allocation of Urban Public Investment in Colombia, South America: An Exploratory Linear Programming Model." Urban and Regional Report no. 78–3. World Bank, Washington, D.C. Processed.

Turvey, Ralph, and Dennis Anderson. 1977. *Electricity Economics.* Baltimore, Md.: Johns Hopkins University Press.

United Nations. 1970. *Administrative Aspects of Urbanization.* New York: Department of Economic and Social Affairs.

————. 1976. *Compendium of Housing Statistics 1972–1974.* New York.

————. 1978. *Non-Conventional Financing of Housing for Low-Income Households.* New York: Department of International and Social Affairs.

U. S. Agency for International Development (USAID). 1976. "Guidelines for Formulating Projects to Benefit the Urban Poor in the Developing Countries." Washington, D.C.: PADCO, Inc.

U.S. Department of Housing and Urban Development. 1973. *A Study of the Financial Practices of Governments in Metropolitan Areas.* Washington, D.C. Processed.

Valverde, Nelson A. 1978. "Bogota City Study: The Available Data." Urban and Regional Report no. 79–6. World Bank, Washington, D.C. Processed.

Vernez, Georges. 1973. "Pirate Settlements, Housing Construction by Incremental Development and Low Income Housing Policies in Bogota, Colombia." New York City Rand Institute, New York. Processed.

Viloria, Leandro A. and Associates. 1977. "Traffic Congestion in Metro Manila." SEATAC, Manila. Processed.

Vlieger, C. A. de, A. R. Manuel, G. A. Vierstra, and M. C. Onland-van Schendelen. 1975. "Drinking Water Supply by Public Hydrants in Developing Countries. Draft Final Report." International Reference Centre for Community Water Supply (IRC), The Hague. Processed.

Walters, Alan. 1968. *The Economics of Road User Charges.* Baltimore, Md.: Johns Hopkins University Press.

————. 1979a. "The Benefits of Mini-buses." *Journal of Transport Economics and Policy*, vol. 13(3), September, pp. 320–34.

————. 1979b. *Costs and Scale of Bus Services.* World Bank Staff Working Paper no. 325. Washington, D.C.

Ward, Barbara. 1976. *The Home of Man.* New York: Norton.

Warford, Jeremy J., and DeAnne Julius. 1977. "The Multiple Objectives of Water Rate Policy in Less Developed Countries." *Water Supply and Management*, vol. 1, pp. 335–42.

Watson, Peter L., and Edward P. Holland. 1978. *Relieving Traffic Congestion: The Singapore Area License Scheme.* World Bank Staff Working Paper no. 281. Washington, D.C.

Webb, Richard. 1976. *On the Statistical Mapping of Urban Poverty and Employment.* World Bank Staff Working Paper no. 227. Washington, D.C.

Wheaton, William C. 1978. "Housing Policies and Urban Markets in LDCs: Egypt." Paper prepared for the AEA Annual Meeting, Chicago, Ill. Processed.

World Bank. 1972. *Urbanization.* Sector Working Paper. Washington, D.C.

————. 1973. "Pricing in Power and Water Supply." Public Utilities Department Note 5. Washington, D.C. Processed.

————. 1974a. *Education.* Sector Working Paper. Washington, D.C.

————. 1974b. "Sites and Survey Projects: Survey and Analysis of Urbanization Standards and On-Site Infrastructure." Transportation and Urban Projects Department. Washington, D.C. Processed.

————. 1975a. *Health.* Sector Policy Paper. Washington, D.C.

————. 1975b. *Urban Transport.* Sector Policy Paper. Washington, D.C.

————. 1975c. *Housing.* Sector Policy Paper. Washington, D.C.

———. 1975d. *Integrating Women into Development*. Washington, D.C.

———. 1978a. *Employment and Development of Small Enterprises*. Sector Policy Paper. Washington, D.C.

———. 1978b. *World Development Report, 1978*. New York: Oxford University Press.

———. 1979a. *World Development Report, 1979*. New York: Oxford University Press.

———. 1979b. "Report on the Sixth Annual Conference on Monitoring and Evaluation of Shelter Programs for the Urban Poor." Urban and Regional Economics Division, Washington, D.C. Processed.

———. 1979c. *Recognizing the "Invisible" Woman in Development: The World Bank's Experience*. Washington, D.C.

———. 1980a. *World Development Report, 1980*. New York: Oxford University Press.

———. 1980b. *Education*. Sector Policy Paper. Washington, D.C.

———. 1980c. *Health*. Sector Policy Paper. Washington, D.C.

———. 1980d. *Shelter*. Poverty and Basic Needs Series. Washington, D.C.

———. 1980e. *Water Supply and Waste Disposal*. Poverty and Basic Needs Series. Washington, D.C.

Yap, Lorene Y. P. 1975. *Internal Migration in Less Developed Countries: A Survey of the Literature*. World Bank Staff Working Paper no. 215. Washington, D.C.

Zahavi, Yacov. 1976. *Travel Characteristics in Cities of Developing and Developed Countries*. World Bank Staff Working Paper no. 230. Washington, D.C.

Index

Page numbers in italics indicate tabular matter.

225

The full range of World Bank publications, both free and for sale, is described in the *Catalog of World Bank Publications*; the continuing research program is outlined in *World Bank Research Program: Abstracts of Current Studies*. Both booklets are updated annually; the most recent edition of each is available without charge from the Publications Distribution Unit (Dept. B), The World Bank, 1818 H Street, N.W., Washington, D.C. 20433, U.S.A.

Johannes F. Linn is senior economist in the East Asia and Pacific Regional Office of the World Bank.